INFORMATION FROM THE
SPIRIT GUIDES

REPORTED BY
ALISON LEA-LODGE

LEA-LODGE BOOKS

Copyright © Alison Lea-Lodge, 2005

Published by Lea-Lodge Books
PO Box 447
Brighton
BN1 1SL

Text set in Baskerville

Cover designed by Thurbans Publishing Services, Farnham, Surrey GU9 8TD

Printed in Great Britain by Antony Rowe Ltd, Bumpers Farm, Chippenham, Wiltshire SN14 6LH

ISBN 0 9548831 0 1

Distributed by Gazelle Book Services, White Cross Mills, Hightown, Lancaster, Lancashire LA1 4XS

No part of this book may be reproduced by any means, nor transmitted, nor translated into a machine language, without the written permission of the publisher.

The majority of names given to living people in this book have been changed to protect their identiy, and any accidental similarity is purely co-incidental.

Dedication

I dedicate this book, the most important project of my life to:

My four gurus each of them selfless and good, and to whom I owe more than I can say. Thomas, my medical guru, Catherine my psychic guru, Julian my Christian guru, and Geshe my Buddhist guru. They are all modest – even secretive – about their supernatural power, which is evidence that they are truly spiritual people.

Also to my Spiritual Family and Friends whose kindness in passing on their knowledge has enabled me to write this book. Please be aware that you, the reader, also have people in the next world who care for you even if you are not conscious of it.

A friend in this world, Margaret, so kind and caring. She has unwavering faith in this project and has supported me through thick and thin over more than twenty years.

Lastly, Richard Joseph, author and publisher, and his wife Elizabeth. Richard received a dramatic miracle healing as a young man, has been able to work on my text with empathy, and provide all technical skills needed to produce a book which we hope will bring deep feelings of peace and reassurances to our readers.

Alison
February 2005

Contents

Glossary	6
Introduction	7
My Struggle	9
The Mother Experience	32
My Spiritual Family and Spiritual Friends	59
Psychic Attacks	79
Visitations after Death	92
Hauntings	100
Messages from Spirit Helpers	110
The Spirits' Advice for me	134
Dowsing – Using a Pendulum	143
Medical Matters	150
The Power of Prayer	172
Healing	195
The Use of Visualisation	204
Beaming Positive Energies	213
The Fluidity of Matter	227
Astrology	229
Crystal Energies	231
Death and Dying	233
Helping those who have Died	239
Special People, Special Places	244
More Examples of Serendipity	259
Dreams	275
The Bardo	291
Reincarnation	295

GLOSSARY

Explanations are simplistic and relate to this book only

The Bardo	Time spent between incarnations
Dharma	the teachings of Budda and inner realizations attained by depending on them
Dowser	One who practices dowsing
Dowsing	To use a pendulum or stick to gain information or locate water
Emanations	Positive vibrations produced from an energy source
Incarnations	Different lives by one human or animal spirit spent on earth
Ju-Ju	West African charm with supernatural powers
Karma	the law of cause and effect in which all our actions are the causes and all our experiences are the effects
Kundalini	A yoga term – latent female energy
Mantra	Repeated phrase (if in a spiritual context for spiritual purposes. Literally 'mind protection'.)
Pendulum	Weight on a thin cord used in place of a dowser's stick. (To pendulum (v.): to employ this technique.)
Rebarbative	unattractive and objectionable
Reiki	The Japanese practice of spiritual healing
Sadana	a Buddhist ritual that is a method for attaining spiritual realizations
Seminary	A training college for priests or rabbis
Tantra	special Buddhist instructions whereby we imagine we have already achieved the future result (enlightenment).
Tantric	employing this method

Introduction

Writing this book has been the most important event in my life, although I am just an instrument used by the spirits for getting their messages onto the earth.

Why was I selected for the task? I was told that although I was low-grade in terms of spiritual development I was blissfully easy to communicate with. My motivation was good. I could be trusted to report honestly the information I was given, and not to misuse it in any way. While I regret being well down the ladder, spiritually speaking, this enables me to assure prospective readers that I am very ordinary and have plenty of failings. This, I was told, would help me to build bridges between myself and my readers. I am under instructions to give details of the nasty experiences I have had in my life, again so that fellow sufferers can identify with me. The events also explain why my psychic talents had to blossom.

I am not a spiritualist. While interested in inter-faith matters and attend Christian and Buddhist meetings, I am very critical of organised religions and know that getting involved with them is anything but a guarantee that one will improve and become Godly. A real, profound, and meaningful spirituality can only be found deep in the hearts of very special people, and many of those have nothing to do with churches or other places dubbed sacred by the people who use them.

One Christmas Eve *The Times* printed an account by a journalist who had always been an atheist but who, surrounded by superb countryside, had received an all enveloping revelation that God existed. I wish I could report that I have had such a profound and absolute experience, but I have not.

The world is full of busy people. I have arranged this book so that you can find, as easily as possible, the subjects which interest you most. Because of the layout a few events are mentioned, briefly, more than once if relevant. Skip the autobiographical details by all means if you wish to, as other subjects have a much greater interest and significance.

There are just one or two things you need to know, firstly the names of my four gurus. I have received healings and psychic messages from all of them. They were all instrumental in saving my life – this might sound dramatic, but it is true.

They are: Thomas, my medical guru, a homœopath who has healed many terminally ill; Catherine, my psychic guru, who applies her talents to helping everyone she knows although she is nearer ninety than eighty; Julian, one-time chief exorcist of the Church of England who believed an amazing and ghastly story which I told him, and rescued me; and my Tibetan Buddhist monk, the founder of the New Kadampa Tradition, with whom I have had paranormal experiences and who has a fine record in miracle healings.

Then there are a wealth of names – each and every one a spirit who has made contact with me and given me messages. I will list them, the members of my spiritual family and spiritual friends: Mr. Skinner, Betty, David, Leopold, Patrick, Sarah, Great Auntie Louie, Anthony, Ellen, Ivor, Eliza, Mervyn, the Anonymous Christian Science Lady, Winifred, the Discreet Homosexual Christian Science Man, my New Man, Thomas's friend, my Biographer, my Hindu, Mr Binay Sen, the Rev. John Keys Fraser, Angela, Dorothy Kerin, Margaret King, Dakota, Veronica, Rosemary, Thomas's father, my Frances, Jill's Frances, Violet, and Thomas Cordingley (my grandfather, not my guru). If I write that I was told something, then it was by a spirit. I have changed the names where I felt this to be sensible.

As you read please remember that while I have been told amazing things I am very much 'Jo Ordinary'. I expect, if we met, we would get along together very comfortably.

MY STRUGGLE

• *Autobiographical details of the nastiest things in my life...* • *Abuse as a child (More of this in the Mother Experience.)* • *The stress in my marriage* • *The discovery I had cancer.* • *How I cope with some of the less attractive aspects of old age, demonstrated by my husband.*

My spirit guides, particularly Betty, have told me I must give an account of the unhappy parts of my life. I do not think I bear grudges, so when I criticize or complain about how I have been treated by a number of people I want it to be understood that I am just giving an account of what happened, so that you may have some empathy with me.

For most of my life I have been lucky. My parents saw fit to give me a good education, at least up to A level standard, and I was able to get reasonably good jobs during a time when the country was enjoying full employment. I started work when I was eighteen and saved enough money to buy my first car by the following year. It was a 1956 Ford Popular, price £45. I took out my first mortgage for a house when I was twenty-six – which for a single female in 1972, was very go-head. I have never had to face real financial hardship, nothing worse than having to be careful and sensible. I have always been extremely self-sufficient and need my own space, but I have always had as many friends as I wanted.

* * *

But everyone suffers misfortunes. My first was to be born to a mother who did not want me – she had been pushed into the pregnancy by my father's family, who hoped for an heir. This was just as big a disaster for her as for me, since bringing me up committed much of her time to a way of life she did not want. However, she really should not have been a mother, since she abused me.

I suppose I must have been about two or three when the episodes of abuse took place – definitely before I reached school age. I remember being dragged into the bathroom and standing there, being subjected to the most unspeakable and desperately painful things she did to me. I was also aware of the reaction produced in her. Years later I understood that what was utterly loathsome to me brought about an evil and warped ecstasy in her.

Understandably, I think, I grew up hating lesbians. Looking back I dread to think of the number of times I recoiled from the 'advances' of harmless, warm-hearted women, who happened to put a hand on my shoulder or gave me a friendly handshake. I would go away into a corner and shake like a wet dog.

But now I see even the ghastly perverts who attack children as pitiable. The driving force in their lives – sex – makes them hated by society because they are twisted, yet the same drive in normal people is an advantage and an asset. I doubt if there are many pædophiles who have an easy choice in the matter of expressing their proclivities, and most of us would have been incapable of ignoring our own sex drives and remaining completely celibate even if our desires were, in the eyes of Mr Average, totally unacceptable. Those who are a danger to children should be locked up – but more to protect children than as a punishment.

A fuller account of my experiences with my mother is given in the chapter Mother Experience – when I felt I had to dredge up memories to convince the man who delivered her un-rested soul, that she really hated me as much as I claimed.

* * *

The second major misfortune of my life was an unhappy marriage. I know that this experience was absolutely vital in the blueprint of my life and that without it none of the meaningful things that have happened to me could have taken place – so in fact I should be grateful for it.

When I married my husband I absolutely adored him. He was unsuitably old for me, unlike the goodly number of earlier boy-friends who had been mostly of my age, or unremarkably older or younger. After my experience as a child I knew that I did not want children. A couple of extremely nice and well – placed boy-friends suffered the pain of breaking up because I knew it would be unfair to get seriously involved with anyone who had the conventional desire to procreate. I could not discuss this subject with any of them, either I ditched them, or I was sufficiently unpleasant that they ditched me!!

I was forty when I married, and for two years I found marriage blissful. I was so happy and relaxed that I even stopped having the truly terrible migraines which I had suffered from since my teens – and which occurred once a month. On a regular basis I lost half a stone in three days.

However, good things do not last for ever. Before proposing to me, my husband had proposed to a woman who had been among the team of nurses who had cared for his first wife until she died. This woman, she was still married when the proposition was put to her, had initially turned him down, saying she was young and still in the market for a young stud. Then she did her sums, and decided that he was worth pursuing after all. But by this time Timothy was engaged to me.

We married in January, and at the Christmas immediately preceding our second wedding anniversary, she sent him a card with a photograph of herself and the most 'come on' message I have ever seen. Had any ex-boy friend of mine written in this way I would have been furious. For me, marriage really did mean forsaking all others and the word divorce did not come into my vocabulary. For life meant for life.

Timothy's views were very different. He waited until I was out of the house one evening and telephoned her. I knew nothing of this and when I returned home he rounded on me with a verbal hatred and violence which I would not have believed was in the capacity of any human being on earth.

I was completely traumatised. I had given up my old way of life for my husband, stopped work, and my friends had become our friends. On that fateful night I learned two things. He had married me because I was in better position, financially, and that I had married the sort of person I most despised – one who marries for material gain. I also learned that my love had been less than perfect in that it was not unconditional. I no longer loved one who had made it obvious that he had never loved me.

Looking back I could see that Timothy's ideas echoed those of his mother. No girls her 'boys' brought home were ever good enough, while she was keen to get her daughters married and was prepared to be much less fussy. Timothy believed that being male made him automatically superior. A woman's role was as the uneducated and subservient bearer of men's children, and when I appeared, unmarried, childless and almost forty, he viewed me as a freak who should be privileged to be his doormat and eternally grateful to him for enabling me to relinquish my spinster status.

My view of unmarried women could not have been more different. I married in bright pink – at my age I had had a fairly full and interesting life and white would have been thoroughly inappropriate.

How did I get involved with Timothy? He and his late first wife had been good friends to an aunt who lived halfway across the country. When his first wife died the aunt was too old to travel to the funeral and I volunteered to represent her. Timothy told me not to, as I would not have known the people there, but that I would be welcome to visit him for lunch sometime later. I took up this invitation, and from that moment knew that my destiny was to marry him.

Because of the family connection I felt that 'vetting' had been done for me. On the handful of occasions when I had seen Timothy and his first wife I liked them, and they had been kind to the family – his wife in particular was very generous, though the poor woman's health degenerated into a terrible state, with progressive brain hæmorrhages.

I was given another reason why I fell for Timothy. It was later explained to me that the spirits of his dead uncle and aunt – who had cared for Timothy's brother when he was dying – had influenced me, putting the appropriate ideas into my mind.

* * *

With the benefit of hindsight, I should have seen the obvious signs of Timothy's complete lack of regard for me. I had declined his offer of an engagement ring, I do not like jewellery, but my wish to have a good – quality wedding ring was met with the response that he was not paying that sort of money – and he could pick up a second hand one in an auction sale for thirty pounds. Our joint search for a ring ended dramatically when a shop holding a sale produced horribly scratched goods which, luckily, were far too small for me anyway. In the end I bought the ring during my office lunchtime. Alone.

Just after we married I found that he opened my post, read it, and if it was of no interest to him, put it in the bin without showing it to me. I objected, and he objected to my objection. Still I remained blind! I was no longer to read a book. If I tried to he took delight in constantly interrupting me and then take it from me, partly read, and read it himself. If I objected his response was, "You want me to read what you read, don't you?" Particularly after the hiatus in our marriage he appeared to dedicate his life to finding niggling little ways to oppose or upset me. The garden path needed repairing, and I had said I would like little gaps to be left among the stones so that small plants could be introduced. He went out, mixed cement, and covered the whole area. Having told me not to walk on it he then trod on it himself, leaving his large footprint indelibly on the path and definitely no flowers.

Knowing that my car radio was always tuned to Radio 4 he always altered it to a pop station. If we went out in the car together and he returned first he would let himself in and then twist the central locking again so that my door was shut and, struggling with bags of shopping, I had to open it myself. If we were in a hurry and had gone our separate ways, but needed to meet up again, he deliberately had me searching for him by not being at the agreed venue. I am very allergic to bleach so he claimed the mugs were stained so he could leave them with bleach in them over-night.

I did most of the driving and he placed all the stress on me that he could by timing each leg of the journey – I was supposed to better my time each time we went on the same route. A speeding conviction had its advantages: here was my excuse to slow down.

I once asked his sister what Timothy had been like as a child. Expecting her to recount his love of or hatred of rice pudding, or some other bit of family trivia, I was little prepared for her reply. The only thing she could remember was that he was a very spiteful child, the sort of child other children did well to keep away from. Suddenly his behaviour came into focus. Spite was at the core of his being.

I recalled one occasion when I had requested him to dig anywhere on the allotment apart from one small area where I had my beloved foxgloves. He went straight there, dug them up, and put them on the weed heap. Amazingly they survived when I recovered them and re-planted them.

He once urged me to take an ordinary electric fire with me when I was working, outside, on a hole in the caravan roof, during a rainstorm... nice try, Timothy. Even women are a little too well educated to fall for that one! If he knew I planned to take a bath he had one, and deliberately ensured that all the towels were damp.

Timothy's first wife had been involved with a lot of jumble sales. The area where they lived was fairly upmarket, and expensive labels found their way onto stalls in support of the Conservatives or moneyraising church events. A lot of her clothes came from this source.

At the start of my marriage he made clear to me that I should dress out of charity shops. I was very hurt by this. Having worked from the age of eighteen until a few months after I married I was used to getting what I wanted, new clothes from normal clothing shops, though I was never a snappy or extravagant dresser. However, I managed to turn this around. If one only paid a few pounds for something one could buy more items, and risk getting things which might only be worn occasionally. However, much of my life was lived on the allotment, on the beach, or sculpting, so that smart clothes were rarely worn. I gradually became more and more scruffy.

Things got to the point where Timothy objected. But by this time I was set in my ways, and he had lost the opportunity to have a welldressed wife. At one point he gave me £50 and told me to change my wardrobe! Actually, the money bought quite a few things from the charity shops but, in the last year of the twentieth century, this princely sum would not, normally, have gone far.

* * *

The topic of which Timothy never tired was that he lost the lower part of his right leg during the war, when the house where he was living was bombed. His first wife suffered similar injuries. Luckily both of them kept their knee joints, their artificial legs fitted well, and they both led full and normal lives.

The invalidity benefit they received, through their war injuries, was very considerable over the years and must have amounted, annually, to at least as much as many hardworking people earned.

Timothy loved the preferential treatment he got from

being classified as disabled. When his first wife was dying he bought beds where the ends could be adjusted electronically. One came with him when he moved in with me.

When we were first married we had a normal four foot six bed. Fitments which we had built into the bedroom left a space large enough for one five foot wide. Timothy suddenly decided that he must have the special three foot bed back. I was confined to a two foot strip of latex laid on a wooden board which we built.

Not long after I discovered that I had cancer. I suddenly took a look at my sleeping arrangements. I never got a good night's sleep. If Timothy woke up he automatically shook the bed so that I was disturbed, too.

How had I let this happen to me? When I was a child I moved from a cot to a three-foot-six bed – my parents believing in having a goodsized sleeping area. Now, aged fortysix, I was reduced to a child-sized bed. I announced that I must be able to rest. In fact the endless shaking to which Timothy subjected me was far worse than the cramped conditions and I moved to the spare room. Later I went into another room, where I was surrounded by bits of sculpture and general scruff but where I also had my little Buddhist and inter-faith shrine, before which I could meditate.

Shortly afterwards Timothy gave away his special bed, and bought himself an ordinary though extremely expensive double one.

Of course, a person who criticises someone who is perfect, is automatically in the wrong. I had arranged to give a little dinner party at a time when, it later transpired, I was to be in the throws of having radiotherapy. Some people walk through this treatment and are completely unaffected, but I felt very tired and below par.

Not knowing how I would be on the day I warned Timothy that, if I felt really weak, he would have to be ready to take us all to a meal in a restaurant.

A few days before the event one of the guests rang up, on

behalf of them all, to find out if I was really fit enough to feed everyone. Timothy answered the phone. He assured the caller that I was fine and then, having put the phone down, reported what he had said. I remarked that it would have been nice to have been consulted, and for this criticism I had to put up with a huge sulk for the rest of the day.

* * *

As he got older Timothy became more and more attention seeking. During one spell away he claimed to have fallen and broken his arm. A friend who was keeping an eye on him from a distance was doubtful, as were the doctors when, a day or two later, there was not even a little bruise to show for his real or invented accident.

On another occasion he came in from the garden and said, in hushed tones, that he had some bad news. He had felt one leg give out, and the ligaments or cartilages must have snapped. I immediately said we must get an appointment with the doctor, and he flew into a rage and absolutely hit the roof! He must have hoped that I would accept his word and, if possible, wait on him even more hand, foot, and finger without even seeking medical help. There was no trace of a limp, and the matter was never referred to again.

One day he did his customary 'poor me' act, and took himself up to bed. He has done this probably about three times a week on average throughout the many years of our marriage. I took him up a coffee and there he was, not breathing. He had a very good colour, and an expression of minute concentration, just like a small child who screws up his face to prove he is asleep. I thought, 'He must breathe soon,' and watched until he was reduced to a sudden gasp. I put the coffee by the side of the bed and ran from the room. Luckily I was going out. I jumped into the car and exploded with laughter. For once his behaviour had been really funny, rather than aggravating and exhausting.

That ruse having failed it was not long before he tried his old trick of claiming to be too ill to eat, or too upset if I had dared to make a criticism real or implied. Credibility was lost however when I noticed that, while I had been out, copious quantities of roast pork had vanished from the fridge.

After the experiences with my mother and the apparently contrasting happiness of home life during the first two years of marriage, the current unhappiness was (almost) overwhelming. Often I prayed to God to kill me. He nearly answered my prayer. It is a common story, sadly. One day in the bath I found a lump. It was small, hard, and I knew instinctively it was bad news. Flat-chested women are at an advantage. Little lumps are more likely to be noticed and they are less likely to be dismissed as fatty lumps by the doctors.

I had been feeling ill for at least two years. I hate doctors, hospitals and dentists, but I untypically took myself to the doctor and said I wanted a check up. He looked dumbstruck, and all the tests came back as more than a little satisfactory. Except one. A hospital test showed that the lump was, indeed, malignant.

Initially my doctor, while sending me to the hospital, had said he felt that the lump was harmless. My visit to the hospital, where a biopsy was taken, kept me in the dark and I assumed my doctor was right, though I was surprised. I wrote and turned down the appointment for a mammogram saying I believed I was clear. The surgeon sent a kind letter saying he thought I was wrong, and I needed treatment.

His letter arrived while I was at work. I had returned to work, but part-time, after my marriage had become unbearable and Timothy, collecting me from the office, had brought it with him. As I read it I cannot describe the white hot ice cold heat of sheer terror that ran through me, filled me, and petrified me. I was about to die. I broke the news to Timothy. He said smugly that he had sensed the letter was highly personal. Predictably he expressed no sympathy or regret.

I found myself on the escalator of hospital visits, surgery, and those ghastly tests to see how far the malignancy might have spread. At the top of my list of the most stressful occasions I put up with, was the wait of some weeks and then the queuing with my peer group to find out if the cells had infected the lymph. Mercifully, we were all clear. But radiotherapy followed just to make sure there was nothing nasty left behind around the scar.

* * *

It was, I think, early October when I told Timothy I had to have a cancer operation. His response was that it must be put off until January so it did not spoil Christmas. He then gave me a detailed rundown of a hernia operation he had had years earlier.

Not long after we got the news I overheard him answering a phone call from a member of his family. At the end of a normal, mundane conversation he threw in the line, "Alison's got cancer". I heard a gasp at the other end of the phone. His matter-of-fact tone sounded terrible. The caller said something, and he repeated the statement. Later this relative made a point of phoning me and saying I had been thought of with love... there are, indeed, many kind people in the world and one should not be upset by the others.

My experience with his attitude was not unusual. I was furious to learn of husbands who saw their wives' life-threatening illness simply in terms of inconvenience to themselves – maimed boobs being less attractive.

While I was in hospital he visited me very briefly once a day in the morning. Never did he bring me flowers or a get-well card. Once there was a mix-up and the main part of my supper did not arrive. Cancer made me thin but did not diminish my appetite, and I asked him to bring me extra rations. I had left food in the house for him and the next day I recognised a by then rather stale bit of bread returned to me as his main offering.

I was pleased about the brevity of his visits. When you believe you are dying you do not wish to see people who do not care for you. In fact I, and I think other people, tended to go through a phase when we were most relaxed surrounded by other cancer patients. The healthy can appear, rightly or wrongly, to be slightly smug or patronising. They are well, and have not succumbed to an illness which will almost certainly lead to a quick demise... a frequent misunderstanding.

Friends were wonderful. They more than compensated for Timothy and surrounded me with love, prayers, lovely cards, fruit and flowers. My special friend Elizabeth and her daughter drove many miles to see me loaded with gifts including a lovely frothy book about a cat, one of our mutual enthusiasms, and red roses.

* * *

When we got married Timothy and I were both members of the Church of England. The wedding ceremony was in a delightful little church close to a manor house. The vicar who married us was a great favourite, very kind and sincere. Unfortunately he retired. We had been fairly regular members of his congregation and kept going after he left. However, we were unimpressed by his successor.

I had always been keen on inter-faith matters. I went to an excellent Church of England school that encouraged an interest in other faiths and I heard about a group that had the belief one should accept that there was truth in all religions.

We got involved. I joined at a time when Timothy was away so he would feel no pressure to quit the Church of England, of which he had been a member for many years. However, he soon followed me. We got heavily involved. The Political Sect, as I am going to call it, was few in number. It ranged from the very wealthy to the very poor and numbered professionals and reformed alcoholics and drug addicts among its members. Immediately we were given a warm welcome and started working for them.

But it was not all that long before I sensed there was something wrong. The atmosphere was not right. The level of spirituality was low and there was a strange preoccupation with worldly matters. Rules and regulations ensured that if someone's marriage hit the rocks there was involvement by the group. I had never had an acrimonious break up with a boy friend but I learned about it now. I found it squalid. Then there were punishments arranged for any who committed petty crimes or who came before the country's courts for serious offences.

It struck me as odd that such rules should be considered necessary. The Church of England had never viewed its congregation as budding criminals. But possibly they had, as it were, a different catchment area. Despite the small congregation I saw punishments brought into action. Somewhere I used to hear, 'Judge not that ye be not judged.' It sounded attractive. Having become dissatisfied with the absence of spiritual succour in the Political Sect's activities I decided to find out about meditation. The Buddhists, I thought, would be the experts in this field. I was right, the moment I walked through the door the atmosphere of peace and love was tangible and I knew that I wanted to discover more about them and their philosophy than just the meditation.

* * *

One night there was a fundraising event put on by the Political Sect. It was terrible. It started much later than it was billed, the content was poor, and then a considerable time was spent haranguing us into committing large sums of money for their cause. And what was their cause? They wanted to complete a building from which they plan to rule the world as a one party state. I hasten to add I did not know this at the time, I am indebted to a well researched TV programme for enlightening me.

At that night's entertainment I sat there, feeling unclean to have got involved with this so-called religious group. I knew I must leave it at once.

My opportunity came swiftly. By attending a Buddhist festival I would be breaking the Political Sect's rules. While one was supposed to accept the truth of other religions one should not actually be of them. For instance a former Christian was not supposed to go on receiving Communion. As I left for the festival I posted a letter to the Sect stating I had left and become a Buddhist.

Interestingly, wishing to keep a tight hold of the members, numbers of people signed up to the alleged faith are well documented. The local members obviously did not want to reveal that I, a previously enthusiastic worker, had quit, and I discovered my name on a voting paper years later.

I do not regret my time with the Political Sect. We learn by our mistakes, and the whole of life is a learning curve. Had I stayed with the Church of England I would probably not have been sufficiently dissatisfied to have turned to Buddhism, and that is where so much that is good in my life has come from, my wonderful Tibetan monk and his teachings and followers.

Timothy has never made a mistake. He says he knew what he was doing when he joined the Sect and he remains with them. We find ourselves at opposite ends of the spectrum of materialism. Over the years Timothy has made a point of telling me that according to certain of his friends in the Political Sect, the anti-cancer drug I take becomes ineffective after a maximum of five years. This is rubbish – Thomas knew of a woman on it for nineteen years, who died only after her prescription was stopped, and one specialist said he had patients who had been on it for more than a decade and would not dream of taking them off it. However, wishing to line up a third wife, my tenacity in remaining alive has been a source of irritation to him.

He cannot help being the way he is. Once I compared

notes with a neighbour in the throws of a divorce. Her sister, a nurse, had thought it likely that my neighbour's husband, so similar to Timothy, was suffering from Asperger's Syndrome, a sort of junior form of autism. Timothy's sister said once she believed he had never loved anyone, which was sad. When his brother, the one person on earth I thought he might love, died he showed little sorrow.

I was not singled out for uncaring treatment. Once we visited a dear friend, Jennifer, who had been diagnosed with cancer. Just before we had arrived she had been told the hospital were not planning to give her treatment – she was having to face death. But Timothy's response to this news, which must have been so devastating, was to hold forth about problems he was having with the plumbing of a caravan we owned. All I could do was to apologise to the family who, perfect officers and gentlemen, were very nice about it.

* * *

Timothy once told me that his first wife had said to him, "I hate you." She had never retracted it, and he knew she meant it. As, by all accounts, she was a kind and generous lady I find comfort in the fact that she, too, had problems in coping with him as her husband. He once told me that when he married his first wife he remembers no love – just a sense of partnership... and the fact that they built up a home together, initially aided by the fact she, who was the older, earned more than he did.

When the poor woman eventually died Timothy told me that there was a great sense of peace in the room. He is sufficiently psychic to have been able to sense if she had returned – but she did not. I, too, await my release.

* * *

That all sounded bitter. I am not – just thoroughly tested.

Only the cancer experience brought about a combination of circumstances, my giving up work for the second time and thus having more time to do other things, and the necessary development of my psychic potential to enable me to communicate and get information from friends in the next world.

All the nasty things in my life have been meant to happen, and I have always had the innate knowledge that while circumstances might push me to the brink, I will never be sent more than I can cope with. I believe this law applies to everyone. Many of us are on a steep learning curve. It is often not a pleasant experience, but we should feel privileged to have been seen as fit material to receive such teachings.

Even so, I lash out against misfortunes when they happen, swearing like a trooper as I go, and often losing it and rebelling against my lot. Yes, there is ample evidence that, as I have been told, I am low-grade, in spiritual terms... though I am hoping to improve!

* * *

Why should the cancer experience result in the blossoming of my psychic powers, I hear you ask. For some seventeen years after her death, and three years after my cancer operation, I was aware of my mother's discarnate spirit attacking me, telling me I was dying, and doing everything in its power to bring about the recurrence of the cancer.

This was the most terrifying experience of my life, and while I knew what was happening, I thought that if I sought help I would be labelled schizophrenic, which would neither rescue me, nor pacify my mother's disturbed soul. But help was at hand.

I discovered I was living five minutes' walk away from my future guru Julian who, as luck would have it, was the Church of England's chief exorcist. When I met him, I told him my tale of woe, and to my enormous relief he believed me. (Of course he believed me! His powers of perception were such that he was far more aware of what was happening than I was!) He agreed to take the case to the Church of England's deliverance group, saying with a dry reticence, "There is a psychic link which must be broken..." I am pretty sure that they spent many hours of hard prayer on behalf of myself and my mother, and I will never forget that they saved my life.

If you are interested in the episode on the deliverance of my mother's disturbed soul, and the blossoming of the (necessary) latent psychic powers that I possessed, you may like to read the chapter on her deliverance, *The Mother Experience*.

I must report that this event in my life found Timothy at his very best. He also had psychic powers, and believed me, and was very supportive.

* * *

As I have mentioned, I had survived child abuse, a bad marriage, and cancer. Another instalment awaited me.

Timothy was a lot older than I was, and I was now going to experience a role similar to that of an adult child coping with an extremely difficult old parent. Throughout much of this I felt a kind of unreality. I was aware I was being sent the experience, once again, to build bridges so that fellow sufferers could identify with me. So be it!

One day, as we walked along, my beloved spouse remarked, "I may be older than you are, but you are the greater wreck." At this point I was pleased to see that Buddhism had kicked in. My silent observation, that this was not a particularly pleasant thing to say, was just that – an observation. I felt nothing, and was emotionally completely disconnected. However, from his side, pride had come before a fall.

Within a week or two he had gone into hospital with pneumonia. He collapsed, could not get up – my attempts to lift him, a dead weight of twelve stone, proved fruitless – and a paramedic called an ambulance. The diagnosis was made quickly in the Accident and Emergency department of the local hospital, and he was put on antibiotics. He responded well, and immediately.

However, while he should have been out of hospital quickly, he decided to play up. One day he declared that he had a routine – he went and washed and shaved himself early before the ward got busy and he had a walk, too. The following day he said he was not going to follow the routine, and he insisted on lying flat on his back in bed, and refused to sit up or walk. The antibiotics ended, back came the pneumonia, and eventually a blood clot formed in the lower part of his leg. Because it was below the knee there was no danger, but he had to have an intravenous drug to dissolve it.

During this time other aspects of his behaviour also left a lot to be desired. The nurses were angels. But he could not resist commenting, loudly, that one of the nurses who had a slightly built-up shoe had a club foot, and another who walked with apparent difficulty, had "Trouble with her hips." How these two lovely and possibly sensitive young ladies coped with such a patient I know not, but they went on being angels.

Then offerings from visitors were criticised and I was ordered to take them home. Some fruit ended up with other patients, but those who visited regularly must have wondered where their cards and gifts had gone....

* * *

Two visitors drove fifty miles, a round trip of a hundred, to see him. After initially appearing pleased he decided to make a scene, so he pretended he was going to be sick which he never was and they delicately withdrew. A great waste of time and petrol for people who led busy lives.

He was much interested in the fact that a couple of men who showed signs of senility spent their time pulling their catheters out of themselves. When I, opening a carton of Ribena, inadvertently squeezed the middle so a few drops fell on his sheet he made a terrible fuss. I said that the hospital was used to worse than that. He retorted, "Not from me they're not!"

At first when I visited I took him the *Daily Mail* – I suggested that a tabloid might be easier to manage than a broadsheet. This was fine, then one day I discovered that the man in the next bed, and Timothy, both wanted to do the *Daily Telegraph* crossword comparing notes and finishing it together. The day I forgot this and brought up the *Mail* my name was mud. I went and got a *Telegraph*, and another patient was happy to have the unwanted *Mail*.

One day, not long after I had arrived to visit Timothy, he declared that he wanted to lie down and rest. I had to pull the curtains round his bed. Meanwhile, I passed the time of day with the nurses. When I was about to leave one said that a friend had just phoned, with a message for Timothy, so I volunteered to take it to him. When I parted the curtains there he was sitting bolt upright which he had previously refused to do and tackling the *Telegraph* crossword.

Eventually the hospital got fed up with him. He was bed-blocking and was being completely unco-operative, so he was shifted to a geriatric ward of another hospital. His attitude became more and more unpleasant.

* * *

Co-incidentally a friend, Roger, was in the same ward – they were almost opposite each other. I was glad to have – as I discretely expressed it to him – "A friendly face to greet me." Roger was quite astute and had Timothy well weighed-up. "He doesn't try it on with me," he said, "but he does with other people."

We had asparagus in our garden, and I brought small hot helpings of it, with melted butter, for Timothy. Initially he was pleased, but the day came when that, too, was waved away! Should I give it to Roger? I asked. When he agreed I knew he would probably change his mind...which he did, but not before the asparagus had been consumed on the opposite side of the ward. I have to admit that I felt a mixture of amusement, and a 'Serve you right'!

Worse was to follow. His mobility had been affected because he had not been on his feet and walking for some weeks, though he was still perfectly capable of getting up and down the ward if he chose to. He has always greatly loved his disabled status, and he made the most of the fact that there was a raised loo seat in one of the loos. But one day it was not there. He told me with satisfaction that when he found it was missing he had sat down without taking his pyjamas down, and "It exploded everywhere." He walked the full length of the ward in this mess as a way of punishing the nurses.

There were other incidents, and one night they, apparently, plugged him with some device so that there would be no problems during the night. He claimed that 'it' had not been fitted properly... I was not convinced.

Instead of making progress he appeared to be getting much worse. He refused to eat or move, or speak... the day came when I saw a doctor, and said I wanted to hear the truth. Had the man said that something terminal had been discovered I would have believed him. However, I was told that Timothy was 'Not seriously ill.' But the doctor, seeing how he was, and failing to realize that what he was observing was a typical Timothy 'mood', had wrongly diagnosed depression, and put him on an antidepressant drug. I advocated taking him off, but the doctor said he wanted to see what effect the drug had.

One day Timothy told me that the hospital were seriously concerned about his health on three counts his prostate, his neck, and his appendix. When I told the nurses they fell about laughing. The doctor had found only one slight physical problem which, as he put it, "Is the only thing he does not complain about." No treatment was regarded as appropriate, or necessary. He flatly refused even to attempt to walk until one day when, forgetting his protestations that he was not able to do anything, he got up and walked down the ward. That was it. He was discharged within hours. One of his tricks had been, if he was forced to stand, to pretend to fall over. The nurses got fed up with this, and one told him that if he did fall over she was not prepared to lift him up, he would just have to lie there. He grumbled enormously about this, claiming that he should have tender loving care. The same nurse was, of course, extremely kind to the genuinely ill.

When I was told he was being discharged, I asked what would happen if I found I could not manage. Absolutely no pressure was put on me, and I was told I should simply say I could not cope, and he would be re-admitted as a 'failed discharge'. I do not admit defeat easily, and I stuck it out. I was to discover why the nurses pointedly told me, "He is not incontinent, and he has a brain." The pattern of dirty behaviour continued. I had managed to get a commode from the Red Cross, but had not realised that he would insist on a raised loo seat. I was unable to get one at the weekend, although I tried three places. I was punished. I went into the loo and saw his underwear on the floor. It had been screwed up. Further investigation revealed that he had deliberately messed in it first. A similar offering was found in the bedroom.

He would walk past two loos to use the commode, so that I would have to empty it. Once he claimed there was no paper by the commode, in fact there was a loo roll at his elbow, a box of tissues on the bed, and a handbasin with a cloth beside the commode. But he got straight back onto the bed with disgusting results.

Soon after he got home he said, "We don't have any blue towels, do we?" I was a bit puzzled until I remembered articles which looked like huge panty-liners which were put on the chairs and beds of those who might have accidents. Had we got some, he pointed out, "I could have diarrhoea in the bed and you would just have to wash out the towels."

Once he was home I kept urging him to start walking again, and get back the use of his legs. Consequently, one night after he had done nothing during the day I pointed out that he had failed to exercise. He said that it was my fault because I had not taken him out, and there was nowhere he could walk at home. This was a complete lie. However, it was a lovely evening, so I said we could go out at once. This was not what he wanted to hear. He got as far as the car and then true to form deliberately fell over. I knew he was capable of getting up and I knew equally that he would refuse to. Hoping that no one was about to have a heart attack and genuinely needing an emergency call, I had no option but to ring for an ambulance. What a waste of public money! He was simply assisted back to his bedroom.

* * *

I continued to visit Roger who eventually, sadly, died in the ward. I had got familiar with other patients, too, and of course the nurses knew me. They never asked after Timothy, but just said, "How are you managing?" We laughed about it. One of Timothy's cries was, "I can't lift my arms." I did an imitation of him wailing his message, and the nurses were delighted. "She's got him off to a T!" they exclaimed. One of the other patients asked how I was coping.

"Difficult." I said dryly.

"We noticed," he said, equally dryly.

Few patients manage to be disliked by doctors, nurses, and fellow patients, but Timothy achieved this. However, there was some excuse for his behaviour. The anti-depressant drug had what our G.P. described as 'A devastating effect,' and he took him off it at once. Within weeks Timothy was returning to near normal.

A friend and distant relative who was a professional and very experienced nurse explained that such drugs removed a person's inhibitions, and a heart drug which he was being prescribed, though only in a minute dosage, would have had a similar effect. Such behaviour had its roots in the desire to re-live the time when the mother had all one's attention. This was endorsed by Timothy's life-long jealousy of his little sister, although his junior by a full six years.

    I was told by my spirit guides, particularly Betty, to write these seedy details, again to build bridges with those who have to cope with the ghastly behaviour which can accompany old age, and then concentrate on getting into a state of equanimity with Timothy. As a Buddhist one aims to view all creatures with compassion, and to have a relationship with all living beings, without feeling close to some, out of attachment, or distant from others, out of hatred. It works if you can do it!

The Mother Experience

* *Guru Thomas discovers my mother's hatred making me more likely to succumb to the cancer virus.* • *I sense my mother's spirit working to make my cancer return.* • *I try to help with prayer.* • *She is too strong for me.* • *Guru Catherine helps me.* • *The Church of England's Chief Exorcist rescues me.* • *I discover my psychic powers and talk to my dead family.* • *While my childhood was in some ways unhappy in others it was normal.* • *Once my mother found the Grace of God I expected my psychic powers to vanish.*

I am not going to pretend that I was sorry when my mother died, but I was genuinely very sad at what I saw as her wasted life. She was the only one of three sisters to have a good professional training, but she gave up teaching when she married and, apart from a little part-time work at my father's art school, taken only because he could not find anyone else who was properly qualified, she chose to put her unmistakable talents to no good use.

She married and had one daughter whom she did not want, and she ended up loved by neither myself nor my father – though he was solidly loyal towards her so far as I was concerned. However, I knew her snobbishness really got under his skin, and there was ample evidence that he had an affair. I do not condone this, but I do understand his need to escape. After all, I left home for a job nearly two hundred miles away, just a few months after getting my A levels – and he didn't have that option!

When she died she had been ill for a long time, so handicapped that she had been unable to get out of bed on her own for three years, and no one, not even her sisters, expressed sorrow, saying that her illness had gone on for much too long anyway. Her funeral, a very good service, was conducted by her sisters' minister. So far as I was concerned she had been laid to rest and I got on with my life.

I rarely thought about her. I had known unhappiness at her hands but my experiences enabled me to understand and empathise with others who had problems with their mothers, and, hopefully, to help them. I have always felt a bad experience was much more acceptable, if it could be seen to have a purpose. But, seventeen years after her death, I was to discover that she had still not left me.

* * *

Through a chain of coincidences, which I would call fate, I had heard about a wonderful healer called Thomas. We had become friends with a couple, the Hansons, who had benefited greatly from his talents.

The husband had gone to the doctor as he was feeling unwell, and had been referred to a hospital to be given the shattering news that he had terminal cancer in the lung, stomach, and abdomen. He was offered chemotherapy, with the message that this would possibly extend his life by a few months, but he would feel extremely ill all the time. He declined the treatment and was referred to a hospice.

A doctor at the hospice asked him if he wanted to fight the disease. If so, he should see Thomas since the doctor could give a list of names of people as long as his arm who had been written off by conventional medicine but who had gone to Thomas, and had either been cured or who were still walking about and leading normal lives many years later.

Thomas was a homœopath. He had worked as a physiotherapist but felt he wanted to help his patients more than he could with physical exercise. He trained using a Vega machine. This device, invented by a brilliant German who was both a doctor and a dentist, enables each patient to be seen as an individual, diagnosing and treating by using electrical means to ascertain how each organ and part of the body is functioning, and what it needs to correct it, if defective.

Our friend went to Thomas, and later scans proved that he had become completely free of cancer. His wife also benefitted. Her arthritis was so bad that, although only about forty, she could not wash her hair herself, her arms not being sufficiently mobile. The cause of her arthritis, Thomas established, was a build up of toxins in her system caused by childhood illnesses. She was cleansed of them and her arthritis vanished. After hearing of this I found myself in awe of this amazing man. The moment I was diagnosed with cancer I made an appointment to see him. This is usually the last resort of the dying – at our meeting he looked at me with disbelief – for I was still *waiting* for my operation.

When I was very ill, I needed to see him every six weeks. This was the time it took for his remedies to kick in. He said nothing about being able to cure me but told me firmly to go under the surgeon's knife as quickly as possible.

After the operation, Thomas still found that I could have had a recurrence at any time. Weeks later, when checking me, he kept asking which side the lump had been on – it was the right – and he found another problem on the left. He told me to go and seek chemotherapy quickly. However, he also gave me a very large quantity of a strong homœopathic remedy. Taking it was an amazing experience. I have never known my body to crave any substance as it did that one. Amazingly the cancer vanished – Thomas certainly never made any claims that it would – and when I no longer had to take the remedy, I felt quite bereft. Apparently Mr Hanson had also been aware of the beneficial powers of the stuff. The flavour was weird. Not particularly edible, but it just felt completely right. The nearest I can get to describing its taste is to say it reminded me of the smell of surgical spirit, but it wasn't really like that, either. I never had the chemotherapy.

At times I could tell that Thomas got a bit fed up with me. He felt I should have been able to build up a greater resistance to the possible return of the cancer than I did. Contrary to what you may imagine he is a robust countryman. He begins every day with a good solid traditional English breakfast – none of your delicate vegetarian diet for him.

As time passed by I did become stronger, and he and the hospital found me fit. I am in his debt for life. He discovered that I needed the pure, and more expensive, version of a drug, and to take it in larger quantities than were being prescribed. I managed to persuade my G.P. to let me have what I needed, so a big thank you to him, too.

* * *

Why do some people get cancer at a relatively early age? Guru Thomas found that usually there was a genetic weakness or some other logical reason. With me he was puzzled, and curious to find an answer.

At one of our meetings, he lolled back in his chair and began to ask questions.

"I don't believe any of this, but I'll try anything!" he said. "Let's just see if there was anything in your childhood."

He first tested the time between being two and five. Everything went wild. It continued to go wild from the time of conception up to prep. school, when things got a bit better.

Quite involuntarily, I was shaking like a leaf, from head to foot, and had the sensation of being lightheaded – there was a also tremendous feeling of relief. He noticed.

"Oh look – you've gone all shaky!"

That was the understatement of the year. It was a weird sort of euphoria, which remained with me for the rest of the day.

A few visits later I was sitting in his waiting room, and feeling particularly well and positive. 'Not even Ma could spoil this,' I thought.

I went into his surgery, and the Vega machine went mad. It indicated that I was the sickest person alive. I could only be apologetic, and explained that my mother must have been around. Thomas knew – and said that if the reading had been right I would not have been alive!

I went for an annual routine check at the hospital, again feeling fine. A female doctor prodded me for a few seconds.

"You've got a lump in your lymph," she said abruptly and any further checks were ignored. "You'll have a mammogram in six weeks."

Being dismissed as a disaster area I returned to the state of terror. I telephoned Thomas who said he did not believe the cancer had returned, I was far too healthy. He said the lump was a build up of mess in the immune system. He sent me a homœopathic remedy, and it vanished. But the seed of doubt had been sown, and the next six weeks were a nightmare. Eventually a very disgruntled radiographer who was looking for something that was not there, accused me of checking myself... I was called back over and over again as the negatives were studied again and again. I did not relax until I had the final letter giving me the all clear. I was a fool not to have had absolute trust in Thomas, but at that stage I panicked all too easily.

Interestingly, my best friend Elizabeth appeared unconcerned when I told her about the lump, and afterwards explained, "I did not think your mother would give up that easily." Prophetic words indeed.

* * *

I was at a Buddhist festival, the highlight of which was to be an empowerment. This is a ceremony performed by the guru which, through prayer, brings about a closer bonding between those taking part and which ever Buddha has been chosen. This should have been one of the spiritual highlights of my life. On the eve of the event we went to bed with pieces of red wool tied around our left arms, and full of expectation.

I don't go to bed and sleep I go to bed and die. Movement is almost unheard of, but when I woke up the wool was down around my wrist. It had been tampered with. I knew who was responsible – I could feel my mother's extremely hostile and destructive presence bearing down on me.

As you can imagine, the festival was spoiled, and when I got home there was no let up. Instead I could sense my mother working to bring about a recurrence of the cancer. Symptoms which had been there first time around returned, but much exaggerated. I did not actually hear voices, but she was constantly implanting the thought in my brain: 'you are dying, you are going to die.'

What could I do? I thought if I approached anyone for help I would almost certainly be labelled schizophrenic. This would do no good. My mother would kill me – I had a horror of her somehow spiriting my soul away to some ghastly realm of evil – and she would still be free to harm other people. I could see that this was a spiritual problem, and it could therefore only be answered by a spiritual solution.

I was at a loss to know what to do but I did two things, I gathered together a photograph of her, a piece of embroidery she had done, and a gold watch my grandfather had given her for her twenty-first birthday, which she had worn for most of her life. I took them to Holy Communion services in an attempt to encourage her to stop trying to harm me, and move on. I also drew up a programme of prayers which I said morning and night. Luckily, I had inherited a good collection of books of prayers so I pendulumed these to see which would be 'right' and, predictably, they were weighted towards the mother and child theme, one was *A Woman's Plea Against Sterility*. But I was aware that I was losing the battle. My mother was stronger than I was.

The first symptom when I had breast cancer, but did not realise it, was that there was a slight discharge, looking rather like cotton wool, from my nipples. This had happened in adolescence, and I was amused to think that the hormones must be stirring once more... but then I found the lump and, like many women, knew instinctively that it was a nasty one.

While I could feel my mother's strength seeking to overpower me a discharge came from my nipples greater than ever before. Looking back, I now realise that it never occurred to me to seek ordinary medical help. I suppose I must have known innately that it would have no relevance. Physically I was at my lowest, and sinking fast.

But one night the phone rang. It was my psychic medical guru, Thomas. His awareness told him of my condition.

"You are not doing too well, are you?" he stated, and went on to tell me that he had found that I had lost all resistance to the cancer. However, I was comforted to hear from him, as he has great healing powers, and on that occasion he found that by using the energies of the Buddha Green Tara, and spinning a prayer wheel, he could raise my resistance from nothing to over ninety per cent.

I lived to fight another day – but still had no idea how I could set about sorting out my mother's troubled and hostile, positively murderous, spirit, and send it on its way. My prayer sessions continued but were, I could feel, completely inadequate. I also felt very, very alone. This was not something I could discuss with people. If I had done so, and made too much fuss in the wrong quarters, I might end up in a looney bin, before inevitably dying. Dying with the knowledge that my mother would be free to damage other people, too. I was terrified.

* * *

At least I knew one other person who would believe me and who, perhaps, could help. This was my psychic guru, Catherine. I contacted her, and soon received a phone call to say that I was right about my mother. She had a link with her, and the thing had been so ghastly that she had had to escape from the house and take 'it' into the garden.

Catherine could not come up with a remedy to sort out my mother, but she did have advice for me to try to improve my health. She recommended that I go to Burrswood, a house of healing in Kent. My immediate feeling was one of scepticism, but she was quite definite, so I decided to go.

On arrival I went to the bookshop, which appeared a good way to find out about the place. There, a very pleasant lady volunteer chatted to me. "Why was I there? And how had I heard about Burrswood?" she asked. I thought for a moment, before briefly recounting the details of the attack. If I was expecting her to cross herself and fly from the room I was disappointed! But if I wanted help, then I had come to the right place. Her response was magnificent.

"Oh my goodness, you can't deal with that on your own!" She then walked across the shop, saying that they had a little book which I definitely needed, and which was in great demand at that time. It was the *The Armour of God* and it gave a number of prayers of protection. I bought a copy and from then on, for many, many months, recited the whole lot morning and night.

The lady also made a few enquiries and said that one of the priests would talk to me. I did not take up her offer, which perhaps I should have done but the book was ideal, and I shall always be grateful to her. According to Catherine I have a 'thing' with Burrswood, and I believe it. One morning I woke up and saw, like a banner across the bedroom, the name 'Dorothy Kerin' – the founder of Burrswood.

The trip to Burrswood had been a very great help, and on my return I contacted Catherine to thank her. She was elderly, and lived about forty miles away, so I suggested that I could drive to see her and take her out for lunch. She was amazed that I wished to thank her, and insisted that we have lunch at her home. It would be easier to talk there. Timothy and I therefore found ourselves seated round her table, having a really delicious vegetarian lunch.

At one point I was telling her that, although I knew my mother had hated me, it was still a shock to know that her antipathy had remained so obdurate. There had been two occasions previously when members of our family had been visited by those who had passed on, but these experiences had been motivated by love, and a desire to help. I was about to tell her how my father had once appeared to me to give me some comfort, and help a dear friend of mine who was dying horribly, when I suddenly changed tack. I told Catherine how my grandfather, Thomas Cordingley, had appeared to his oldest daughter to tell her that she must not try to save her mother, my grandfather's widow, as 'I am ready for her now.' When my grandmother died her daughter was able to tell the rest of the family about her father's visit, which was very comforting.

As I recounted this, Timothy exclaimed, "He's here. I can see him... Mr. Cordingley!" My grandfather was floating above my head. As he manifested I, who did not see him, felt a sensation like a little electrical charge taking place in my brain. I have felt this often since, when 'talking' to those whose bodies have died, but whose capacity for communication is still very much alive.

Back home I produced photographs of my grandfather, who died years before I was born, and Timothy confirmed this was the man he had seen, although he had manifested in a younger form. I reasoned that, possibly, my grandfather wished to be involved, and help. This proved to be the correct. For many weeks, I was able to talk freely and fully with members of the family, my grand-parents and aunts, who all set about trying to help both me and my mother.

It is difficult to describe what I felt, how I knew what was happening. The only easy bit is to express the absolute terror. Imagine that you are a little tune being played on a violin. There is nothing wonderful about the tune, but it is harmless, and reasonably pleasant. Then there starts up the large, discordant sound of a heavy orchestra with masses of percussion, brass, and every other instrument being hit, blown, or bowed as loudly as possible. They are not trying to play together, but to drown each other out. Through it all you try to hang onto your little tune.

* * *

Then fate intervened. I met a lady at the local Buddhist Centre who was a Roman Catholic, but who had worked in the field of trying to sort out disturbed psychic phenomena. I could tell her about my problem. She said that I lived in the right place. A man who was probably the most gifted person in the country in this field – the Church of England's chief exorcist – was our local vicar. I did not know him, but I lost no time in writing to him.

In addition to having to cope with the immediate danger, I was shocked that my mother, who had never liked me, had managed to sustain such an enormous hatred of me for so long. I can honestly say I am not vindictive nor do I bear grudges. I try to take the view that what is past is past. Once my mother had died I had put bad memories behind me, but now I felt I must dredge them up, and explain the history to the vicar to convince him. I spoke the truth or I would be dead, and my mother's disturbed soul would still be on the loose.

* * *

I had suffered from every childhood illness possible and now see that my home life was probably partly responsible. When I was two, I had whooping cough but my mother did not consult the doctor until I was almost better. When my father discovered I had been ill, he was angry. This was out of character, and made a deep impression on me.

The next year I had what the doctor, who could find no fluid in my lung, called borderline pneumonia. I coughed with each breath I took. I was prescribed the then fashionable drug 'M and B'. One night I wanted hot milk and while my mother tried to quieten me, my father went to get it. However hot it was in reality, it felt cold to me. My mother urged him to make the drink hotter, but there was near panic in his voice as he said that if it was any hotter the bubbles would still be on it – it was boiling. No doubt the drugs were having side effects. He was very distressed at my suffering.

Apart from the sexual abuse my mother was also a great believer in corporal punishment. Daily, I would be dragged into the hall, so she could enjoy herself smacking my bottom, and any pretext would do. By contrast my father smacked me only once, the lightest of light taps on one hand after I disobeyed him by touching a piece of his students' work, which he had brought home. He had told me not to touch it, and that if I touched it again he would smack me. I did not believe him, touched it again, and his hand gently hit mine. I was distraught, and went running to my mother.

* * *

I think one of the problems with their marriage was that my mother, the youngest and definitely the most spoilt and indulged of three sisters, could not cope with being married to a man whose work as headmaster of an art school was the most important thing in his life and also kept him from home for long hours. As well as starting at 9.00 a.m., evening classes did not finish until 9.00 p.m. I used to go home for lunch when I was at preparatory school; I later learnt that that was because we would otherwise only have seen each other at weekends. My mother did not work and I was her responsibility.

As a small child I was told that babies were born because of love, a theory that puzzled me considerably. Then I discovered that some were born because of 'accidents'. My parents had been married for seven years before I arrived. It appeared to me that they must have got complacent, having got away with it for so long, and been careless with the contraceptives they were using, and I was the result. No wonder she resented me! I suddenly saw her as positively human.

But when she told me I had been the result of fertility treatment I was completely traumatized. They had consulted specialist Austrian Jewish refugee doctors in London, and been subjected to various treatments. How had it all gone so horribly wrong? What was it about me that made me so unlovable? I felt great guilt at the failed relationship.

While my mother was pregnant her size increased not at all, although I weighed 7lbs at birth. The first two toes on each foot were crossed over each other because I had been packed so tightly but they straightened out when I learned to walk.

Her jealousy of me manifested itself both in hatred, and in her wishing to deny me things. She also did everything in her power to suppress any sign of femininity in me. As a little girl I was put into boy's swimming trunks and when I particularly wanted a pretty pink dressing gown, she insisted that I have one in a dark and ugly colour.

I got on well with a neighbour's little boy and we played together happily. No doubt envious over his sex she constantly made vindictive remarks about him but it did not spoil our relationship, and we had our early Freudian experiences together!

* * *

Once, when I was older, we were on a bus and there was a screaming child among the passengers. I was told I behaved like that twice. On the first occasion, my mother removed me from a bus and made to walk the last two miles home – a long way for one so young.

The second time took place when we were on our way to stay with relatives. Our car had broken down and we were travelling by train. My parents put my little tricycle, they were made of metal in those days, on the luggage rack which in that era was mounted above the seats, but the tricycle was insecure, and fell down onto my head. I screamed, out of shock as much as the pain, and made a scene. My mother told me that I made a terrible noise but that the other member of the compartment, a man in R.A.F. uniform, was very nice about it. Apparently he was quite concerned for me, a response beyond my mother's comprehension.

* * *

Just before my tenth birthday I was the third child in the school to get toxic jaundice, apparently introduced by a doctor's daughter. Just as I was supposed to have recovered from this, I started being sick again. Jaundice can recur, but I was not yellow, and appendicitis was diagnosed. Our family doctor loved children, and still held in his memory the pathetic picture of myself as a little waif alone in a private ward having her tonsils and adenoids out. He hated the idea of me having to go to hospital again, and postponed the event – with dire consequences. The last night I was at home I was being sick continuously and when the following evening the operation took place it was discovered that peritonitis had set in. I was very, very ill indeed.

Don't ever believe that sick children do not know how sick they are. I remember thinking quite coolly that if someone told me I was about to die I would believe them and also not mind in the slightest.

I recovered, but never felt quite the same again. Tonsils, adenoids and the appendix, are all lymph tissue. With these gone, much of my immune system was lost.

I had had time off school because of this illness, and this was the run-up to the old Eleven Plus exam. Early one morning I heard my mother crying. She was telling my father that she was afraid I would fail the exam. I knew that if I did not pass the exam, she would be far more upset than if I had died. I was seen as a great inconvenience.

When I was at preparatory school she interfered hugely. I had to be the star of every drama production, come very high up in the class, and win medals at sports day. Actually,

I produced the goods rather well, especially considering that I am sure all this was not natural to me, though at the time I was persuaded that it was.

When I went to public school she lost her grasp. It was out of town and, like most women at that time, she did not drive. On the whole I did sufficiently well, but when I was in the sixth form I had a really rough ride. I was not naturally academic, my father had just had a very severe stroke, and the deputy head who was also the senior English teacher made my life a complete hell. In every class she had one or two 'hates' that she would plague and mock, and in our reduced A level class I was the sole butt of her nastiness.

In those days standards were high, B grades were excellent, and Cs very respectable. It was confidently expected that I would fail the lot, but I managed to pass in all three subjects. I remember sitting down in the examination hall with no expectation of passing, but thinking that at least the examiners would not have a down on me.

My mother opened the envelope with the results while I was in the garden, and she came out and gave me a great lesbian hug. I had justified myself and she could now be unpleasant to the parents of the students who had failed – there were plenty – and I found myself wondering, 'Was it worth it?' My revulsion was enormous.

My friend Tamsin was very academic and went on to get a first class degree – a rare thing in those days – so my mother had ample opportunity for more nastiness and jealousy.

* * *

My first job, taken a couple of months after the A level results came out, was almost two hundred miles away. I went into digs, my father driving me there, while my mother stayed at home. We grabbed the first place we saw, which provided bed and breakfast for summer visitors and which was empty during the winter. The people were kind, but the room was just big enough to take a double bed and not much else.

I returned home for a holiday and invited Tamsin round for the evening. I had brought an old car and, as she did not have one, I was going to drive her home. When we had eaten, we relaxed and talked about a wide range of subjects, just as we used to. Quite early on my mother appeared in a dressing gown, demanding that the girl leave, as she 'couldn't help worrying', whether I would get back home safely. Stunned into silence, we reluctantly obeyed.

When I got home I flipped, telling my mother that, 'I could have been living in a brothel for all that you knew or cared – which was quite true. My humiliation was enormous.

I remembered how my mother tried to turn my father against me. She claimed I had taken a pair of scissors from her workbox but I had never stolen anything in my life. When her silver napkin ring changed shape, it must have got squashed as the drawer was closed, I was blamed again. Not, of course, to my face so I could defend myself. I just overheard her telling my father of my alleged wrong doings.

Her arthritis was also my fault, I had given her a hot water bottle which leaked. I remember her telling someone that arthritis was not always genetic, so I would not have to feel I would get it automatically, but I could feel she was wishing it onto me. The friend sounded horrified!

Although at a conscious level I spent my childhood thinking that things were more-or-less ordinary in the mother-daughter relationship, I remember fantasising that my parents were killed, and I was adopted by Tamsin's parents. I knew her mother, who was like a lioness with her cubs, would never love me, but I still felt I would be better off with them than I was at home. By this time I was in my early teens, and my father and I had become estranged.

Looking back I saw little glimpses of how things might have been. Once, at a children's party when I was, possibly, about eight, I had a bad cough. My little hostess's mother took me to one side and gave me a jelly sweet, to try to soothe my throat. I remember feeling her kindness towards me, and a sort of surprise that anyone could be so caring.

In imagination I pretended that my mother had died and my father presented me with a bright, happy, vivacious stepmother, the sort of person with whom one could have fun. In short, I imagined what it would be like to live with a woman who was the antithesis of my mother. I even imagined that this lovely lady would encourage me, and see me as someone who could become attractive.

An unmarried great aunt died, and left me £30. My mother told me that the money would be in trust for me until I was eighteen. So when I was eighteen I asked for it. It transpired that my mother had been sent a cheque which she had cashed and used herself. At preparatory school we had all been expected to buy National Savings Stamps – these savings had gone the same way. I went to school feeling traumatised and unclean. For the first nine months of my existence I had been in the womb of a woman prepared to steal from a child. I gazed round the other girls at morning prayers, the nice, wellgroomed offspring of doctors and solicitors, and felt a complete alien. Their mothers would have been incapable of such an action.

My feeling of guilt and dirtiness lasted for quite some time. Then I reasoned myself out of that state of mind by realising that the fact I was so shocked, indicated that I was not like my mother. Had I been like her I would have seen myself, through her eyes, as fair game.

I never had the money as such, but when I bought my first car my father replaced the most rusty of its wings. It cost £30 and that was his way of giving me what I was owed without his admitting my mother had been wrong.

But while she hated me, there was a weird ambivalence. She saw me as her property. After she died I discovered she kept my milk teeth and carried them round with her in her bag, along with my medical card. Three years before she died she got septicaemia, and was not expected to live. I was told late one night, and travelled to see her the following day. Apparently she had kept the whole ward awake screaming, 'I want my Alison.'

I was on a coach, on the way to visit her, when she died. Suddenly, as we drove along the motorway, there was a bang and smoke started coming up into the coach from some part of the engine or transmission. The poor driver had a nasty scare, quickly stopping on the hard shoulder, and applying the fire extinguisher. There was no real emergency, however, and a relief coach picked us up quickly.

So far as I could calculate it, this incident took place at the same time that my mother died. When I returned to work I remember telling people, who knew we had not got on, that my mother's last act was to try to bump me off! I realised that such a comment should not have been made so lightly.

So, having dredged up ghastly memories, I wrote to the man who was to become another of my gurus, Julian, the Church of England's chief exorcist, trying to convince him that my mother's spirit was trying to kill me, and that there had been a history leading towards this outcome. Even I had difficulty in seeing how my experiences with her could result in quite so much destructive hatred.

* * *

As I sat alone at the typewriter I felt my mother was with me. In her lifetime she had had a certain way of sulking if she did not get her own way. I could feel her opposing this attempt to write about my experiences. To record them was both cathartic and an attempt to survive.

People who had known her when she was young said she was pretty – she had long dark hair and a prominent nose, but as she aged I was really only conscious of what I saw as her ugly expressions.

Julian was wonderful. He believed me. He explained that

there was clearly a strong psychic link between myself and my mother, and that this link was energized by the thoughts I had of her evil intentions and unkind acts, and it must be broken. He asked to borrow something which had a strong connection with her, like a photograph. I still had the package containing the watch, a piece of embroidery, and the photograph which I had taken to the Communion Services I had attended.

Rather than just drop these in to the vicarage I took them along to a service. While they were next to me on the pew I could feel some pretty ghastly vibes coming off them.

Julian took the items, and I watched his face. I fancied that he did feel something and if he did, then my allegations were sure to be vindicated. "We have someone who can tell how we are doing by the feelings that come off them," he said. The relief that I was going to be helped was enormous, but I did feel a bit anxious about the time scale. I felt the matter needed to be dealt with urgently.

Just after this Timothy and I went away for a week in Wales. Towards the end of the two hundred and eighty mile journey we left the main roads, and took to country lanes, which were all very familiar to me. As I drove along I noticed for the first and only time that the 'Give Way' signs at the junctions of the even more minor roads which joined us could be read from my road, because of the angle at which they had been placed. Mesmerized by this, I ignored a 'Stop' sign which did apply to me, and had to stand on the brakes as never before when I realised my mistake. Some poor motorist had a nasty shock, but luckily we avoided a collision.

I was shaken, I do not usually do this sort of thing. Later wondering... I dowsed, and was told that my mother had set-up the situation. I was also told that I had been protected by a particular Buddhist prayer which I said daily.

Afterwards, I remembered the contrast in my parents attitude when I had learned to drive, and bought my first car. My father had confidence in me, his only reservation being that I tended to exceed the speed limit, while my mother sneered and poked fun at me, implying that I might well not make it to where I was going. I can say with honesty that I was a good driver when young, with many boyfriends feeling that my judgement and reactions were excellent.

Each day, while away, I carried out a programme of prayers morning and night, to try to help my mother and protect myself. Husband Timothy fully understood and accepted the situation – members of his family are psychic and, of course, he had seen my grandfather floating above me.

Towards the end of my time away I had a feeling that things had changed. I dowsed, asking if my mother's power to do me serious damage had been reduced. Previously the answer had always been 'No', but suddenly the reply was 'Yes'. However, I was told she could still make harmful mischief. This state persisted for a few days. Then again in answer to questioning, my guides told me that while my mother still wished to harm me, she was no longer able to.

We came home, and Timothy went down with bronchitis. However, one evening he got out of his sick-bed to tell me he had a message he must give to me. It was, "Your mother will not be troubling you again. She has found the Grace of God." This sounded too glib by half, but when I pendulumed I was told that this was true... in fact she had forgotten that I had ever existed. The psychic link had, indeed, been broken.

* * *

I asked Julian if I could see him for a few minutes when I collected my mother's possessions that I had lent him. I wondered how the link had been broken. He would not tell me this, but instead he offered, as a sort of part explanation of how the healing had taken place, a reference to the Communion service in which there are the words, 'Do this in remembrance of Me.' His opinion was that the word 'remembrance' was inaccurate as there is no equivalent to give a true interpretation. It did not mean to re-enact, but in the present sense, which is why Roman Catholics believe in the actual 'body and blood'.

He added that in the expression, 'In my Father's house are many mansions...' mansions is also wrong because the English language has no suitable word. The true meaning covered all the different kinds of rooms and lodging places used by all different sorts of people on their way to make a pilgrimage. The emphasis needed to be on the diversity of these places, from the squalid to the grand.

* * *

Both before and after the events that allowed my mother's soul to rest in peace, I had many conversations with dead members of the family. I discovered much about their thoughts and feelings. I was also able to remedy many misunderstandings. I had much to apologize for, but found that those on the other side fully understood and were not judgemental. I learned that when I was a child, although they were always loyal to my mother, they had been, in fact, extremely concerned about my welfare.

Neither of my parents wanted a child but they succumbed to pressure applied by my father's family who wanted my parents to produce an heir. Conception was difficult but thanks to a programme of fertility treatment, I was conceived. When I arrived, I was definitely second best. I remembered my mother telling me that when I was born my paternal grandmother had said, "Never mind, perhaps it will be a boy next time." My mother had retorted that she was very satisfied with her little girl. She wasn't, but her response was more than understandable! My mother's family, apparently, were all set to welcome *any* baby, but there was never any pressure to procreate from that quarter.

Once I arrived my mother spent all her time keeping me from my father's family. They scarcely knew me. When my mother and I visited them, a few times a year, it was just for lunch, so our time with them was always brief. If I made any favourable comments about the meal my mother immediately slapped me down. Once my grandfather had died, and before my grandmother got too old to travel, my grandmother and aunt used to come to us for Christmas. My mother resented this but for me they were a welcome diversion.

I remember one period when I suffered a painful earache. My tonsils and adenoids were diseased because, I think, of my father's continuous pipesmoking habit. My grand-mother nursed me and I found her lap a wonderfully comfortable place, not a bit like my mother's. Looking back, I think it was just a case of her having normal maternal instincts, and compassion. She might have preferred boys to girls but she was a wonderful, encouraging, and unselfish mother to my aunt. My mother's family, my grandmother and two single aunts who lived together, spoilt me rotten. I was no different to other children, for I loved the goodies they gave me but I admit that I was not as lovingly disposed to them as I should have been. Later, I was able to apologize about this, which felt good. Little had I known how anxious they really were about my mother's behaviour towards me, and how they were keen to make me feel that they cared about me.

Although my father had not wanted a child, it was love at first sight in the private maternity home where I was born. My mother recalled how, with amazement, he told her, "She's the pick of the nursery!" I don't suppose I was for one moment, but I have since heard that such a response is the result of normal bonding. Once I asked the spirits for my mother's reaction; but could get no answer except that she had wished me evil throughout my life.

The fact that my father loved me aroused more hatred and jealousy in my mother. The youngest of three sisters, she wanted to stay the spoilt baby of the family forever, and have no competition. I never loved my mother, which is really not challenge even if the results are questionable.

My figure was female, bent, with the knees almost together and the feet splayed apart in a slightly crouching and uncomfortable 'in-movement' position. The arms were in a strained and stiff attitude which I associated with people suffering from extreme cases of cerebral palsy. There was a large, witchlike nose and chin. The mouth was open as though issuing a curse uttered in fear and hatred. The breasts, flung into different directions by the body's movement, showed how ill at ease the figure would be if confronted with the role of suckler.

The sculpture had succeeded, anguish was indeed portrayed. Then I realised that I had captured all too accurately what had been my mother's inner consciousness in the twisted and rebarbative figure. With this recognition came the knowledge that I must get rid of the thing. I wrapped it up thoroughly, and the dustmen took it away.

I have little idea how aware my mother was of her own state. But I do remember her once saying that she liked the music of Wagner because, "It's the violence in my nature." When she uttered this comment, she had such a sparkle in her eyes that it left a lasting impression.

So all was well? My mother was healed, and I was rescued, but, as one hears so often in cases where someone was abused as a child, all could not be resolved so neatly. One major problem was that my mother had done her best to bring me up with her set of values. She was a snob, and she would crawl round anyone with money. She gloried in and sneered at the misfortunes of others, and relished their failure. I did the same, often, though I did reject some of her tendencies. I did not value money as she did, but felt humiliated that we did not have as much money as some of my peer group. I was a confused, messed up child.

In fairness, I believe I have made a huge effort to sort myself out and become a less ghastly person. I can credit myself with quite a bit of improvement. However, sometime after my mother had gone for good, I was aware that my progress was pathetic. I needed to dig myself out of the pit in which I found myself as I knew I was not doing well on my own.

* * *

I was booked to go to another Buddhist festival where our Guru – my Guru – would be one of the teachers. I knew that while I could certainly not ask to see him personally, I might be able to get close enough to him as he came in to give his teaching, and that might give me the opportunity. I felt like the woman who touched the hem of Jesus's robe... I felt something must happen. Actually, I was wrong in assuming I could not see him on a personal basis; he does not make himself exclusive and is often available to his followers, but I was one of well over a thousand people present.

My plan worked. I sat at the end of a row, and as he came by me our eyes met. I was momentarily paralysed. My eyes filled with tears. In a split second and with absolute love he had read my soul, and silently gave me a message which was, 'Suffering and guilt'. This, then, was the state of my mind that was blocking my progress.

This insight led me to go to confession. I made an appointment and went before Julian who, I knew, must know hugely intimate things about my life. It is the greatest tribute to him when I say that I was happy to trust him with them. I told him how I lost my virginity to a married man. How, like my mother, I had revelled in getting one up on others, enjoyed seeing them suffer or being humiliated... It sounded terrible, but I expect it would have been just about impossible to shock or surprise him. I told him about my failed marriage and my negative feelings towards my husband, too. After confession things happened.

For a day or two I felt totally exhausted, but it was a very pleasant form of exhaustion. I wondered if it meant my body was packing up, and I would die. Possibly the tension of staying alive to try to make reparations for the person I was, had been released, and I would just sink... if this was to be the case, I could face death with more equanimity than before. But my physical and spiritual health improved and a perceptive friend Isabel later noticed that I was a 'different' person.

I asked my guides where my relationship with my father stood in all this. He had been a wonderful father when I was a child, he genuinely loved me, but he lost interest and became almost hostile as I grew older. He died when I was twenty-four. I was told that my relationship with him played no part in my 'suffering and guilt' syndrome.

A Christian Scientist spirit told me that I should be optimistic about my health and there was no need for me to go on receiving punishment. It was pointed out that my two years of really good health had been at the start of my marriage, when I believed myself to be loveable. However, in fact, I had not been loved as I imagined, so it was not the fact of being loved which proved the controlling factor, but my perception, even though it was erroneous. In other words, the controlling factor was my mind.

My Christian Scientist told me that if one really accepted the love of Christ one could remain healthy no matter what people thought of one, or how they treated one. People have become sicker as they have become less aware of the love of God. With the love of God anything is possible.

Buddhists are masters of accepting that one's perception is the only true reality for oneself. I should have been able to sort myself out completely, but somehow I don't even try. Is it laziness? Self punishment? or the fact that I can cope, after a fashion, with the way things are? I do not know. But I would advise other people to do as I say, not as I do, because I would like other people to succeed where I have failed.

* * *

Looking back I am still mindblown by my 'mother episode'. After all, with all the problems, my mother did, nonetheless, produce me, and feed and clothe me. She was an excellent cook, and she did a lot of good home baking on behalf of her family. She used to make me clothing, too, summer dresses and shorts. Like the other children I had birthday parties, and the abuse ended before I went to school. Had she been that much worse than many other mothers? Why, on dying, could she not decide to move on, but opt to let mortal hatred continue as an obsession? The family had believed they had raised her as a Christian. We all have faults, but they were certainly not bad people. And, as a child, she was loved and spoilt rotten. She believed herself to be very special.

There may have been one clue. When, three years before her death, my mother was expecting to die, and was drifting in and out of consciousness, she said to me, "There is nothing there." She thought death meant annihilation. I knew that she wished to deprive me of my belief in God and the afterlife, so I just said nothing: there was nothing I could say.

Years later I heard that my mother had once considered becoming a Roman Catholic. Her mother and sisters had been Presbyterian, which later became the United Reformed Church, but she was sent to a convent. This had always struck me as a strange choice, since even the middle-of-the-road Church of England was too 'high' for the rest of her family. Ideas she got fed at school must have presented a conflict. I was always told that she had been a bright pupil, and a cousin of hers once said that the school had wanted their star pupil to become a convert. But I never heard a word of this from my mother, who always focused, critically, on the Catholics being a superstitious lot.

On the rare occasions that my parents went to church it was to the Anglican Parish Church, but I could feel my mother's disapproval of it. I was always a solid member of the Church of England. My father's family had been active church people for many generations and were nicer people, I decided. My mother's family came home from church discussing the hats people had been wearing – a trip to church meant dressing up – and gossiping. Even at the age of eight I knew this was not what one's religion should be about. And when I went to a church school, the dye was cast. She would have resented this. However, the whole ghastly experience was now behind me. Life should now settle down, I decided, and my psychic activities would be a thing of the past. They had served their purpose.

* * *

How wrong can you be? For about three weeks our old cat, Norman, focused on Something just above my right shoulder every time he got on my lap. What I was unaware of, he was clearly able to see, or at least perceive. If there really was something there, a discarnate spirit wishing to made contact with me, I should perhaps make myself available... and so I started talking to Mr. Skinner, the first of my 'Spiritual Family and Spiritual Friends.' I gradually found myself surrounded by wonderful loving and caring people. People to whom I felt very close.

My Spiritual Family and Spriritual Friends

A list and descriptions of the spirit people who have given me the information for this book

Until forced into psychic matters by the need to have my mother's disturbed soul 'delivered', to use the Church of England's terminology, I had believed that it was very wrong to have contact with the spirit world. I knew that once people had died their souls had other places to go to, and other things to do. I still hold to this view. But sometimes the spirits of those who have died want to get in touch with us, and then it may well be equally wrong and unhelpful to deny them contact. This part of my book lists and describes my spiritual family and friends with whom I came into contact.

– *Mr Skinner* –

Mr Skinner had been a relative of, and roughly the same generation as, my great grandfather. His life in that incarnation had been an unhappy one. By nature he was quiet and restrained, destined not to be very ambitious or successful. His wife was probably brighter than he was, she certainly thought she was, and she made her dissatisfaction with him very plain, completely destroying what little self confidence he had had.

I was given a precise picture of Mr Skinner, and could even see a slight family likeness to my great grandfather. He was slightly plump, my grandfather was more muscular and stocky rather than carrying fat, with a face shaped between round and oval, and slightly wavy lightish brown hair cut fairly short. His clothes were typical of his era, about 1850 give or take 20 years.

Mr Skinner was very reticent. I never knew his Christian name. As I have mentioned in the section on reincarnation we both worked to try to help a middle-aged lady with mental health problems and, understandably, a less-than-wonderful marriage. Mr Skinner did brilliantly. His level of success did much to restore his self esteem, and he has since reincarnated in Africa as a black baby who will be materially successful and spiritually a wonderful example to all races of patience, honesty, and justice.

– *Betty* –

Also mentioned in the section on reincarnation, and one of the most wonderful, closest, and greatly valued members of my spiritual family was Betty. When I first became aware of her presence my response was completely offbeam. I was sent a picture of her as a dull church-going female, a little shorter than average, slightly plump, with a pleasant but character-less face. Her features were regular, her eyes blue, and her short, graying hair mostly obscured by a neat but nondescript hat. Her wardrobe consisted of dowdy skirts and blouses. Never would she wear trousers or anything bright and jolly.

Why, I puzzled, should I be involved with someone like this, exactly the sort of person with whom I would find it almost impossible to empathise. But how wrong I could be? Appearances are deceptive, and beneath this boring exterior was someone truly remarkable.

Knowing, no doubt, that we were going to have a lot to do with each other, and understanding my difficulty, Betty arranged to come to me one night in what I can best describe as a dream-vision. She put her face close to mine, and I saw tremendous humour and a really strong personality which would be able to respond to any challenge. She exuded joy and was stifling an amused smile.

Betty, it transpired, had been my mother in what had probably been my happiest incarnation, while I was married to Anthony, and living in Ireland. I had been less than a wonderful daughter, taking her for granted and being selfish, but her love for me never wavered. There remains a great and deep love for each other at a profound level, for, though I had failings in our previous incarnation together, I was not really bad, and did care for my then mother in my own way, deficient though it was.

One night the bedroom curtains were disturbed, with one opening twice, after I had closed it. The culprit turned out to be an anonymous male, who was a friend of Betty's. I gathered that she had a rather soft spot for him. He would not tell me his name, he did not want to be prayed for, and the advice he gave me was rather cheeky... and I did not follow it! But the fact Betty approved of him showed me another aspect to her character. I told this visitor that I would refer to him as 'The Joker in the pack', and he was satisfied with that.

– *David* –

When I first saw David he was a striking young man, full of energy, with very dark, wavy hair. He had been a healer while he lived, and had continued this work since his death. I once saw him in a second image from the same incarnation. He was possibly of retirement age, not old, but greatly weakened through illness. His hair was thin and grey, and he moved with caution aware of his own frailty which I think was caused by a heart condition.

I had been very privileged to have had contact with David in two of our previous incarnations as he has always been far more advanced, spiritually, than I have been. He showed great spiritual strength and healing abilities.

I have to admit that sometimes the temptation to try to contact valued friends in the next world does get too much for me. On 22 June 2000, after I had had difficulty tracking him down I was told that David was attached to an embryo of between two and three months, but was still able to travel about. In his future life's blueprint he would probably become a teacher, possibly in Manchester, and would face a tough situation. He would definitely be born in England.

Later on I was told that although David was now a baby he could visit me while he slept. This was at a sub or unconscious level. Not everyone can do this, I was told. There had to be a strong desire to link up with members of a spiritual family. I had always understood he was an advanced being. After Mr Skinner, Betty, and David, came Leopold.

– *Leopold* –

While the others had been Christians and Protestants, Leopold was Jewish. He was to be visualized as slim and finely featured, with wavy, neat grey hair. He had been through the terrible refugee experience like so many of his race, and had been classed as a displaced person or, in legal terms, 'Nationality Doubtful'.

He still had the aura of one who had had an unhappy life. With his awareness of great suffering and an excellent brain his contribution had to be unique.

Over the years Leopold has visited me infrequently. However, his absence enabled me to see, all the more clearly, when he did reappear, the tremendous change in the man. He had become wonderfully happy and optimistic. His face was stronger and he was robust, much more confident, and exuded a very strong motivation. Apparently he had linked up with a different incarnation, in which he was much happier. He had also been working as a healer and had had excellent results, which had made him extremely joyful.

Later on I did Leopold a great disservice, I am ashamed to say. We had heard about a medium healer who worked with a spirit who had been a Rabbi. After meeting the medium, and seeing him in action, I was doubtful whether he was genuine. I had the opportunity of subjecting myself to his attentions, but was unsure whether to go to his surgery, or not.

In general terms I asked for advice, and Leopold appeared. We had not been in touch for ages. but he said that I should be treated by the medium, and so I went. I felt I had had help, though I was still suspicious because of the money paid relative to the time spent with each patient. However, another advisor felt that I had not been wise to get involved, and that while one aspect of my health had benefited another, and one more serious, had not. I was disposed to believe the advisor, and thought Leopold might have been wrong. However, still unsure I consulted my psychic Guru, Catherine, and she found that both the medium and the spirit Rabbi were good, genuine, and positive.

I voiced many apologies to poor Leopold and just hope that if he heard himself being doubted he also heard my regret at questioning his judgement and very kind advice.

Perhaps not surprisingly Leopold appeared slightly younger during his visits after he had linked into his happier incarnation. When he was depressed he appeared to be, possibly, in his sixties or early seventies, but he lost this semblance of age, and became about forty-five. His hair, which had been greying but thin, became white but beautifully healthy and wavy.

Apparently Leopold healed in his own way, he taught people and enabled them to take control of their own health, and heal themselves, by assisting them to progress spiritually. He worked with individuals, and not groups, thus positively influencing the lives of those on earth today.

From time to time I have had conflicting messages about whether or not Leopold wanted to reincarnate. On one occasion he wanted to reincarnate to teach, spiritually, at a grass roots level, perhaps as a school teacher, but on another occasion I heard that he was very busy, and content to be, between lives. Early on he was in a healing process, recovering from the traumas he had experienced by being Jewish.

Once I had the message that he was involved in helping a lovely girl that I had met at a Buddhist festival. Our beds had been side by side in the marquee where we slept. She had an inherited wasting disease and had already outlived the doctors gloomy predictions by many years. She was very special – a good, brave, and delightful person.

A couple of weeks after I got this message, when I was feeling particularly low, I received a card from her. She had got a job abroad and was about to leave the country. She wondered if I remembered her...

– Patrick –

Patrick was a whispy-bearded, midgreying haired student-type who had run into middle age. His style of dress was soft grey woollies and sandals. Gentle and compassionate, he was the sort of man who would be heavily into opposing insecticides, and in favour of recycling. He would be incapable of joining the rat race, and was so unforceful in personality that if one entered a room where he was sitting one would possibly be unaware of his presence.

I was told that there was a possibility that Patrick might reincarnate, and be born to someone I would meet in the future.

– Sarah –

Sarah had a joyful presence. She had been a selfless, warm, and very giving wife and mother, gunning for her children with boundless enthusiasm. She had not received the gratitude she deserved from her family, but did not let the careless way they treated her deflect her from giving them all the love and care that she could.

She was a little above average in height with straight dark

shoulder-length hair which tended to get greasy rather quickly, and a wonderful open, happy, welcoming face. She paid little attention to the clothes she wore, she was far too busy trying to help everyone she knew get what was best for them and she radiated true warmth.

We have had little contact over the years, but she was happy for me to describe her as a member of my spiritual family. For a time I attempted absent healing by reading a collection of prayers. If she was with me she liked me to hear them spoken out loud, not read silently.

– Louie –

Great Auntie Louie, mentioned in the section on reincarnation, came next, and I learned of the help she had given me in trying to protect me from my mother. With her arrival I could not resist looking through old family photos. There she was, a widow, with my grandfather, her brother-in-law, elderly and with a jolly smile. The picture of her as a posed and better looking younger woman was far less attractive to me.

– Anthony –

Not long after her arrival I was reunited with my beloved Anthony, also described in the section on reincarnation.

– Ellen –

One night I linked up with a new friend, who said I was to visualize her during her life spent as Ellen, though this was not her most recent incarnation. I was guided to see her as a lively and well-preserved sixty-year old with fairish, wavy, fairly short hair, and a round/square as opposed to long oval face.

She was pleasant, kind, and thoughtful, with a good sense of humour. Not a family person, she had been the unmarried daughter who cared for her parents, her role had been everyone's favourite aunty by adoption. She had died, aged sixty-nine, of pneumonia, but was to he visualized at sixty as this had been the time during her life when she had been most fulfilled. This incarnation had been spent in England, and she had a deep love for the country.

Ellen had had a more recent life as a German/American woman, Ingrid. She had lived in Boston so that she could learn about Christian Science, and help others by using its principals but this life had not been happy, and she had always felt a foreigner in a strange land. She had died, aged sixty-four, twelve years before Ellen contacted me, which was in 1998. There had also been a twelve year gap between her incarnations as Ellen and Ingrid. She said she would help me with my health problems, particularly with my defective immune system.

Her presence is beautiful, and I was very happy when, one night, she came to me to say specifically that I could regard her as one of my spiritual family and friends, rather than just a passing visitor.

– *Ivor* –

A new man, Ivor, visited one night. I learned that he had been born in 1935 and had died, aged sixty, of a brain haemorrhage. This was about two and a half years before he contacted me, in March 1998. He told me his father had been in a reserved occupation during the war.

– *Eliza* –

Another visitor was Eliza. She was small, slight, and had fair to sandy coloured hair. Her features were quite sharp, and she was strong. Eliza told me that four lifetimes ago she had been a gardener. I discovered this one night when I was guided in the choice of healing remedies, and was aware that her knowledge of these matters was considerable. It now manifested as a deep instinct, an inner knowledge of the properties of plants.

Eliza had died in 1974, aged 71, of pneumonia. She said she had been a Christian Scientist in her last life. Christian Scientists believe that we are all made in the image of God and are perfect. Only a wrong perception (which they call 'mortal mind' as opposed to the correct 'Divine mind') or a belief in sin, which also has no real existence, can cause perceived illness. They avoid doctors etc. and often heal themselves, or seek the help of Christian Science practitioners who apply an awareness of their correct and whole state to them, and thus bring about a cure.

Eliza said that she had cured her illnesses by Christian Science methods throughout her life, but that the fatal pneumonia had been her response to unhappiness.

– *Mervyn* –

Another Christian Scientist visitor was Mervyn. He said he had been a relative of Mr Skinner's but had had a much more recent incarnation, living in the twentieth century. He appeared as a young man, but was eighty-eight when he died. He had been the manager of a retail store somewhere in North America. He regretted not taking his religion more seriously during his life, and was now trying to help people reach their own spiritual potential.

Mervyn also said he had been a cousin of Patrick's, two incarnations back. Over and over again I found that lives and spirits were interwoven.

– *My Hindu* –

In an effort to do some absent healing I decided to get together suitable prayers from all the different religions. Most of my letters were answered, but I was unable to get any response from the Hindus. Some lovely Indian students then tipped me off that one of their main books was the *Bhagavad Gita*. I bought a copy, and asked my guides if I could take a passage from this as my Hindu contribution. To my amazement the answer was negative. However, I saw that The Upernishads were described as the Hindu's equivalent to the *New Testament*, so I invested in a volume. This time there was a positive indication, although the chosen text was certainly not what I would have expected. The subject, the progress of the soul after death, had not been included in any of the other prayers, and the message was that the soul could inhabit anything it chose, if this was right for it.

It turned out that I had been helped by the soul of an Indian Hindu. He had died 12 years previously, aged 84 and, during his life, had been a trader with a shop. He had not been religious, and moral scruples had not restricted his way of making money. While less corrupt than many he had done things which he knew to be wrong, and he was now making amends by working to raise spiritual awareness on earth, in the hope that the world would become a better place.

Unlike most Indians he had no plans for reincarnation, since he had his mission. He would not give his name, nor the part of India where he had lived, but he did say that he would guide me to people and people to me, and be helpful.

– *Mr Binay Ranjan Sen* –

One night I had a distinguished visitation. I had been asking about the contrast and similarity between medicine and spiritual healing. Medicine, I was told, was a physical thing, purely mimicking the effect of greater spiritual energies. In one of my favourite books, *The Autobiography of a Yogi* by Paramahansa Yogananda there is an account of people who have lived without food. These included the relatively well-known example of the Roman Catholic nun Teresa Neuman. This phenomena, which I have encountered again recently, and which involved a lady of about my own age living today, has always appeared to me to be the epitomé of a demonstration of the power of spiritual sustenance.

As I tried to find out about these things I was aware that someone with a great knowledge of these matters was with me, and I managed to find out who it was. One of the photographs in Paramahansa Yogananda's book is of the yogi a few hours before he died. He is shown with Mr Binay Ranjan Sen, who had been the Indian Ambassador to the United States, and who had given the eulogy at the funeral on March 11, 1952. It was Mr Sen who had come to help me to understand the power of the mind when there was faith in the strength of the spirit.

– My New Man, Thomas's friend , and Winifred –

Sometimes spiritual visitors give no names or details. One I dubbed 'my new man' while another was identified as being a friend of Guru Thomas's. Another about whom I knew little was Winifred. She had been an aunt figure in a previous life and also had a link with Alice, who is mentioned in the chapter on Reincarnations.

– My Biographer –

One night I felt a very gentle presence, a man with a naturally refined nature, quiet and benevolent, and from a well-educated background. In stature he was a little larger than average with a strong oval to square shaped face, light brown, wavy, thinning hair, and blue eyes. He was slightly plump, and non-aggressively strong in build. His dress was relaxed but smart, a good quality sports jacket and trousers. One felt he would never panic, always behave well, and had a great deal of awareness. He said he was a biographer who had died a few years earlier and he wished to remain anonymous. He appeared as a man of, possibly, forty. He agreed to help me write this book.

– *Angela* –

The vicar who married us was an excellent man, very kind and sincere. He had a wife who was a positive angel, all the more so because she was definitely a realist and was equal to all circumstances. Not long after the vicar retired she got cancer, and died in quite a short time. On hearing this I was horrified – thinking that the husband would be quite incapable of looking after himself. In fact, he coped excellently, and told us that he had known instinctively how ill his wife, Angela, was before the diagnosis, and had a great feeling of *déjà vu* through the whole episode, which had enabled him to come to terms so well with her death.

One evening he telephoned me. When I put the phone down I felt complete ecstasy, an elation which was not at all an appropriate response to a pleasant but fairly routine phone call. I climbed upstairs, and went to bed. The light was still on when I felt a beautiful presence manifest above me. While I could see nothing I was aware of a wonderful, alive range of autumn colours, and, at the same time, felt being beamed towards me all the finest and most loving feelings a mother might have for a child.

This experience gave me an insight into the ultimate of a mother's best feelings. There was protection, then a letting go, watching the child leave home to make a life of its own, but always being there to provide support if necessary. There was a whole range of sentiments, all wholly positive, selfless, and quite wonderful, with a natural fullness and absolute generosity, calm, giving, and non-invasive. This was Angela's gift to me.

I had often thought that the children of this couple were favoured indeed, a more stable and caring home it would be impossible to find. Angela's capacity for love was so great that she opened her arms and her heart and embraced me as though I were her own child, to give me the great gift of a love which I had not previously experienced in my present life, although I was nearing my half-century at the time!

When I told the vicar about this he said that, after Angela's funeral, a number of people had told him they had seen her floating above them. I feel sure this was her way of reassuring them, and giving them her blessing. Her concern was completely in character.

– Dorothy Kerin –

I regard Dorothy Kerin who founded Burrswood and who is mentioned in the chapter on Special People and Special Places, and as one who worked to protect me from my mother, as another member of my spiritual family.

I have never had to ask for a description many books have been written about her. She received miracle healings during her lifetime in one case giving her attendant doctor the surprise of his life – and herself gave many miracle healings. While Burrswood was partly given over to conventional medicine it remained magical. Angels were known to be seen by different people, once when a book with the names of ill people was being taken up to be laid on the altar of the church there.

– Rev. John Keys-Fraser –

One night I was in the bathroom, washing before going to bed, when I was aware of a male presence. The vibes were very like those of my father, but he had moved away and I knew we would not have contact again.

I received a deep inner conviction that all would be well and that I would be cared for. Once in the bedroom I asked who the presence had been. There came into my mind the picture of the Rev John Keys-Fraser, who had been vicar of Scarborough in the latter part of the 1960s. I had been going through a rough time and I remember him giving a very comforting sermon full of assurance that we really were being looked after. Our eyes met for a second, and I felt his message really was for me.

Was it really the case that the vicar was with me, or was it just a flash back of memory? I was told that he was with me indeed and that his mission was to offer people faith, comfort, and reassurance. This had been the purpose of his immediate past life and it had continued since his death. There was also the thought that sin really would be forgiven.

In addition to my spiritual family I have another category for visitors. These are friends who give a blessing but do not envisage an on-going relationship.

– *Veronica* –

One night I felt a new presence, and was told it was someone whose funeral I had attended. I felt this was needle-in-a-haystack detective work, and asked for a name to come into my mind. This happened, and I felt again Veronica, a lovely lady I had known for most of my life. She and her husband had both been on my father's staff, and we were all very fond of the family. They had one daughter. Veronica, had suffered from chronic asthma all her life. Memories of my childhood included anxious telephone calls to the local hospital enquiring about her condition, for she appeared to get near fatal pneumonia on a regular basis.

Veronica was a magnificent and talented individual. She was extremely artistic, frequently having beautiful woodcuts exhibited at the Royal Academy Summer Exhibition. She was among the most tolerant and genuinely caring people I have ever known. She kept in touch with me after I had left home and at Christmas, when I would return home, I would be invited round for a meal at which no trouble was spared to make me feel really wanted.

During her lifetime, Veronica was mildly eccentric. I saw that she had retained a highly original way of looking at things when, one night after we had renewed contact after her death, she suggested what energies might be used to help people... she certainly put a new but far from unreasonable slant on the exercise.

– *Rosemary* –

Rosemary, predictably, came to visit shortly after her death. (You will find more about Rosemary in the chapter Special People Special Places.) We had shared psychic experiences. She had retained the radiance she had had in life but the quality of it had deepened. She told me there was a great endless well of healing energy, that all illnesses could be cured, and no medical knowledge was necessary. She promised to help a very ill friend of mine.

I did not expect further communication or get it. She was the sort of person who would definitely move on and progress in her own way.

– *Christian Scientists* –

l have found that, if I am getting involved with a group, spirits from their number tend to come and visit me. I acquired 'an anonymous Christian Science lady' and a man who described himself as having been a 'discrete homosexual'. He had once tried to have a girlfriend with disastrous results, and just enjoyed the company of other men. Another Christian Scientist did not even reveal which sex he or she had been.

The lady said she had died about three years earlier, in 1994. She was familiar with me although I had not previously been in contact with her.

– *Dakota* –

Some Christian Spiritualists in Eastbourne with whom I had been in correspondence once supplied me with a list of tapes, in which mediums were recorded revealing accounts of spiritual truths about the world and the after-life. Some personalities in the next world gave biographical details of the lives they had led on earth, their transitions into death, and the world in which they now lived. I did nothing at the time, but I got a pyschic tap on the shoulder by a Red Indian guide, Dakota, advising me that I must take action and investigate quite a long time afterwards. I did, and the tapes were brilliant. There was none of the " 'ello Eth, it's Sid 'ere', in fact personal messages were discouraged. These were communications of a general and much more profound nature.

– *My Corinthian Man* –

Another group with a representative who contacted me from the other side were the Corinthians, which places great importance on healing. They are a Christian group, and some of them are interested in spiritualism.

– *Jack* –

Jack had been a fellow commuter for some years and although he took redundancy, it was a sort of early retirement because he was handicapped and his condition was deteriorating. We kept in touch.

When he died, I was unable to go to his funeral, so I dedicated some Buddhist prayers for him instead. He had had a very good and active brain, and very definite opinions to go with it. While I doubt if he was really an atheist, he usually took this standpoint, more or less, if religion or the possibility of an afterlife came into the conversation.

I did the prayers quietly in my bedroom, sitting on the bed. His presence was so strong that I felt the need to move up in order for him to sit down beside me. I could tell he was pleased that I was doing the prayers, but he was viewing the whole thing with immense humour. His personality had not changed at all but, freed from his troublesome body, there was a great feeling of being relaxed and at ease.

When I returned downstairs my husband exclaimed how strongly he had felt Jack's presence, and what a lovely presence it had been!

– *Two distant cousins* –

Steve came to visit me shortly after his death. Details about him are included in a later chapter, *The Bardo, Life Between Lives*. Then Helen, an old lady who had been instrumental in my discovering that I had now much-valued younger relatives living near me died. As she lived hundreds of miles away we spent a couple of nights at her flat. The morning after her funeral, as we were having breakfast, a most beautiful double rainbow manifested, and remained for a long time, so we could appreciate it. While I resisted the temptation to try to draw this lady down to earth I must admit I was delighted when she did send me one message.

– *Frances* –

I very nearly lost Frances, another of my spiritual family. I have to confess I completely messed up the relationship just after she came to visit me. Apparently we had met between lives, in earth time between 1917 and 1945. I had a very clear picture of her. She was of average height with dark hair cut short at the sides and bushy on top, a prominent nose and deep set dark blue eyes under strong dark eyebrows. She was of medium build, shapely, and strong. She was positive, reliable, and efficient, and her manner energetic.

Frances had been a healer in a previous life when she had been a psychologist. She was able to *read* me after we had been together for only a day or two. However, I was going through a spell of feeling ill and, concerned that I might not survive to note down the contents of this book, I asked if she could keep me alive for the purpose.

She was, rightly, horrified by this request which was well outside her orbit, and fled, outraged. I thought I would never hear from her again, but I did.

After 'September 11', when most of the spiritual family had deserted me to devote their energies to more crucial work on the world stage, Leopold, who had been given a reserved occupation because of his terrible experiences in the last war persuaded her to return to me.

I was struck how, in the meantime, she had changed. I could feel she was much more at peace with herself and was stronger, calmer, and more relaxed. There was an explanation for this – she had become a Christian Scientist. Their teachings were obviously a balm to her soul.

– Jill's Frances –

Frances was a well starred name at this time. Another family member of the name appeared. She had helped Guru Catherine's daughter Jill, so I named her Jill's Frances.

Jill's Frances had been a lady from a socially elevated family. A Lutheran Austrian, she had been a nurse during the First World War. She was tallish, slim, with slightly wavy gray hair, and she had died in 1960, aged seventy five.

– Violet –

I also gained another new friend, Violet. She had died in the 1950s, at the age of forty but her appearance was that of a woman of thirty. She had worked in an import/export business, married late in life but her husband turned out to be both selfish and unsympathetic. She was never a very happy person and there were no children. Her father had been a senior figure in a clothing factory in London during the Depression and, although her mother had been a housewife, and did not work, the family had fared much better than many others in those hard times. Violet had been a member of the Church of England during that incarnation but had previously been a Roman Catholic. Now she was not interested in religion: she was into spiritual awareness.

Since dying, Violet had been training as a healer, and she said she would be working on my migraines by trying to remove the deep-seated imprints which had established the complaint. It is difficult, after decades of suffering, but she really did appear to be making a difference. They had reduced from manifesting every four weeks to every six, but as I write this, the gaps have reached eight weeks – and once all the classic signs of an impending migraine suddenly vanished, an unheard of event.

– *Thomas Cordingly* –

I was delighted that grandfather Thomas Cordingley returned. My grandmother had gone on her way, he had stayed behind, in spiritual terms, to help her and now he could move on. He had no idea what had happened to my mother or where she had gone.

* * *

Before moving on I must record the great gift I was given before 'September 11', when my spiritual family were still around me.

My husband was away at the time, and I became aware that two people were with me, my wonderful husband of my early incarnation and first love of my present life, Anthony – and Betty, then called Catherine, who had been my mother all those years ago. I was then called Sarah, a selfish and unappreciative mother, although I had genuinely loved my husband and children. But Betty and Anthony had endless patience and their love for me never wavered.

Now they had returned and for a day I felt thoroughly

cherished in the heart of a loving family and in a way which I never experienced in this lifetime.

I marvelled that, when I had cancer, I was absolutely terrified of dying, while, with Betty and Anthony with me I wished I could leave this world at once, and have them at my side for ever. This, of course, would not have been possible. We all have individual spiritual paths.

I started to feel tired, psychic contact can have this effect, and Anthony and Betty became distant. I was told I must get on with my present life, apply myself, and prove that their faith in me was well-founded.

I could not be blind to the coincidence that, in this life, both my mother and husband, who might have been expected to care for me, did not, and I was given one day when spiritual beings who had had the same relationship but who had loved me deeply came back and gave me their beautiful gift. When they left I felt bereft.

Anthony did return once more. As I was writing notes for this book I found I was lapsing into a rather ponderous style, not my own – instinctively I knew it was Anthony helping me. There have been times when my biographer, Ellen, and someone else, who wants to remain anonymous, have also had a hand in the writing of this book. I find that when I have no spiritual assistance I have a much harder task. I was warned that my spiritual family could not cluster round me forever as they had important work to do, and I accept it is right for them to be deployed elsewhere, where their help is greatly needed. There are great tragedies on the world stage.

PSYCHIC ATTACKS

● *A schizophrenic, cured by the casting out of devils* ● *Nurses and doctors believe the voices their patients hear are those of genuine spirits, not hallucinations.* ● *Spirits traveling with a schizophrenic.* ● *A friend is attacked psychically by her dead husband.* ● *A child is attacked by a spirit.* ● *A hostile friend of my mother's, and how to help in controlling her.* ● *Through her attack I am open to illness.* ● *How the psychic influence works on the body.* ● *Thomas is attacked and I try to help.* ● *My cat becomes disturbed.* ● *A verbal outburst is psychically encouraged.* ● *The drunk and unconscious are vulnerable.* ● *The word God banishes a mischievous spirit.* ● *The well-motivated can be the focus of attacks.* ● *A friend performs an exorcism.* ● *A good and knowledgeable entity speaks through me - an amazing experience.*

When I was young the thought of being involved in psychic attacks would not have occurred to me. I accepted that there was indeed power in voodoo and other traditional, if rather ethnic, forms of curses but I did not expect to find anything closer to home.

One of the most impressive messages given by a distant but much admired relative at her funeral was 'Death makes no difference at all'. People were to think about her and talk about her after her death in exactly the same way that they had before. This illustrated a big truth.

When people's bodies die their minds continue without any magical change. A kind and lovely person remains kind, while a mind which has wished to harm others will continue to have the same extremely harmful and unpleasant motivation. People's psychic powers appear to be the same whether they are alive, or have moved into that equally active plane which we inappropriately call death.

I have been given proof of this. In fact, if I wanted proof of life after death this would serve brilliantly, though anyone wishing for only nice stories would be in for a disappointment. Possibly we should not so much fear the malevolent as be aware of its potential, and derive comfort and assurance from the fact that there are the most loving and wonderful spirits out there who wish to help us.

Julian pointed out that the psychic is neutral, it is the use to which it is put which determines whether it is good or evil. The experience I had of my mother's attack upon me was a gross one, many spirits are mischievous rather than seriously wishing evil on anyone, but even in minor cases damage can be done. I shall describe a few other instances of psychic attacks to illustrate how the phenomena can manifest. This may make you wonder if you have felt the results of such an attack, good or bad, but failed to recognize it as such.

My Guru Catherine had a daughter, Jill. Born retarded, there were no other problems until Jill was in her teens, when she became schizophrenic. The family were very supportive, but the time came when her violence made her a danger to herself and her family and, regretfully, they had to arrange for her to live in a home.

Her condition stabilized to some extent, and they risked having her at home at weekends, though they dreaded it. Time went on, and well into middle age Jill developed an ulcer on her leg. All sorts of conventional medical remedies were tried, but nothing worked. Catherine decided to call in a spiritual healer, to see if he could help.

To everyone's relief and amazement Jill loved having her healing sessions every Saturday. She sat in an obvious state of bliss, and was as good as gold as the man laid his hands on her head.

Then something amazing happened. Her schizophrenia vanished. His work completed, the healer stopped coming and the mental condition never returned.

Years later Catherine was talking to a nurse she had met socially. The nurse, who worked with mental patients, explained how they were discovering that much mental sickness could be cured by prayer. Jill was by no means the only schizophrenic whose illness had suddenly ended. In fact, there was even a college where those wishing to learn to help the mentally ill through a spiritual approach could train and get a properly acknowledged qualification. Those involved were rushed off their feet for the work load was enormous.

Catherine decided she must contact the healer who had cured Jill, and she told him about the work the nurse was doing. "That," said the healer, "is exactly what I did with Jill." He had realised that there was a spirit attachment and had, in my friend's words, "Cast out devils, just like it says in the Bible." She expressed surprise that the healer had not told her what he had done, but he explained that not many mothers wished to be told that their daughters had been possessed by demons.

I remembered the time when my Guru Julian had been talking to me about his work in delivering my mother's disturbed spirit. The telephone had rung. He answered it, and afterwards said that his group had numerous calls from doctors and nurses, who were caring for schizophrenics, saying that they were convinced that the voices the patients reported hearing were actually there, and were those of distressed or harmful discarnate spirits, and some were asking for help. Julian was among those who wrote a book *Deliverance* which I found very interesting.

There is another book, *Healing the Family Tree* by a missionary doctor who witnessed little Chinese ladies praying for and curing those whom western medicos would have labelled schizophrenic, and he started using their methods. Dr. McAll's experiences are recounted in the book, available, like *Deliverance*, from S.P.C.K. bookshops.

I met Cynthia who had been labelled schizophrenic, and who believed that she could be helped because, she alleged, she had two spirits which were with her, and were the cause of her trouble. Her condition was fairly serious, in that while she took medication she was rational, but she claimed it made her fat, and she often stopped taking it, and within a month or two she would be back in a mental home.

While she tried to make out there was a great similarity between us, with her spirits and my mother, there was in fact a great divide. While I knew that my mother must be moved on, she saw her two spirits as companions. One, she acknowledged, had malicious intentions, making her see the television distort into horrible pictures to frighten her and getting up to other mischief, while the other called her, 'God', and claimed to be a friend. If she took her medication the spirits had difficulty contacting her. Cynthia had been told by the second spirit that together they could be healers. To my horror the woman had even had patients and had charged them for her services! On one occasion she insisted on putting her hands on my head – hoping to convince me I could start using her 'professionally'. Being psychic I decided to tune in, and see what I could feel. It was horrible! Depressed, depressing, and oppressive! I felt I was being suffocated. Had the healing gone on for any length of time I would have had to make an excuse, and run for the garden!

When I got home I asked my guides about the spirits and the woman concerned. Rather predictably I was told that the obviously bad spirit was bad indeed, but that the other was just as damaging. She would have liked to be a healer, but was totally unsuitable, and by kidding the woman about non-existent powers and turning her into a charlatan, and by telling her that she was 'God', she was doing a lot of harm.

Thomas was of the opinion that the woman was genuinely mentally sick. I think the fact she was happy to be called 'God' suggests that he was correct.

I told a Buddhist about Elizabeth who was having great problems. She knew that her late husband, he had been dead for some years, was trying to poison her by now adult children's minds, against her. My contact suggested that a particular kind of blue stone could offer protection and told me where I could find a shop specializing in crystals. She also advised me to buy the book *Handbook for Lightworkers*.

I went to the shop, and they were very happy to let me dowse to find out which piece of stone would be best for my friend. They did not have the book in stock, but I must have been meant to get it since my favourite bookshop provided it at once. Glancing through its pages it was as though I was looking at a foreign language I was clueless as to what the author was talking about. However, I extracted the scrap of information I needed for myself. Moldavite, a green stone, had its origin outside the planet and had the ability to judge right and wrong, and give protection accordingly.

My friend reported that her blue stone worked, and so did my green one, which I bought at the same shop, again choosing it by using the pendulum.

I wondered why my friend's husband had been behaving the way he had and was told that about three hundred years ago she and her husband had been brother and sister. The sister (my friend) married but the brother remained single and was jealous of his brother-in-law. My friend was being helped by her parents, who had been dead for some years, and they had tried to persuade her late husband to stop causing problems, but he was not receptive. He was guilty of cruelty and mischief, but stopped short at being evil, I was told.

My advisor said that Elizabeth should also get rid of a ring which her husband had given her. I found this message difficult to pass on, but Elizabeth appeared to know instinctively what I was referring to, and she parted with it without a second thought.

A girl I had met when she was a small child had become mentally ill. Julia had been the apple of everyone's eye, attractive, sociable without being at all pushy, and beautifully behaved. Tragically, her mother died when she was five. Her family did their best for her but were aware that such a trauma might present problems later, although she appeared to cope well at the time.

Sadly, their worst fears were realised. Somehow the grieving for her mother, which manifested when she reached puberty, surprising and at times, it showed. Whenever I spoke to her family I was expecting to be criticised because of this, but they never commented or remarked on my attitude. After her death my grandmother had done her best to help me, and protect me.

However, I did not maintain contact with the family. My aunts vanished as soon as my mother's unrested soul had been delivered, and my grandmother who had controlled her daughters lives, had prevented them having boy-friends and marrying, told me that she did not approve of Buddhism. I had had more than enough invasions into my life. So, telling my grandfather, Thomas Cordingly, with whom I would have liked to keep in contact, of my reasons, I told him I loved him, would remember him forever, and said goodbye.

* * *

Years later, after members of my spiritual family had deserted to try to calm down world events following September 11th, [a reference to the attack by terrorists on the Twin Towers in New York 2001 causing the deaths of 2,752 people.] my grandfather returned to me. He was on his own. He had moved to a lower spiritual plane to help my grandmother, but could now move on. I sensed him one night, seeing in my mind's eye a roundish area in front of and above me. It was a little like a cut area of polished stone with a light area on the outside, a darker circle within this, and then a soft, calm, vibrant grey colour in the middle.

* * *

Some time later I was given an interesting insight into how much I had known about my mother's state of mind, at a sub or even unconscious level. I had decided, as an exercise in sculpture, to portray 'Anguish'. Expressing extremes of emotion, or experience, in art is always an interesting turned to self-hatred and attempted suicide. The psychiatrist, under whose care she had been even before the suicide attempt, regarded the pattern of behaviour as quite normal.

I could not accept this. Surely not every child who loses a parent ends up in a potentially fatal state of self-loathing. I asked my spirit guides what was going on, and was told that a mischievous spirit, (a relative of her dead mother's) felt Julia was not making the grade as a living memorial to her mother, and implanted the idea in Julia's mind that she was responsible for the death.

The prayers of myself and others were not strong enough to prevent Julia ending up as a resident patient in a mental hospital. However, Leopold said he would try to help. As a Jewish refugee he had experience of understanding grief and inappropriate guilt, and he hoped for an improvement in Julia's condition in six months from that time.

I was told that if the worst happened, and a subsequent attempt at suicide was successful Julia would either reincarnate quickly, or continue to have necessary experiences in the bardo (the state between lives).

Some time after my mother left me I established that another discarnate spirit was attacking me, and trying to influence me. This was June, a friend my mother had made in the bardo. They worked together. June was understandably angry that her friend had been sent elsewhere, and wished to damage me and keep up the negative work my mother had been doing.

Anthony advised me that I must tell June to 'Go towards the light' and I must recite the Lord's Prayer, God be in my head, and Christ be with me, for protection.

Later I was told that I must visualize putting June into an amœba-shaped bubble. This would stretch in any direction so she was not restricted, but she would be unable to reach and damage anyone. I had to beam at her a line contained in a translation of the Lord's Prayer by N. Douglas Klotz: 'From you is born all ruling will, the power and the life to do, the song that beautifies all, from age to age it renews'. It was particularly the second half of this piece, 'the song that beautifies all, from age to age it renews' that was important. I could see why.

When I was asked to help sort out June I was very concerned since I knew I was not qualified to make decisions in this kind of case. I was told I need not worry, and I would be guided. My main concern was that I would not know when it would be safe to let June out of her bubble, and send her on her way. I need not have worried, my friends came to me with a clear message several weeks later, I could feel things had changed, to say I need not concern myself with June any more. I had completed my contribution.

In *Deliverance* there is talk of 'binding and releasing' of spirits. I asked my guides whether I had seen an example of this, and was told that I had. My spiritual friend Winifred said she knew the person who had been involved in June's case. She indicated pages in *Deliverance* which she suggested I read. They covered details of how the paranormal should be dealt with, and prayer material.

Psychic attacks, and the effort needed to dispel them, often cause physical trouble. This time I had succumbed to the current popular 'flu, as I thought. In fact it was a more serious bacteriological infection. The thing dragged on, and the degree of exhaustion was great. I was told that my work with June had been achieved by using my psychic energy, so I was naturally depleted. My illness had started with a tickly throat that progressed to days of being very sick. I lost a lot of weight which did not want to go back on, and then I came out in an itchy rash, large swollen areas just about everywhere, feet, top of thighs, back, wrists, face, neck, calves etc. Clearly my defective immune system was completely overloaded. This had started as a psychic attack from June.

Patrick told me this had been allowed to happen, the fact I was ill over Christmas was just bad luck, as I had needed to protect others who were also suffering June's attacks. While I went through this suffering my spiritual family deserted me, and apparently there was a strong need for me to work off bad kharma.

I had been anxious that I would be too ill to attend a Buddhist empowerment for which I had booked, but Patrick assured me I would manage it. He was right, but I was not well when I returned home.

Patrick then told me about psychic attacks. They work on the mental processes, the control mechanism of the brain, to dictate to the body, what will happen. Someone who is unbelieving of this possibility can be just as likely to fall a victim. Few people would identify problems as psychic attacks – they would just be seen as having become ill. Products in the system might be made toxic, like a plague of boils, possibly harmless waste products might be adversely transformed in this way.

Purification can be used as an antidote. *In The Armour of God*, a little book of protective prayers I got from Burrswood, there is a line about the 'promised indwelling of the Holy Spirit,' and Vajrasattva, the Buddha of purification, can be employed. As a bad spirit uses the victim's energy another suitable antidote should be used, possibly Green Tara, the Buddha of active compassion, or a robust psalm carrying the message that God provides energy and sustenance.

I had made things worse for myself by my lack of faith. I felt so ill, I even wondered if I would keel over. It was also unhelpful that some people I knew expected me to be ill (statistically my cancer should have returned), while in fact the most important way to help the victim of a psychic attack is to be totally positive.

One night I was told that bad spirits could latch onto those who suffered from guilt or mental distress much more easily than those who were strong.

Information gathered by experts in the field of vulnerability have stressed that we are at risk while we sleep, and some have found that unconsciousness, for instance brought about by a general anaesthetic administered in hospital, can be risky. When mental control is lost through the abuse of drink or drugs the person concerned can also be laid open for a psychic attack.

Psychic attacks can come from the living or the dead. Thomas went through a spell when he could help his patients but not himself. I asked my guides and was told a curse had been put on him. He had greatly helped a patient who was understandably grateful, but the patient's partner became jealous and their relationship deteriorated. The patient's partner was punishing Thomas psychically.

What could I do? I had to advise Thomas to read parts of the book *Armour of God* for his own protection, and pray for the one who was hating him by reciting the *Nunc Dimittis* (Now lettest thou thy servant depart in peace...). Thomas was advised to be even more spiritual in his approach to healing.

My advisor was someone who had had a connection with Thomas in a previous incarnation. This anonymous male was now heavily into all religions. He had an over-view of Thomas's work and wanted to help. Later he told me that Thomas's antagonist had stopped working against him but had left a bad legacy and it would take a long time for Thomas to get well.

I had always been the person to whom our rescued cat could most easily relate. Holly fled from friends who visited the house, and was lukewarm towards my husband. But with me she nestled down in bed, and was loving and relaxed.

My husband went away for about ten days and, during this time, our old cat Norman became extremely demanding. He had always preferred men to women, but made do with me at every possible opportunity and, because of his age and the fact that he was missing my husband's lap, I let him get away with it. Holly got a bit less attention during the day, but still had priority during the night.

Once my husband returned Holly threw a complete

wobbly. If I went near her she lashed out and swore. She stopped sleeping with me. She made a few overtures towards my husband, though not many. There was a strange expression in her eyes, and an ambivalence. If she got on my lap she would stay for only a few minutes, then get off.

I sought help from my friends upstairs. It was so sad that Holly, who had not had the love she needed in the past, was rejecting the affection that was available now.

My spirit friend Rosemary, another cat lover, came to my aid. She said she had been able to make a suggestion, psychically, to Holly. It was possible to put an idea into the mind of a human or an animal, and cats and dogs tended to be very psychic. Holly soon returned to her normal loving ways. (Rosemary appears in the chapter *Special People*.)

Possibly, though, she had been feeling something else. I had been aware of not being in good shape myself, and it was a while before I established that, once again, I was being bogled by something mischievous, resulting in my having the sort of negative thoughts I was fighting against.

Co-incidentally, I saw Julian in the distance at a public event. Our eyes met only briefly, but it was enough. I felt wonderful, and the nasty presence vanished.

A mischievous spirit may use the same psychic tubes, as I call it, to do verbal damage. I do not have a particularly volatile temper, but it is there, and I can *lose* it with the best of them on occasions.

But once I responded in a completely 'over the top' way to a very minor annoyance. I saw a child messing about and interfering with things that he definitely should not have been. Instead of just asking him to leave them alone, and go away, I started shouting in a way that was unwarranted. Afterwards I realised that I had not been on my own when generating the outburst.

I have heard experts say that mischievous spirits have a field day in pubs and places where people, through alcohol, drugs, or any other influence, lose control of themselves, and can easily be taken over. Rows, fights, and violence are often the result.

Of course, if one knows one gets nasty after a few drinks the solution is to drink fruit juice – one cannot shed responsibility for one's actions if one knows inebriation will lead to trouble.

Sometimes nasty visitations are brief and easily dealt with. On one occasion I was about to petition on behalf of friends when I felt a hostile presence. I told it in no uncertain terms that my prayers were between myself, God, and the people I was trying to help. At the word 'God' it fled! Clearly Goodness was a much stronger energy on this occasion, and inspired fear.

At another session I was in contact with Sarah, a member of the spiritual family, when I felt something adverse arrive. I used *The Armour of God* to dispel it.

Guru Catherine believes that the more one tries to do good the more bad or mischievous entities try to prevent one. Sometimes when she uses her pendulum, and it is almost always being used to discover a way of helping someone, it goes haywire and sends obviously wrong messages. Once or twice I have had similar experiences.

A lack of concentration is frequently a problem with me and I have been told by my guides that this can be induced by spirits wishing to impede me. I was told that, for me, a visualization combining the love and light of both Christ and the Buddhas would be an appropriate way of sealing myself off from such influences.

After the 'mother experience' I was understandably very aware of the dangers of hostile discarnate spirits, and when I heard that Catherine's nurse friend was involved in helping so called schizophrenics with spirit attachment work I was concerned for her safety. She assured me that they were aware of this, and took precautions, bathing themselves in light. She also gave the following prayer which anyone can use at anytime.

The light of God surrounds me, the power of God protects me, the presence of God watches over me, the love of God enfolds me, and wherever I am God is.

Teresa, a Roman Catholic friend who was both knowledgeable in theological matters and extremely aware spiritually, told me how she had, though she did not describe it as such, carried out an exorcism.

A lady with a great conscience and of a naturally caring disposition, she had always made a point of visiting sick friends and acquaintances. Among these people was a woman who was terminally ill with a wasting disease. Sometimes, when she visited, her husband was there, too. To her disgust and embarrassment, he would start a tirade against his dying wife, saying how old and ugly she looked, and then compared her with her visitor, Teresa, whom he found much more attractive.

This placed my friend in a dilemma – should she stop visiting to avoid this happening, or should she continue, even if the husband was so obnoxious and his comments hurtful to his wife. A priest advised her that she should continue, for the sake of the wife, who must already have known what a nasty man her husband was, and would also know she could trust Teresa completely.

One day, as usual, the tirade started again. Teresa had had enough. In thought, (she could certainly not speak the words), she said, "In the name of Jesus Christ of Nazareth, come out of that man." Suddenly the husband's abusive criticism ceased, and she never again heard him vilify his wife. After the wife died he made advances to Teresa, who made it very clear she was not interested.

* * *

Psychic communication can, however, be very positive. I have referred to Jasmuheen – the lady who lives without food or drink – in the chapter on *Medical Matters*. When I heard her speak, she appeared with no notes at all, although she was able to keep up an informative and inspiring dialogue for the whole evening. She explained this by saying that her guides helped her. They had never let her down, and could instruct her in what she should say. Make no mistake, psychic communication from those who know more than we do, can be wonderful and positive.

I was once with a group studying both Christian and Buddhist religions. The teacher representing Christianity was excellent whereas the alleged Buddhist was hopeless. He simply hadn't a clue, and I suspected he had been too lazy to do any preparation for the session. This was a great pity as among those present were Christian priests who had come especially to learn about Buddhism.

There were periods of discussion. Some topic was raised, and I felt I must put forward a legitimate Buddhist view. I opened my mouth and listened with wonder while the most amazing and profound exposition of Buddhist philosophy poured fluently from my lips. Even as whoever-it-was (it was certainly not me) spoke, I wished I had had the teaching on tape. There was too much said, and spoken far too quickly for me to begin to remember it all. I recognised all the ideas and advice from the excellent Buddhist teachings I had received but, even if I had had time to think first, there was no way I could have expressed the philosophy so well.

After I finished, the silence was stunning. Someone eventually blurted out a comment to the effect that they had received some great wisdom. They had, but unfortunately it had not come from me. It came through me, but not from me. This was the first and so far as I am aware the only time that I have been used in this way. I felt a fraud, but could hardly go into a rambling explanation of how I was a bit psychic.

My great regret was that the account was so much above my level that I could remember little, and wished I had been able to take notes!

Visitations After Death

● A beautiful paranormal experience. ● A man killed when his son was a baby, supports his family decades later ● A great aunt visits me ● My father returns to help a dying friend ● A late husband and fiance together visit a bereaved lady. ● Children are saved by a benevolent nun. ● People can manifest in their old haunts while they die in another.

Paranormal spiritual experiences can be very beautiful – more beautiful than it is possible to describe in ordinary words. The first Christmas I returned home, after going away to work, I slept in my old bed as usual with our lovely rescued cat Topper at my feet. (He only came inside the bedclothes if it was really cold!).

On Christmas morning I awoke and was immediately aware of a most wonderful presence in the room. It stayed for quite a time. Had I been able to cut a cubic metre in the air I would have made contact with it, though I could not see it.

Topper woke up. He immediately turned towards it, and I could see he was focussing middle distance – he could actually see something I could only sense. The presence remained. I tried to feel which sex it was – but it had left such conventions behind. Could it be a dead relative returning to wish me well? I could feel no answer, only the perfection of an absolute and perfect love. I remember thinking, 'If this is God, this is more than enough for me.'

A rescued animal, our cat was extremely nervous. Even cat-loving friends who came to the house only caught a brief sight of him as he slunk away in a state of disapproval and fear. But this being he also perceived as wonderful.

Eventually the presence left, quite slowly, and the room returned to normal. It felt terrible. The vibes had been so beautiful while the spiritual manifestation was present.

Topper had actually seen the departure. He was distraught, hunting for it. He went behind the dressing table, behind the curtains, and did everything in his power to track it down – it was quite a while before he could get back his equilibrium. I just felt I had been so lucky to be made aware that something which manifested as perfect love could exist. Life had changed a little bit – forever.

* * *

My Guru Thomas never knew his father as he was killed in the war when Thomas was a baby, however, the father materialized and visited Thomas's wife when she was alone. She had suffered the distress of miscarrying twin daughters when she was five months pregnant and he materialised to show her twin daughters as two happy young women, one as a bride and the other as, presumably, a bridesmaid. The message was one of comfort, as the twins were fine.

He also told her about his death. As a wounded soldier he had been carried off the field but, unaware of the gravity of his injuries, was fully expecting to be back in action shortly. When he had to accept the fact he had died it was, he said, the most traumatic experience he had ever had. Military records confirmed the nature of his death, and his cheerfulness. He said that manifesting in human form was very uncomfortable and he would not do so again.

Understandably there was scepticism when Thomas's wife told the family of her experience. Thomas's mother was doubtful – until her daughter-in-law revealed that her father-in-law had had an unusual feature – a wobbly eye. After that revelation, Thomas had never been told of this peculiarity, the truth of the experience was accepted.

* * *

My maternal grandmother, a widow, spent many years

being ill while her two older daughters, who both worked, devoted most of their time and money to making her comfortable and giving her the best of everything. During one of her bouts of illness it looked as if she would not survive – but she did.

However, some time later the elder of my aunts awoke one night to find her father, my grandfather Thomas Cordingly, who had been dead for about ten years, at her side. He said, "Don't try to save mother. I am ready for her now." My aunt told no one, but shortly afterwards my grandmother died, quite suddenly. It was a great comfort to the family to know of my grandfather's visitation and message. It was also observed that he had chosen to contact the daughter who had always been his favourite.

* * *

The first time I saw a ghost I must have been about nine. In fact I have only ever seen – and heard – two. I have often been aware of presences and receive, mentally, an image of their appearance, but I do not see them manifest externally.

I was staying with my mother's sisters. Two of them lived alone in a house which they previously shared with their old aunt – my grandmother's sister. They had three cats, the youngest of which had belonged to the old aunt. They were all female, and the two older ones produced kittens at regular intervals. The other one had been spayed and, perhaps because she was jealous of the others, she was an animal with anti-social tendencies spitting and scratching for no good reason. As a small child I had learned to avoid her!

For the first time I was deemed old enough to sleep in a room on my own, a little bedroom outside which, I believed, my great aunt had had her last stroke. I went to bed and fell asleep unremarkably. In the middle of the night I awoke suddenly. I have always been a passive sleeper, when I get out of bed in the morning it looks almost untouched, but I found that all the bedclothes had been pulled back. There was the loud sound of a cat purring, very close to me, and a voice said, "Get in there with Alison." I woke up in a state of great alarm, and watched the dark shadow of a figure move towards and through the door.

   I screamed! I raised the house! I was judged too young to sleep on my own after that. Only later, when I finally recognised that the voice had been that of my poor old aunt, and that she had achieved the impossible, of making her old cat loving and friendly, did I much regret the fuss I had made. She had not meant to upset me. She had been fond of me, and wished me and the cat well. But I doubt if many children would have been as cool, calm, and collected as I wished I had been. I was sorry, though, that I had responded as I did.

* * *

The other ghost I actually saw was another family member, and the one with whom I had been closest – my father.

   Losing him had been traumatic. There had been a lot of love between us when I was a child, but by the time I was into my teens much of this appeared to have evaporated. I had picked up my mother's snobbish and materialistic attitudes, sadly lots of people get a warped satisfaction from sneering at and feeling superior to other people – and he was fed up with both of us.

   I left school and home when I was eighteen, but, by that time, he had a mistress. I marvel at what might or might not have taken place as he had had a very severe stroke, and I would not have thought he would have had any sexual capacity left. We were pretty distant. But there still had been, in the past, a lot of love.

   Some years after he had died a senior work colleague became very ill with facial cancer. I was very fond of this man – in fact I had the feeling that if I ever needed to talk to someone I could have confided in him. This was a strange thought since at that time it was beyond my imagination that I would ever confide in anyone. I also thought that if I got married, though I had no intention of doing that either, I would like him to stand in for my father, and give me away.

The colleague, Robert, had always had a small growth, but this suddenly became enormous. I realised, with hindsight, that it would probably not have been regarded as viable to remove it because to take away all the malignant tissue would have been too disfiguring.

But crisis point had been reached and an operation was inevitable. Robert did not want to die. He was desperate to stay alive, and would do anything. The surgeons had to remove half his face in an effort to save him. The results were horrendous. The first time I saw him, behind the plastic mask, my one fear was that he might read an adverse reaction in my expression. But the thing that was really terrible was not the physical appearance but his fear of death, his frantic clinging to life.

Always having a belief in prayer I prayed and prayed. It did no good. He got sicker and sicker. I was very upset.

One night I woke up. My father, his younger self as he had been when he and I were at our closest, was bending over me. "Why don't you ask me?" he asked in kindly tones, although there was a hint of annoyance – I had forgotten that he had a slight West Country accent! Yes, of course he did. The sound of his voice was so comforting that, when I woke up in the morning, I cursed myself because I had still not asked my father for help – I had gone straight off to sleep again.

But the prayer was answered. Robert found spiritual peace and there was the calm of acceptance. Fear vanished. When I heard that he had died I knew that it was right. I could not be sorry, just marvel that everything had fallen so perfectly and purely into place.

My father certainly had a belief in God and Christ, but he never mentioned it. However, when he heard of other people's accounts of supernatural experiences he was completely sceptical. He did, however, expect everyone else to believe that, when he was a little boy, an uncle who had just died came to visit him when he was in his bedroom. He did not actually see his uncle, but he could feel his presence!

* * *

I was extremely fortunate that one of Timothy's sisters had no difficulty in dealing with the knowledge that a priest had had to come to my aid in sorting out my mother's spiritual condition, or in the fact I was so strongly aware that things were wrong. Felicity told me of a very vivid experience she had had.

She had been left a widow at a relatively young age. While her husband was ill the family doctor visited the house regularly. He was unattached, and after the husband died a closer friendship blossomed. The couple were as good as engaged when the doctor suffered a fatal heart attack. Poor Felicity was distraught. She had lost two men within a very short space of time.

As she grieved she was aware of the presence of both men with her. Her husband, she could feel, was annoyed at her affection for the other man, still seeing her as his property. The doctor, no doubt sensitive to the fact she was recently widowed when their relationship started, had always told her that if he found he was not wanted he would just fade away. As she was aware of her husband's disapproval she became aware also that the doctor was doing just as he had promised, and he just faded away.

* * *

One of my aunts had the knack of getting to know some very interesting people. One was a lady who was married and had a couple of children. They lived in a big old house on a site which had been a religious institution. Appreciating that small children are ill at ease sleeping alone in big rooms, they arranged for them to share a bedroom.

Imagined playmates have featured large in the lives of many small children, and when her offspring told their mother of a kind and friendly lady who visited them after they were in bed she was happy that they had settled on creating a very agreeable character to keep them company. She played along with their game, asking in the morning if their friend had visited the night before, and sometimes getting a positive, sometimes a negative, answer.

One night the couple were going up to bed, when, to her annoyance as it was very late, the mother heard chattering and laughter from the children's room. She swung open the door, but froze when she saw the figure of a nun seated by the beds. Sensing she was observed, the nun turned to her, and raised her hand in an 'All is well' gesture. The mother silently withdrew.

The next day the children were jubilant. "You saw the lady who visits us," they exclaimed and, wisely, their mother gave no indication that anything unusual was happening. The nun continued to visit while the children were small, but as they grew up she left them.

The time was the 1930s. The war loomed, and the family felt that their big house was not going to be a suitable home for the war years, as the father would be away a lot. They had contacts in America, and were delighted when they received an offer from friends to give a home to their children for the duration of the war – however long that would be. The father was pleased that he had managed to get berths on a large liner which was due to take many favoured little evacuees across the Atlantic.

The mother was alone when the door of the room opened and the nun stood there. "Don't let the children travel to America. Let them stay here, and I will look after them. If you let them go you will regret it for the rest of your lives." Having delivered her message she departed. The parents were in agreement that, whoever the nun was, she loved their children, and her advice would have been given for their benefit. The arrangements were cancelled – which was extremely lucky. The liner never arrived in America. It was torpedoed and sunk with the loss of a great number of lives, many of them children.

The family stayed in the house, and had a happily uneventful war. While the nun never appeared again, they felt confident that she offered them her protection.

* * *

A rather difficult old lady lived in the same town as I did, and sometimes I would see her in the street. A friend, Janet, used to help her with her garden. Eventually the elderly one had to leave the family home she was so attached to, and be cared for professionally.

One day I was travelling a few yards from the house where she had lived for many years when I saw her – then realised this was not possible, since she had been in a rest home for some time and was definitely not fit enough to be out walking on her own. How odd – in spite of being unusually tall and thin she must have had a double.

In fact she had died – and the local newspaper indicated her death had been about the time I had thought I had seen her. Not long after I saw Janet. She told me that there had been an amazing event – she had seen the old lady near her old home around the time of her death.

I told a friend from Sierra Leone about this, and she said that in her village (and no doubt many other villages) the dying were often seen in the street. Locals would remark on seeing the image of the very sick woman – who in reality lay prostrated on her deathbed – and observe, "She is already on her way." The whole thing was an accepted phenomenon.

HAUNTINGS

● *Assistance.* ● *A commuter's haunted house.* ● *Evil happenings at a haunted cottage.* ● *A huge country house is bought and the consequences.* ● *A little love nest has its problems.* ● *The lady did not leave.* ● *The spirit of the house expressed her opinions.* ● *A group of mischief-making spirits at work.* ● *An unwelcoming church.* ● *A bedroom with tragic associations.* ● *The lady who will not leave the family hotel.*

I have been preparing this section about hauntings. As I have been writing words have flowed easily, and I have remembered things I had forgotten for years. It is past midnight. Should I stop and go to bed, or make use of the moment when the work has been going with such ease?

I decide to ask my guides. Have I been getting help? 'Yes'. Is it from one of my spiritual family or friends? 'No'. Is it someone who was ever involved in the Church of England's deliverance of unrested souls work? 'No'. It transpired it was someone who had had a great interest in the paranormal. The main reason why this section is important, and must be written, is that people must be made aware that those who have died without peace should be helped, and that places rendered uncomfortable because they are haunted can be made pleasant and free from the problem.

Such work is not to be taken lightly. Anyone can pray it is true, and prayer helps, but for a major problem professional help should be sought. While many spirits are just distressed or rather mischievous some can be worse, and the most evil – though mercifully very rare – can be dangerous.

Anyone who is aware of such a problem can contact the vicar of their local Anglican Church. For all areas there is a priest in charge of this sort of work. He will do his best and if he is unable to resolve matters he will call upon others with greater strength in this field. Do not live with, or ignore, distressed paranormal activity. Let there be a healing with peace both to the unhappy discarnate spirit, and to the household as a whole.

As you will see, I have not always known what I know now. For instance when I discovered a haunted church I fled in terror, and had no idea that I should have made the vicar aware of the problem, and asked for his help. Remember that, after death, people are much the same as they were on earth. They are just as capable of being confused, unhappy, and ill at ease, and they are no more likely to enjoy this condition than we are. So get someone to help them and release them into the next world where their experiences can be so much more positive, and they can be happy. Bring compassion to bear.

* * *

For quite a few years I was a regular commuter. On the whole, I enjoyed it. In those days the trains were fairly plentiful, and ran on time, and one could doze, read, or do what one fancied. A few fellow travellers became friends.

One, Samuel, was an extremely nice married man with a family of whom he was very fond. He was rather sweet in that he tried to find me a husband – he could not comprehend that single people could be happy to stay that way!

On one occasion when I was chatting I told him that I had known two people who had sold up and left their homes because they were haunted, and they could not cope with the vibes or things that happened. This announcement was greeted with silence. I added that I had not said that I expected Samuel to believe it, but the people concerned certainly had. After another pause, he said he would tell me something that he and his wife had told almost no one.

They had once lived in a house that was haunted by three generations. It had been an L-shaped chalet bungalow, and on one occasion he had looked through one window, and into another room to see a man sitting in his chair. There were other people who also appeared to take delight in being seen. His three children were not troubled, and the parents were keen to keep the problem from them, in fact to begin with they did not even tell each other.

Things vanished, and then reappeared in strange places where they would never have been put. Life was difficult to put it mildly. When yet another article disappeared without reason, his wife exclaimed, "This house is haunted!" That broke the ice, and thereafter, they both shared their views.

All kinds of mischievous things happened there. One night there was a crash, and a mirror fell off the hall wall, the hook taking a large lump of plaster with it, but in the morning the lump of plaster was missing. Another night, as they lay in bed, the couple felt an evil presence arrive. They were so scared they could not move, even to put out a hand to each other, and Samuel told me that he, literally, felt his hair rise.

At this time their children were young, and in bed when he had his supper after coming home from work. Through the frosted glass door they saw a child pass on the way to the loo. After a few minutes they went to check, and all the children were asleep. The same thing happened the second night. On the third night the same thing happened but with a horrible difference – the child moved as if crippled and in great pain. Alarmed, they went to investigate. All three children were sound asleep. They lost little time in moving house.

Of course, now I would advise them to get in touch with the Church of England. Whatever was happening needed sorting out. Was it a glorified poltergeist phenomena, or maybe something had 'gone wrong' when the previous family lived there? I have no doubt that all could have been resolved.

* * *

At one time I worked with a very nice girl, Rachel. We used to chat together over lunch in the canteen.

Before her marriage her parents had bought a country

cottage. They arrived there but their old cat took one look at the place, foamed at the mouth, and refused to go in. Shortly afterwards the animal died.

Rachel had an attack of 'flu and when she was recovering she left her bed to sit downstairs in the afternoon, with her mother. There was the rattle of the front door lock. Footsteps walked to the back door, and the back door lock rattled. She looked at her mother. "That happens every afternoon at three o'clock," her mother said.

While they lived at the cottage, her brother, a normal, healthy boy, nearly died, and her parent's marriage, which had always been a good one, nearly ended. Their luck returned to normal when they left the cottage.

* * *

When I was a child, we used to see our neighbours, the Vennings regularly. Further down the road lived the Jameses, who were friends of the Vennings.

The Vennings told us that the Jameses were moving – they had bought a huge and magnificent house in the country for a song – only the same amount that would buy a detached four bedroomed house. The Vennings had been taken over to see it, and were greatly impressed, it was a truly imposing edifice with a magnificent front door, and rows of Georgian style windows on either side, a similar symmetry in the many bedroom windows above, and, clearly what must have been servants' quarters with more windows under the roof. The whole was set amid fields. There were no other buildings near.

After being shown the house the Jameses took the Vennings for a drink at the local pub. They had a chance to chat to the locals. One of the old codgers went up to Mr Venning, established that he was with the Jameses, knew that the Jameses had bought the house, and said, "They won't stay there long – too many strange things happen there." Mr Venning put this comment down to sour grapes, and forgot all about it.

The family moved in. In those days few people had televisions, and their chief source of entertainment was the radio. It broke, and the house was in silence. The next morning their schoolboy son came downstairs. "You got the radio working again, last night," he observed, but was told that it was still dead. He went on and on about how it had worked, he had heard a lady singing after he had gone to bed. The family got fed up with him and his persistence, but the matter eventually died down.

Some weeks later they were sitting round the table having dinner when they all heard the most beautiful woman's voice singing ecclesiastical music. The son piped up, "That was the lady that I heard." The sound was definitely coming from within the house but no actual source was ever established.

One morning the wife was doing some housework in a library complete with books which they had bought along with the house. She took out a book, and opened it. As she did so she felt a presence materialise behind her. She found herself rooted to the spot, too fearful to move. Eventually she thought she must do something, so she gradually closed the book, and the presence melted away. That was the final straw and the family moved out.

A couple of years later we saw the house advertised in an upmarket Sunday supplement. The vendor had played down the size of the place, mentioning principal bedrooms, but ignoring the servants' quarters. We heard that the subsequent buyers also moved on quickly.

The known history of the house was interesting. The place stood on the ground (possibly some parts of it still were) of what had been a nunnery. Allegedly, an underground tunnel had run between it and a priory, and one of the nuns had had an affair. As was the routine punishment in those days, she was bricked up, to die of starvation.

* * *

The mother of a school friend said that, when they were first married, she and her husband found themselves a pretty little cottage which became their 'love nest'. However, every night they were disturbed by the sound of banging in the roof. It was a weird noise and they were not enthusiastic about going up there, to have a look.

Eventually sleepless nights goaded them into action. The husband plucked up courage, and opened the door to the loft. He was met with a solid wall of cobwebs. My friend's mother said they had never seen anything like it. There was no way anyone was going to venture any further, but there was no need to, because after the trap door was closed they never heard another sound.

They were both convinced that whatever it was that had been there had been trapped, and they had enabled it to escape.

* * *

Timothy had postings to different places during his working life, so he and his first wife had to move house a number of times over the years.

On one occasion they had a little cottage and, as soon as they moved in, there was a very strong smell of spring flowers. This could not be explained since it was the wrong time of year, there were none in the garden, and no one had upset any bottles of perfume.

They later learned that the old lady who had lived there loved her garden, and masses of bulbs came up in the spring.

One night they were in bed and were suddenly startled by a low but penetrating laugh at the end of their bed – it was a distinctive sound. Shortly afterwards Timothy recounted what had happened to his next door neighbour, and mimicked the laugh. "That is exactly the way the old lady used to laugh who had the cottage before," he said. Although dead she had clearly not quite left it.

There was one unpleasant experience while they were living there. Timothy's wife suddenly had the feeling that something terrible was happening to Timothy. She was so distressed that she found herself leaving the house, and going to the front gate. When Timothy got home he revealed that he had very nearly had what could have been a fatal accident on the way home. The roads were icy, and a pedal cyclist shot out of a minor road and into his path. He braked but skidded, spinning the car round, and narrowly missing a deep cutting at the side of the road.

* * *

A distant relative, Gillian, though basically a kind and caring lady, had a weakness into middle age, men! And that included other people's husbands.

At one time she was living and working in a large country house, mostly caring for the children while their mother pursued her profession in London. My relative lost no time in making overtures to the husband, and she became the talk of the village. Also employed at the house was a cleaning lady who lived locally. The amount of work she had to do, and the minimal time allowed, should have resulted in the house being decidedly dirty, but she claimed that she could manage her job well because she had help. She was aware of a spirit who aided her in her work.

The idea of supernatural help was politely ignored by everyone around. The house was clean, and that was what really mattered.

The spirit of the house was decidedly less well disposed towards Gillian, however. One night after she went to bed she too felt a presence – but an extremely hostile one. Luckily for the family my relative soon moved away, and things, presumably, were able to return to normal.

* * *

A friend reported that there was evidence that a big old house with which she had connections was haunted. The owners had put in domestic staff to keep it running, but things had not gone smoothly and one of the employees had to be asked to leave. There were many reasons for this, all valid, but he was resentful and vindictive.

The haunting particularly upset one good member of staff, who stayed, and others noticed that things happened. In particular newly made beds showed signs of having been disturbed, and things moved about.

I made enquiries from my guides and was told there were possibly as many as five mischief-making spirits who looked for places to haunt. The sacked employee had put the evil eye on the place. I was told that there was a distinction between people who wished ill in a relatively non-threatening manner, and those who worked on the psychic plane.

The mischievous spirits were actually harmless, but should be sorted out and told to go towards the light. Apparently the unpleasant manifestations were also a way in which the karma ripened for the owner of the property.

* * *

While many people have not actually seen a ghost there are few of us who have not sensed feelings in buildings or places. "I couldn't wait to get out of that house!" someone might exclaim, although there is no apparent reason for this. Equally, one might hear, in blissful tones, "Isn't the atmosphere wonderful?"

I will tell you about one of the nastiest experiences which I had. During our last couple of years at school Tamsin and I decided to go Youth Hostelling on bikes. We were utterly clueless. We settled for the Cambridgeshire area because there were few hills but had no idea that a strong wind can prove just as challenging and, with little faith in Youth Hostel food we loaded our bikes with edibles of all kinds until they weighed a ton. We set off, and did rather well to manage thirty miles on our first day.

Among the things we carried was equipment to enable us to rub the brasses in any churches we visited. While I was a Christian and had a belief in God my budding scientist friend Tamsin believed nothing existed unless science knew about it and could explain it. But she was just as interested in brasses as I was. One evening, after our meal at the hostel, we set out with more iron rations to be demolished before turning in for bed. As we peddled along we saw a church on a hill. We made our way up to it, and left our bikes by the porch, we also decided that it would be a good place to enjoy our second supper.

We were well rewarded when we entered the church. The brasses by the altar were magnificent, and included the portrayal of a large family, the children in descending size, and with those who died in infancy shown with skulls for heads. We had left our rubbing equipment at the hostel, so we decided to return the next morning. My friend walked back to the porch, and I had a final look at the brasses.

I became aware of a hostile presence arriving. The feeling got nastier and nastier, and, while not quite running, I made my way down the aisle as quickly as I could. I was nearly at the doorway when my friend turned round and I saw an expression of sheer terror on her face. Once I was outside the church I felt safe. I felt I had rather scored a point – for whatever reason my friend had felt even more afraid than I had – and I calmly suggested that we unpack our food. I was met with the exclamation, "You felt it too, didn't you?" I admitted it, and we jumped on our bikes and pedalled at break-neck speed down the hill. Afterwards, she claimed it must have been the sound of cows in a neighbouring field . . . but sound had never come into it!

* * *

I once met a lady who was an enthusiastic Roman Catholic. She knew I wasn't, and I was therefore rather surprised that she told me the following story. There was a seminary with a bedroom that had problems. A succession of young and hopeful potential priests who slept there committed suicide. Obliged to admit that there was indeed a series of tragic and macabre coincidences, the church eventually stopped using the area as a bedroom and opened it up, decking it with flowers and prayers.

* * *

Timothy and I once spent a night as the only guests in a seaside hotel in South Wales. We rounded off our dinner with a coffee in the lounge, and chatted about someone we knew who believed that she had spirits travelling with her.

Clearly the security man must have overheard us, for at the first opportunity he came across, and said that the hotel was haunted. He was a big strong fellow, but the manifestations clearly spooked him. He would go round at night turning off all the lights, and they would switch themselves on behind him. There was a figure the guests recognised as ghostly – they even knew who she was, the aunt of someone who had owned the hotel – but this did not solve the problem.

He grumbled that intelligent people staying at the hotel who saw things were not to be choked off with banal denials – they knew what they had seen.

That night I tuned in and found the vibes strangely, how can I describe it, energetic and overcharged. However, I did not sense anything hostile. When I got home I sent him details of how to get the Church of England to sort out the problem.

MESSAGES FROM SPIRIT HELPERS

- *An eclectic collection of observations and advice.*

A friend once remarked that the only people who appeared to be completely confident that there was life after death were spiritualists. One night I was told that it was indeed the role of a medium or healer to provide evidence that our consciousness does continue after death and that God given healing energies really do exist.

The messages reported here were all given to me by members of my spiritual family. I offer up their observations and advice as coming from people who have a different overview to that which we have on earth. I make no claims that what is written is correct. In the book *Deliverance* there is the observation that the dead do not necessarily know more than the living. But I hope you will find something informative or at least of interest in what they have to say. A variety of subjects are covered.

A good example, evidence even, that we on earth receive help was given to an older friend, Kenneth who had been in the London Fire Service during the war. He and his group had been called to a building that was burning fiercely, and they had to go into the basement. Before long there was a terrible sound of falling masonry and they realised that the door through which they had entered had been blocked. They were also plunged into darkness. They were trapped and doomed. However, in the gloom appeared a figure in a top hat. He led the men across the room and up a flight of stairs they did not know existed.

A lady who ran a business near my home once told me that throughout her life she had been fearless. She had suffered the tragedy of losing her mother when she was, I think, about thirteen, but her mother continued to care for her. I then heard an amazing list of potentially very serious accidents, of very, very near accidents, in which the lady had been involved – but she always came away from them totally unharmed. She was confident that this would always be the case. On one occasion her mother had sent her the message 'Marry... to prosper' The lady took the advice, did prosper, and the marriage was happy until her husband became ill and died. She was not old, and soon found another partner.

Sarah, who specializes in helping people with matrimonial and similar problems, told me she was helping two of my friends. One had just lost his wife and, in addition to coping with his grief, had to accept that, made obvious by the circumstances of her death, the fact she had been unfaithful to him would become public knowledge.

In the other case a young couple who were blissfully engaged and very much in love had plans for their future happiness destroyed because the girl's parents, from a different ethnic background and living abroad, forbade the marriage. They would not let their daughter return to England after visiting them in their home country.

* * *

Leopold confirmed that people who have died can learn about healing from spirit doctors who have much greater insight after death.

I met a friend's aunt only once, but Ruth was a good and caring lady, and we heard of each other's activities through our mutual friend. She died, and shortly afterwards I felt her with me, one night, and realised that she had returned my energy levels, which had been very depleted, to normal. Our mutual friend was ill at this time, and I was told not to help her as Ruth was doing so. Interestingly the diagnosis was ME, from which there was supposed to be little relief, but at this time my friend did unexpectedly get stronger.

The aunt told me that she was learning to be a healer. Her teacher was a man who had died about two years earlier. While he had not been a healer in his immediate past life, he had in an earlier incarnation. She also asked me to pass on a message to her niece – that she was very happy and very busy. Years later the niece gave me brightly-coloured pullovers that Ruth had knitted, and not long after this my friend's mother, the aunt's sister, who had been ill for a long time, became very ill, and died. I am sure there was more linking up, more love, and more healing.

* * *

One night Patrick and Mervyn wanted to talk to me about angels. Both they, and others, rejected my concept, popularly held, of 'guardian angels'. The objection was that what sounded airy and ethereal was in fact a manifestation of a lot of hard work and effort. Also, there was nothing magical about what the so called angels tried to do, and triumphs and disasters were experienced by them in much the same way as we do on earth.

It was certainly true that a spiritual force from, for example, a dead relative, may wish to help, and would very likely be around at times of danger. Messages might be put into the consciousness of those on earth through a psychic link. For instance, someone's proposed course of action might be a bad one which would result in suffering, possibly a car journey that might end in a crash but, despite suspicions that all may not be well transmitted by the helpers, the plan may be adhered to with the inevitable unhappy outcome.

* * *

'Feelings' and 'gut feelings' are often thoughts received from helpers, though they can also be genuine premonitions by the person concerned. Messages can also be sent to try to guide people to do right things or to try to stop them doing wrong ones. Someone might be encouraged to contact a friend who, unbeknown to him or her, needed help, or might be sent a stab of conscience if tempted to go shoplifting.

I wanted to know why, so far as I could ascertain, many good, pleasant people did not appear to have guardian angels, by whatever name, helping them. I was told that no one was forced to do this work. The lack of volunteers in the after-life meant that many on earth did not have such support although it was needed. People do not suddenly become caring after death. The selfish remain selfish, and will only learn not to be when they become receptive, and this may take a number of incarnations. I was told that if one was praying and petitioning for someone the connection was made in an instant, like electricity. It was like putting a plug into a socket and there was no need to keep pressing the plug into the socket afterwards.

I was concerned that the benefit someone who was being prayed for received was dependent on the strength of the prayer, or the strength of the spirituality of the person doing the praying. Surely, the actual need of the person who was being prayed for was what should count. If this theory was correct it appeared to be unfair. I was told that this was not unfair – God could override events anyway.

Prayer could help with physical aspects, but while support could be given to assisting a person's spiritual state, any real improvement in this direction could only be brought about by the patient. In the end it was the spiritual that counted.

I was told that hate worked at a psychic level, and high-quality love on a spiritual level. The boy-meets-girl more casual love worked on a psychic level.

* * *

One can act as a link. A friend was having to make a very traumatic house move. Various people came to try to support him on the day when he had to leave what had been his home for many years. We had all feared the worst, that he would be very obviously greatly upset. In the event he was robust and matter-of-fact.

Afterwards he admitted he had been anxious about how he would feel, but had been able to take the view that it was time to move on. I discovered he had been helped by my anonymous Christian Science lady.

* * *

The time of death was always significant, I was told, but it did not necessarily relate to a particular point in someone's development being reached. In most cases where there is serious illness or a sudden accident this has happened for a purpose. Very often the event was preordained and will benefit the person spiritually, or aid the learning process even if the opposite appears to be the case.

It was possible for a preordained accident or illness to be postponed because of the effect it might have on third parties, for instance a father might live longer than had been planned for the benefit of his small child.

Although life often has a blue print, I was told that predestination can be over-ridden, though only by spiritual things and, in the case of illness, not with the use of ordinary medicines. Flower remedies and mantras would be more likely to work because today's conventional science precludes spirituality. If predestination is overturned at the time drugs are being taken this will be an unrelated coincidence that has happened only because other factors have come into play.

Spirituality can be provided either by the patient or healer. The practitioner could overcome the patient's will if the patient wished to die but, obviously, could not gainsay God's will. Also keeping a very sick and suffering patient alive at all costs was not necessarily a good thing.

* * *

An apparent miracle healing might indicate nothing truly momentous, it could just be the spiritual strength of the practitioner. As we have too little wisdom to know when to petition and what to petition for – possibly a recovery or a beautiful and peaceful death – we should ask for God's will to be done, as he has knowledge we do not.

* * *

Sarah said that a doctor could not help with an illness brought about by bad karma ripening – only contrition by the patient could bring about a cure. Most people would not know why they were ill, if the cause was karmic.

David told me that karmic illnesses were experiential illnesses. (I had suggested 'real' or 'perceived', but was told 'No'; they were built on experience and observation.) Help would only appear once the karmic cycle was over, when there would have been a spontaneous recovery anyway. If the karmic illness ended in death then the patient would go into the next life more purified.

Two people destined for great spiritual achievements, Mary Baker Eddy the founder of Christian Science and Dorothy Kerin of Burrswood, both performed miracle healings, and suffered terrible ill-health. This was necessary to prepare them for the work that lay ahead.

* * *

Friends had been giving a great deal of support to a woman who was dying of cancer, and was terrified. I asked if I could help, and was told I couldn't and my friends could not help the patient spiritually, either. However, her late husband and her parents were, in fact, caring for her. I asked why she had to suffer so much and was told she needed the experience of this sort of death, and would be helped on the other side. She had to cope with this death experience on her own. Previously there had been a lot of support from her family.

Quite often the job of caring for different people in the same family is shared, and may be exchanged at times, among their dead relatives and friends.

Once I was told, contrary to what I would have expected, that my friend Elizabeth was not being tended by her parents, who often did look after members of their family, but by an uncle and aunt of her son's father-in-law. This couple were not blood relations but had been exceptionally caring friends of the father-in-law when he was a boy. I beamed in, and found them wonderfully strong and dependable.

Elizabeth's parents were busy looking after their other daughter, her family, and grand-daughter.

I was told not to get involved with any of the family's problems. My attempts at help would have been inferior and unnecessary.

When the dead hung around to help those still alive it was not the case that they were earth bound. There were, however, many different reasons why one could be earthbound. One was attachment to things of this world and an inability to accept that one had died. Those who die have many options open to them and if their motivation is good they should find it easier to progress in the afterlife than on earth.

My mother had not been earth bound when she hung about me – her greatest desire had been to harm me and this over-rode all else.

Those who feel uneasy about praying can make their contribution in a different way. We can dedicate whatever we wish, the making of a meal, a country walk, or a prized possession. I attended the funeral of a fellow all-the-year-round swimmer but, instead of going to the funeral feast afterwards, I went and had a dip. The sea was wonderful, and I thought of Amber as I dedicated my swim to her. As though in acknowledgement she led me to a part of the beach where I discovered a plastic football, covered with sand. This is just the sort of childish thing that gives me pleasure. The beach was empty, so its owner must have long since gone. I still have it, and remember her.

* * *

I was told that the dead can help the living and achieve this through the winds, another name for the spirit.

If, however, there is an evil intent coming from the dead to the living, the damage is done, or attempted, by using psychic powers. These operate through suggestion, either conscious or subconscious. An example of this is Voodoo; bad news given by a doctor, if believed, can have the same effect on the body.

The dead can influence one for good or evil, if one is not strong enough to withstand the invasion. The more spiritual one is, the less likely to fall under other adverse influences.

It is uncommon, but possible, for a living person to exercise influence in this way.

All these experiences are received through a psychic channel. This is why spirituality, being stronger, can withstand adverse influences.

People can be led to spirituality by many paths – each person is drawn to his or her spirituality in a unique way. The danger is that people can get confused between the spiritual and the psychic and get caught up in the psychic.

People's spirituality manifests in their state of mind. How they got into this state of mind, whether through organized religion in a group, or in any other way, is not important. The ways are infinite, for instance one might be in the country on a beautiful day and feel God's creative energy.

Anthony informed me that when people die we mourn the loss of the accessibility of their spirituality through their bodies. While we live the spirit expresses itself through speech and actions, and it is this nearness that we miss.

When people die and lose their bodies they at last realise the insubstantiality of the material, and can therefore achieve enhanced spirituality more easily than they were able to while on this earth.

People have dreamed of the dead, or had a vision of them, as assuming a perfect form. They are themselves, but with their material elements exchanged for spiritual.

A friend who befriended a scruffy unwanted cat told me that when the cat had died he had a dream in which the animal appeared before him immaculate, in a beautiful etheric aspect of itself. He felt the cat was telling him that it was all right.

* * *

In the afterlife, I was told, we do not have day and night as on earth, but we can still get tired and need times of rest.

Leopold told me that speech was redundant among the dead, through spirit telepathy he could pick up on other people's thoughts. Communication was just as easy as it had ever been. Hearing, sight, and smell are retained, but not taste as we know it. The experience of tasting was received in a different way.

* * *

I was sent the thought that unhappy marriages are their own sort of war. Men and women who actually went to the extreme of killing their husbands or wives in doing so actually provided them with their wonderful escape into happiness and freedom. And, I contemplated, is there a difference between killing by violence – literally and obviously – or by gradually reducing a partner's will to live through imposing unhappiness which results in terminal illness?

One thing I do know is that where one partner in a marriage is basically good and kind and the other spiteful and destructive there will be no compulsion for the good one to be with the partner in the afterlife. Only where there has been deep spiritual love, or possibly an equal motivation during the life to do good or evil, could the relationship be continued after death – though obviously in a different way.

However, it is difficult to look long term and accept these truths rather than getting caught up with the unjust situation so obviously evident in the here and now.

* * *

We would all like to see a good outcome in the material world, but should try to accept that this will be over almost instantly, while the future embraces eternity.

Many people noticed, and some of the psychic expected, that the going would get tough during the approach to the millennium. Friends who practised different kinds of healing including a homœopath and one who did reiki found that they did not find their patients benefiting as they should. Another who kept a watch on distant friends through psychic awareness found she missed times when they needed help.

David explained that while it was true that, at this time, individual karma was ripening there were also great heavings in the world, though these were not brought about by the millennium as such. There had been overriding forces at work, which made things very difficult.

On another occasion I was told that the world was unhappy because its energies were affected by things such as pollution, the extraction of oil, and the destruction of the rain forests.

Wars are a great evil. Mass killings do an immense amount of harm. I once heard about a soldier who had been court martialled because, on the battlefield, he had suddenly stopped fighting. Before the court he said that he was pulled up short when the figure of Christ appeared before him, and said how angry he was that after all he had taught the people they continued to fight and kill each other.

The charge was dismissed. Would that all military men

were as enlightened as that court must have been.

Fighting is always taking place somewhere in the world, and I asked Ivor about group karma. There is the concept that one is not only affected by one's own actions, but by the actions of one's country, or the group to which one belongs. This could be particularly worrying if one lived in a country where politicians, over whom one appeared to have no control, involved other people in fighting wars although most of the people were against the aggression.

Ivor said that those who were part of a bad group, like soldiers actively working for a bad cause, would suffer as individuals and would tend to return as a group which was going to suffer. Individuals that did not like or take part in the evil going on around them would benefit as individuals. Any individual fighting to kill, no matter what the circumstances, would have attracted bad karma.

A holocaust gas oven operative might get asthma or lung cancer, or someone forcing another to become a refugee would become one himself or perhaps be a member of an unstable family and would have no security.

When Karma ripened the process would not have to involve any awareness of why suffering had to take place, or regret, there would just have to be enough suffering for the 'reaping what one has sown' to balance out.

I wanted to know what effect suicide had on one's karma and was told it was the motive which determined the effect. If one was terminally ill, and putting a great strain on members of the family, and was convinced one could never be useful again, this would not create bad karma. However, suicide aimed at spiting or punishing another person would.

I was told that when someone, whose life has taken a spiritual downward path, dies, the trend is likely to continue if the deterioration was brought about by deliberate actions. Whether life was long or short was unimportant.

* * *

It is the case that most of us will have been better and kinder people than we are now. I was once told that one reason Timothy was the way he was, was that he had been much more able to relate positively to people in a previous life. His subconscious knowledge of this made him dissatisfied with the way he was in this one.

After death, however, there are forces that try to guide us into better ways, just as there are here. However, there is a big difference between there and here, as there are no forces encouraging further deterioration there. All help is on the positive side. People can though, through their own desire, continue to get nastier in the afterlife.

Ellen assisted with the thought that it was wrong to confuse loving someone's faults with loving them. It was untrue that one could only love oneself if one loved one's faults. One should accept faults for what they were.

The idea that we are made in the image of God, was what we should cling to. To tend to associate, indivisably, people with their imperfections was to tend to weld them together. This was not fair on them!

In St. Augustine's words one should 'Hate the sin but love the sinner'. In Christian Science there is the belief that we are all perfect really, being creatures of Divine mind, and in Buddhism there is the belief that there is Buddha nature in each one of us. If we aspire to this concept we can progress, and will find ourselves much happier, and should wish others to do so, too.

The following information was given to me one night by a helper with wonderful vibes who was happy to help but wished to remain anonymous.

There is the saying that there is always someone worse off than oneself, but it is probably more accessible to say 'I have in the past been worse off than I am now'. This will be true because of experiences in past lives, the fact we are fit enough to say this and make the judgement is evidence enough and we tend to relate better to ourselves. This argument also tends to emphasise the immortality and indestructability of the soul, and it is our lack of belief in this which is the cause of so many of today's problems.

* * *

Materialism is a reaction we have when we do not accept that our souls are the only part of us that will continue after death. By surrounding ourselves with possessions we believe we protect ourselves with real things. Erroneously we perceive ourselves and believe others perceive us, as enhanced and strengthened by the material trappings of modern life. This is completely wrong. It is the possessions which are insubstantial, and our soul state which is real and lasting. We pay too much attention to the former at the expense of the latter.

As people degenerate, and get more greedy, they care less for others. But they know, in their heart of hearts, that they are failing. They cannot relate to fellow human beings nor to God, thus cutting themselves off from the love and mercy of both. They do not expect to come under God's care. Like a grown up son or daughter who has incurred parental displeasure and has left home under a cloud they find it difficult to return.

It is probably easiest to be able to be a good person if one has possessions which are adequate for day to day existence but not too much to spare, so material things need not be an issue either way.

There is the wise observation in Buddhism that a total absence of possessions need not indicate a spiritually advanced being. Attachment can raise its head over a lack of wealth as much as an abundance. If someone without is eaten up with jealousy as his neighbour has more there is certainly no virtue in this. It is one's attitude to material things, not the objects themselves which matter.

* * *

In some African countries there is a superstition that twins are a bad thing. If a woman produces them she receives condolences rather than congratulations.

Guru Thomas found that there was something different about twins, and families in which twins existed.

I wondered if I could find out any information. Twins were never unrelated souls, I was told. Usually they were those of people who had previously been very close, like brothers and sisters or husbands and wives. If twins did not get on with each other this was because there was some karmic factor which had to be worked out and resolved, probably there had been trouble between them in the past.

It is a common belief that the soul enters the body at the moment of conception. Could one soul divide into two when twins were produced? I was told this was possible but very rare. I asked if their souls could reunite and was told that this could only happen if one twin died very quickly, before the karmic state had altered. Once there were two individual people each would be creating new karma independently of the other, so their souls could not, again, become one. This information came from one of my conversations with Betty.

Much is made, and always has been made, of exceptionally bright children. I was told we should not get too excited about this manifestation.

Those referred to, often disparagingly, as late developers were often preparing themselves for their work in the afterlife, where it is accepted that life is transitory, while consciousness and action are continuous.

* * *

The energies in places can be built up over the years. However, time need not play a part in this. While some are built up cumulatively others are created by an acute event, like a murder or an event of great joy. Energies can be neutralized subsequently by feelings of indifference.

When this was put to me, I remembered how I had heard stories of dogs refusing to walk along country paths where murders had taken place, and I had also always had a gut feeling that some shrines, particularly Roman Catholic ones where miraculous visions had taken place, were in danger of having their energies dissipated, if sceptical 'Jo Public' made them the subject of irreverent curiosity. Alternatively, a sacred area visited regularly by devout and well-motivated pilgrims would, I always felt, keep or possibly increase its powers. I suspect that although there appears to be doubt that the *Turin Shroud* could, historically, be what has been claimed for generations, it could have been endowed with energies by those travelling many miles to marvel at it.

On the subject of energies of feelings which appear to have been retained for a long time, an aunt told me how she had once been in a place where Roman Catholic martyrs walked on their way to execution, at a time when they were being prosecuted by the Protestants. Suddenly she found that she could have recited the whole of the Latin Mass – something which would normally have been impossible.

* * *

The phenomena of the same discoveries and inventions taking place in different parts of the world at the same time has often been noted. I asked for an explanation and was told it happened through a psychic influence, and could be labelled a manifestation of global consciousness.

This was not the same sort of psychic experience which caused viruses. I was told that the various types of psychic phenomena work in different ways on different parts of the body and mind.

Psychic messages are received in different ways by different people. Rebecca knows that if she feels a pain around her heart someone close to her is in trouble and needs help. She will then pick up the phone and ring round until she has discovered who is suffering and what the problem is. She is a lovely person, and does everything in her power to help them.

Symbolic events will tell her about things like the break up of a friend's marriage. For example one of a pair of earrings which were last seen together in a drawer may inexplicably disappear. There is often a connection between the items concerned and the people about whom she has the message.

Great Auntie Louie told me that when I earthed the physical conditions of other people this was not psychic in origin. There was physical as well as mental telepathy. Epidemics were telepathic. With the psychic one usually needed a linkup, while telepathy was more general.

One morning I was meditating alone when I suddenly felt unwell. There were very acute cramping pains in my stomach. Should I run to the loo? I decided the feeling would soon pass, and I stayed put. A minute later my husband came in to say that our dear old cat, Norman, was very ill and in great distress. He had been heaving, and was obviously not just trying to bring up food or a furball. That proved to be the last day of his life. He knew it, and crept away to die, although we brought him out (wrongly, I now know) and spent his last hours with him, saying good-bye, until the vet arrived to put him to sleep.

We can certainly have an awareness of and telepathy with other beings. A number of my cats have known exactly when I was coming home. My first cat, Topper, remained with my parents when I left home. I used to return to visit about every six weeks. My father used to drive to meet me off the train, a distance of some miles, but my mother realised that it was at the time we greeted each other that Topper's mood changed, and he knew I would soon be home. Many cats await their owners return. Often they are there well before any tell tale signs like the sound of a car engine or foot step.

There was a dramatic example of communication among

my distant ancestors. Bruce was an older son with a drink problem. He went to sea, and ended up in China. One night his little sister woke up crying, and ran to her mother. She found her mother equally distressed. "I know," she said, "Bruce is dead, isn't he?" He was.

* * *

For about a week my ability to dowse vanished. I lost my ability to ask questions, but instead had a predisposed answer and the pendulum swung madly, positively or negatively, accordingly. Why had this happened? As I try to do my dowsing for good reasons I was both perplexed and upset. But I was struck by how easily I could make the pendulum swing, my mental massages were very strong indeed. Was I being told something? When things returned to normal I was told that I was. After death I might be used to plant ideas into people's minds, though nothing definite was decided.

It sounds dubious to try to influence others in any way at all, but I remembered hearing how a group of spiritual helpers had guided a man on a battlefield to take a route where he would be protected from snipers that he did not know existed. He had to go a longer way round, but without the spiritual messages he would have been killed.

For a while I worked with criminals. Many were young and were basically good people, but their parents cared little for them and never took the time or trouble to talk to them or explain things to them. One young and reformed burglar said he hated himself for his past activities. It had been a terrible thing to enter someone else's home, violate it, and steal their things. He had been led by older boys. His mother had died, and his father was an alcoholic. He had never considered the effect of his actions on his victims.

Supposing one could have put reasoning into his thoughts? Made him see the old lady he was robbing was like his grandmother? Much suffering would have been prevented.

One could possibly see a joyrider about to head down a road and to an inevitable fatal crash, killing innocent people, and persuade him to take another route. We have all made bad decisions. Advice in the form of a different opinion might have been useful.

Elizabeth once told me she felt compelled to visit the First World War battlegrounds. This was an unexpected and out of character choice for a holiday venue, but she had had an uncle who had died in France during the great war. There was a strange dichotomy here, in one way she wanted to go, and at the same time she was not all that keen.

I discovered that her late mother, who had been quite a force to be reckoned with, was the one who was keen for her to go, and was implanting the thought in her mind. She thought the uncle had not received enough attention. The uncle himself, however, was indifferent as to whether or not Elizabeth went to France, and the idea eventually dropped.

I wondered whether I could pick up other people's ideas easily and whether other people could pick up mine. I was told that others could pick up on my thoughts – I had noticed how rather unlikely people would raise topics like reincarnation, an awareness of the presence of dead relatives, etc., with me out of the blue, and how often when I investigated a new approach or technique in sculpture someone would say that so-and-so (whom I had never heard of) did something similar. However, I did not pick up other people's ideas particularly quickly. Ordinary thoughts were more on a psychic rather than a telepathic level.

I was then told off for being concerned with trivia, whether I might inadvertently be copying or being copied in my work – and told to take messages more seriously. I could feel an indignant presence, which I established as an anonymous single Christian Science lady.

* * *

As an all-the-year-round swimmer I am reasonably at home in the water and in the right conditions swim quite well. I was having a wonderful time, moments of relaxation and freedom as I enjoyed the gently rolling waves.

Suddenly I was aware of a man hovering over my right shoulder. His vibes told me he was not one of my spiritual family, I did not perceive him as my kind of person and I would not have been his. He had been viewing me with some doubt and his mood was rather heavy, but he said with some respect, "Well, she's a bloody good swimmer."

Who was he? I was told he had a daughter still on this earth and she had been suffering from cancer. He was very unhappy and concerned about her prognosis and had been shown me as an example of one whose life had not been ended by the disease, and was demonstrating fitness.

I was told I must add his daughter (name unknown) to the list of people for whom I am guided to pray. So: 'the daughter of the discarnate spirit who watched me swim'. God knows who I mean!

When people start embracing faiths like Buddhism or Christian Science things tend to happen.

I was driving along a country road and was approaching crossroads where I had the right of way. I saw to my grief that there was a lovely black cat lying in the road, apparently having been hit by a vehicle. Its tail was still waving as it lay terribly injured.

I slowed right down and then saw that I was not looking at a cat but a black dustbin liner. I was just starting off again when out of the minor road ran first one, and then another, beautiful little long-haired dachshund dogs. They were clearly valued pets that had escaped from a nearby house. Had I not misinterpreted what I saw I would almost certainly have hit at least one of them. I felt strongly that someone 'arranged' this.

* * *

I fail dismally to follow much of the excellent advice I have been given during my spiritual quest. Both Christian Science and Buddhism espouse the truth that the only reality that exists is our perception of things. So far as the Scientists are concerned only perfection exists – anything less is our false way of viewing things and Buddhists point out that none of us can change the world around us so we must change the way we see it. Both work!

As one who suffered from the conventional problem of allergies I know that my problems could be overcome by altering the way I see food. I fail. David suggested that I dedicate food, seeing all of it as 'an ocean of nectar', as described in Buddhism, and believing it would provide perfect nutrients, sustain perfect body weight, and at the same time cleanse and purify the body. I failed to do this and David returned, and told me to stop dowsing for good and bad foods. I must change my perception!

There are many Buddhist practices which I would enjoy doing but my time gets crowded with other things. In order to keep in touch with the Buddhas concerned I recite their mantras. On one occasion I had the strong feeling that I should say them out loud, they are usually repeated silently, and I later heard that there had been a number of spirits with me who had no knowledge of Buddhism but were interested. They preferred a spoken to a silent recitation.

I was told that if people rubbish or criticise things they do not understand, while other people derive benefit, then this shows the first group is ignorant and in no position to judge. (Rather obvious, this one, but I know I should report it faithfully.)

* * *

For those of us who are aware of spirits who are travelling with us these people are our friends just as much as those who are here and with us on earth. In fact, because they are not constrained by mortal things, and, assuming that they are benevolent and there to help us, they are preferable to many we meet down here.

If these people suddenly vanish, the feeling is one of great distress. And this is what happened on 11 September 2001. I became aware that my usual group, which I call my spiritual family and spiritual friends, were no longer around me. I felt deserted and, because I often sought their advice when making decisions, seriously bereft.

I asked, and was told, that these spirits whose motive was to help mankind, had taken flight to try to alleviate global matters. My group were trying to prevent the USA from overreacting with violence and hatred in response to the terrorist attack.

Of course, I was not the only one. I first met a lady attached to a spiritualist church. My polite enquiry, about how she was, was met with a stream of distress. Once, previously, I had asked her how she knew good spirits were with her, and she had replied that she just got 'a nice feeling' and advised anyone with the same experience to make the most of it. Her 'nice feelings' had disappeared. I tried to explain that I thought, in the spirit world, it was a case of 'All hands on deck' following the trouble in America, but I am not too sure that she accepted my explanation.

Then I met another friend. Only after we had known each other for some years had she revealed that she had had, ever since she could remember, beautiful and helpful spirits, one on each shoulder. But now they had gone, and in their place was 'something horrible'. Again, I put forward my theory. Then I heard that Guru Thomas – and his father had visited me once or twice and told me that he had been around for Thomas – was having a rough time. I suspect he might also have been in a state of loss.

While we were all very put out to have been deserted I think none of us would have failed to appreciate that there are times when the greater need of others must mean that we take low priority.

Eventually I found that some of the old helpers had come back to me, and I also got new friends, though this was some months after 11 September. In fact, far from bemoaning one's own loss, one should be grateful that there are beings trying to protect us on a global scale. How they deal with the aggression and arrogance of politicians and other selfstyled leaders I do not know, but they can probably help a very great deal with the ordinary people whose lives either are, or may otherwise be, devastated by events.

When looking at the notes, made over many, years, of messages from my spirit guides I found two horribly accurate predictions which had puzzled me at the time.

This book was not intended to be in any way political, but the predictions involved the fate of our country, and some of my guides have gathered together to advise me that I must include what I am going to say. The members of my Spiritual family who contacted me were My Frances, whose crystal clear brain I could feel beaming at me very forcefully, Leopold who had suffered so greatly as a Jew when Hitler came to power, and Patrick. Cuddly, woolly Patrick lost his easy-going attitude and became more focused than I had ever known him. He even managed to show some anger at what had happened.

Before one of the first elections for which Tony Blair stood as prime minister Guru Catherine pendulumed to see for whom she should vote. She was told the Liberal Democrats would be best, the Conservatives were second, and Tony Blair would be 'A disaster'. One has little expectation of politicians, but this language was extreme. Blair won. What did it portend?

Then, at the end of the Buddhists' Spring Festival, 31st May to 3rd June 2002, at Manjushri Mahayana Buddhist Centre in Ulverston, Cumbria, my Guru announced he had something to say to us.

We had received wonderful Buddhist teachings and as

always they were delivered with love, sincerity, and humour. Suddenly he became serious. "You think you live in a democracy," he said. "You do not. The future of the world is in the hands of a very small number of people." Why had he said this?

Millions demonstrated against the proposed war in Iraq. Had there been a referendum there would have been an overwhelming "No". The old, young, rich, poor, D.S.S. job-dodgers, professionals, those of all races, religions, and atheists united in their revulsion at the idea. To their grief, arrogance won the day, 'power' won the day. I say 'power' because true power is spiritual, not material, and lies only in the hands of God. Ultimately love will triumph over hatred. Good people who were slaughtered will progress in joy, while their killers will have to face the consequences of their actions, if not in their present lives then in the next. There is no escape. I know. My spirit guides told me that bad karma created in my last life, when I fought in World War I, made me acutely aware of the present suffering of the Iraqis.

Sitting safely behind their desks the leaders of nations order their forces to take part in the mass murder of civilians which is the established pattern of modern warfare. Remember the saturation bombing of Dresden in World War II, the lethal burning and disfiguring napalm which the Americans rained down on the peasant farmers in Vietnam, and the cluster bombs which we and the Americans used to kill and maim many thousands of Iraqi civilians. Cosily the Allies flew overhead, out of harm's way while below the hospitals to which the horribly injured were taken lacked even the basics of clean water and electricity. (This policy, of destroying the country's infrastructure, was common knowledge in the peace movements even before war was declared.) This was a bullies' war.

Politicians told us we were 'liberating' these victims. The lie was obscene. I heard a statement on Radio 4: 'Wars are between politicians, not people.' How true.

The Pope and the Archbishop of Canterbury, and all the churches they represented, were solidly against the war in Iraq. Blair and Bush claimed to be 'Christians'... A Christian must be someone who tries to follow the teachings of Christ. 'Love your enemy... forgive... turn the other cheek.' Labels don't count. Fundamentalists, whether Jewish, Christian, or Muslim appear to have one common desire – to find excuses to go to war. In so doing they ignore the Great Commandment: Thou shalt not kill.

Blair described the 'end' of his war as 'A glorious victory'. End? Every time we 'took out' a building (spin for destroying it and slaughtering all the civilians in the area) where an arch-terrorist was allegedly hiding we recruited more moderates to the ranks of the enraged extremists. And these men and women will not stand in neat, uniformed rows, easy-kill for the Americans, but will travel the world as disparate individuals, identified only by the mayhem they leave behind.

My common sense logic would be rejected by our leaders. I fear their true attitude is, 'Boy O Boy we paid millions for our weapons of mass destruction, and aren't we going to enjoy using them!' It was our tank busters that were tipped with depleted uranium, not the weapons used by the Iraqis...

With our approach the war on terror can never be won. Only with dialogue, understanding and empathy can peace be achieved. Ghandi told Churchill that the world must follow the Beatitudes, 'Blessed are the peacemakers...' It takes a Hindu to teach a Christian the Christian message.

I felt helpless as we went to war, and unclean to be associated with a country responsible for such evil. Millions shared these feelings on both sides of the Atlantic.

However, I hope that this book will give some comfort and encourage the belief that, whatever appearances, God is with us and is in everything. Neither we nor the victims are alone or deserted. My spirit guides have offered their evidence of this. Please accept it, with their love.

The Spirits' Advice For Me

● *Coping with child abuse.* ● *Ill again but help is at hand.* ● *My body, a guinea pig for spiritual helpers.* ● *I have bad karma which must be worked off.* ● *A helper influences Timothy.* ● *My sight and hearing diminish as I subconsciously wish to withdraw from life.* ● *I am given perfect sight for a minute or two.* ● *Binge eating.* ● *Vegetarianism.* ● *Our inner and outer addictions.* ● *Can an animal spirit travel with another animal?* ● *Psychic work can be draining – we may get help.* ● *Kundalini.* ● *I see people other than in their normal physical selves.*

Having been abused as a child presents an ongoing challenge, but I had all kinds of advice on how to cope. David, a member of my spiritual family, told me that there could be no healing without forgiveness of one's self. Just about everyone who has been abused as a child feels this guilt, which may be inappropriate, but is very real in one's own perception. The hate pushed onto one and the feeling of being unlovable and deserving this is believed at a deep level.

Dorothy Kerin advised me that my belief in my own ugliness was so deeply entrenched – my mother and then my husband had beamed critical and negative thoughts at me – that I now automatically went to charity shops to buy my clothes. My attitude was something I was stuck with and I was not strong enough to shake it off. However, I would not have this problem forever.

Patrick, a spiritual friend, told me to visualize light within me, God and Buddha nature, radiating outwards, and keeping at bay all damaging external factors which were trying, consciously or unconsciously, to exhaust me. Ellen, a member of the spiritual family, urged me to separate myself from the rest of the world (in perception) for protection.

Ellen told me I must spend some of my meditation time on

my own behalf – I needed to get physically stronger. The message that one must work for oneself was confirmed at a Buddhist teaching when we were advised to enjoy time with ourselves. This has to be taken in the context that the whole purpose of Mahayana Buddhism is to gain enlightenment so that one may help all other sentient beings.

Sometimes people suggest that we cannot help others unless we have first sorted out ourselves. I do not go along with this idea. I know I shall never be anywhere near perfect, and if I did not try to help others while in my imperfect state then I could never help anyone. That must be wrong too. One must try to do both, make progress oneself and try to answer the needs of those around one.

* * *

My immune system is a disaster area. Parts have been surgically removed and the rest are either damaged by radiotherapy or seriously overworked. Friends upstairs were trying to help, for instance, Patrick told me to go to bed with the Christian Science belief that all would be well in the morning.

Suffering can be worthwhile if there is a purpose. My body, for example, is faulty and uncomfortable. I have a fat arm from radiotherapy treatment, and for a year after I picked up the MRSA Staphylococcus during a hospital visit, I mistook my extreme illness for 'flu which was popular at the time, I suffered from itchy swellings. Thomas discovered that, in getting to grips with the infection, my immune system reacted by dragging up the cowpox virus I had been given as a child, as an immunisation against smallpox. Live viruses in the system can cause a lot of problems.

While suffering from cowpox I awoke to discover that I felt a lot better, and much of the puffiness had gone. I was aware of a recently dead neighbour, Louisa, with me and healing me. Dorothy Kerin controlled the red and itchy lumps which covered me so I could continue to socialize. Angela assured me that my friends upstairs were practising healing on me.

Over the years I have got fed up with illness but one night I was told that my body was being used as a guinea pig by healers upstairs, to test how things reacted to their treatments. Ah well, so long as there is a purpose!

I was reminded that I had bad karma to burn off, built up during previous lives, I had been dishonest in my dealings when a fisherman and self-centred as a fresco painter when I had forced an employee, suffering from the effects of plaster dust, to keep working. Then during the First World War, my wish was to kill Germans. I asked if joining up and being killed was in that incarnation's blue print, and was told by a rather shocked Angela that nothing like that was ever in a blueprint.

* * *

If our outer addictions are smoking, drinking, and eating too much, then our inner addictions are anger, hatred, resentment, and festering sores of jealousy, greed, materialism, and a desire to score points off, or at least do better than, other people.

* * *

For over twenty years I had provided a Christmas Day meal for friends, but the year came when it appeared that no one would be depending on me. The previous year I had been terribly ill, and I still marvel that I had managed to get the guests fed and watered, and did not let them down. We suddenly realised that we could have a free day, do a few things we enjoyed like going for a leisurely walk, doing a bit of sculpture, and we had a really wonderful day.

I puzzled that Timothy gave me a break. He did not try to wind me up, practise every little bit of spite he could dream up, or complain about his health, endlessly. Surely, this did not happen spontaneously? No, indeed it did not. The specialist in marriage problems among my spiritual family, Sarah, had used her influence. A big 'Thank you', Sarah!

* * *

There was a time, when I became aware that my sight and hearing were diminishing – and that this was not through normal causes. I found my mundane life so unpleasant that I was, through my failing senses, both symbolically and literally withdrawing from it. But Betty, I was told, was trying to help me regain my hitherto good eyesight through thought transference, and by trying to make me feel optimistic.

As I had such a limited focus for reading, I went to Boots (the high street chemist and pharmacy) where I tried their off-the-peg reading glasses. Seeing me investigating the stand one of the assistants said that if I was shortsighted they would not help. How true! They made matters even worse. But as I experimented with other glasses, I suddenly had the gift of perfect vision. Puzzled, I fumbled for the miraculous spectacles that brought about this transformation. But at that moment, I was wearing none at all. Amazed but slightly shaken, I hurriedly left the shop and my sight returned to its poor state. But at least I had seen its potential.

Later, when I asked what had been going on, I was told that Ellen had been with me. She confirmed the reason for my apparent poor sight – my wish to withdraw from my day to day life. Anthony said he had also been there when I was gifted, albeit very briefly, with perfect sight.

One interesting fact is that while my close sight is terrible I can see, beautifully and clearly, more distant scenes. I started wearing glasses at twelve, and have been very shortsighted from the age of thirty-ish. I cannot help seeing the manifestation as symbolic. My immediate life I view with pessimism, but if I look ahead to the distant horizon...

* * *

I have always enjoyed eating, but have never had any serious weight problems, so far. But for a time I became obsessed with overeating. Luckily I prefer reasonably healthy food but even so my overloaded body made me sluggish and ineffective.

As I walked down the aisle of a church before a service and looked up at the figure of Christ above the altar it was as though He rebuked me, telling me I should not be so silly and trivial, and should focus on the more important things I was supposed to do in life. Alas, not even this brought about the cure it should have, though I did modify my habit a little. I discovered that there were two reasons why I started binge eating. One was that it was a response to an anxiety state, and the other was that I was in close physical proximity to someone who was also eating very excessively, again in response to an emotional problem. My telepathic receptors were again working overtime! Confirmation of this link came when the other sufferer moved away, and my desire to eat diminished and then vanished.

However, another lesson came from this experience. Again it was one of our cats that saw someone just above me and it turned out to be Geat Auntie Louie. Her message was that neither the quantity nor nature of the food we eat makes any difference. It is our perception which influences how we respond to it. Hence someone who eats a lot but expects to remain slim and believes he or she is eating correctly will not be damaged, while someone who eats very little, but perceives even this to be unhealthy and fattening is likely to suffer.

Years earlier I had had a short and insignificant spell of binge eating. I was told that it was caused, at one level, by depression, but that I had been sent it so I could empathize with and understand people with the same problem.

I was told that if we could manage to be vegetarian we are

being right in all ways. At the most basic level meat is dearer than other sources of protein, pulses, seeds, nuts, etc., so we are saving ourselves money. But, more meaningfully, in the ecological scale of things ground used for growing crops rather than grazing animals produces much more food. No one in the world need be hungry. The demand for cheap meat results in intensive farming methods and great cruelty to the animals concerned. There is the theory that one can actually pick up the awareness of the distress, fear, and suffering which these creatures have experienced by eating their dead bodies.

Some animals appear to have greater psychic awareness than we have. I have seen a number of cats focussing on things which I could not see. While I could feel a presence, the animal could actually see it.

I remember hearing that, somewhere in Africa, there were or had been people who believed that the spirit of one animal could enter another.

Among the cats we have had was one little female with a rather unhappy life. I made the mistake of letting her have one litter of kittens before having her spayed. Poor little Shirley loved motherhood. Had I left nature alone she would have had litter after litter in a state of bliss, but it was not viable to find homes for endless kittens and the vet advised that, as she had had five in her first litter, she would probably go on having that number. This would drain her, and it would not be in her interest to let all of them live. The idea of murdering healthy little kittens was not attractive.

I realised too late that in having her spayed I had destroyed her main reason for living. The poor little thing lived to about ten, then developed cancer, and had to be put to sleep. A year or two before she died another cat, a large female that had never produced, came to live with us. She was a totally different sort of animal, and despised Shirley openly. As the dominant cat was older, I hoped the first would outlive her, but that was not to be.

Eventually the dominant cat died, and we got Holly from the Cats' Protection League. This little animal had been ill-treated, and she was completely terrified of us and everything else. We followed the usual procedure of keeping her in for a few days and feeding her well. We thought she was beginning to settle but we were wrong. She vanished. We searched everywhere and kept calling her name. At night I put little dishes of food all over the house, expecting to hear the usual little rattle as her name disc knocked against the plates. Then there was nothing – silence – and the food remained uneaten for about four days. She appeared to have gone for good. I was distraught. I know cats well enough to understand how great their suffering can be.

Then, to my immense relief, the food started to disappear again. One night I was in on my own. It was winter, and I turned off all the lights, stayed quiet, and waited to see if Holly believing that she was alone, might appear. To my delight I heard the chink of her disc against the plates.

For some time before this event, the cat flap had been doctored so that while a cat could come in, it would be impossible for it to get out. As soon as I stirred the poor little thing fled. I searched each room of the house thoroughly. There was no sign of her. I looked in possible and impossible places. At last I peered into a tiny corner under the stairs, a few square inches bordered by a wall, the gas meter, and a wooden shoe cleaning box, and hidden behind brushes. I saw two little almond-shaped eyes looking at me. My delight and relief were immeasurable. I fished her out of her little hiding place, and Holly sat on my lap and purred.

Once she had come to accept that she could live with us her little personality, and she had a lot of character, blossomed. She had probably been hiding in her concealed corner all the time she was missing.

But what had happened during the four days?

I noticed that she did many things which my poor,

unhappy, much lamented cat had done – and I wondered. I asked whether it could be possible that the spirit of the dead cat could in some way be harnessed to our current pet, and was told 'Yes'. While the living cat would be unaware of the spirit of the other one it would be as if this was riding with her and in her.

I was not allowed to ask what had happened to the awareness/soul of the first cat between dying and riding with the living cat, but I was just told that Africans had a much greater understanding of animal and plant life than we in the West do. Animals can reincarnate or go to other places – they have no choice in this. But I was told that the lost four days were significant.

* * *

Using psychic energies to try to help people tends to be very tiring. Once when I was feeling particularly drained I was told that I need not try to help Holly. A lady who had been dead between one and two years was caring for her. I asked if she had once been the cat's owner, but was told 'No'.

Quite a few times I was given the message that I should ease off the psychic activity, and use my energies to write down what I had been taught.

Once, on a retreat, I met Jess who appeared to me to be much too energetic, almost to the point of aggression. She was a most unpeaceful person, though she had a very good personality. The subject of releasing energy from the kundalini came up, and it transpired that she had had this experience, and strongly recommended. it. However our teacher advised caution.

I asked my guides whether I would ever experience my kundalini rising and was told I would not, since I had been damaged sexually by my mother. However, I was told that the same energies were available with the help of the Buddha Green Tara and the Medicine Guru.

* * *

There is another way we can receive messages, simply through our own perception. It took me years before I realised that when I saw people I picked up on something other than, and more significant than, their appearance.

A middle-aged couple, were engaged. I knew the man slightly, but his fiancee not at all. I formed the impression that she was young, fair, and bubbly, a really happy soul. I had no contact with them but heard months later, on the grapevine, that although they remained friends the woman had abandoned all thoughts of marriage. I had always thought that the man was rather self-orientated and was not surprised. Then I saw them together again. At first I did not recognise the woman, whom I perceived as old, dark, tired, battered, and utterly wretched. Somewhere along the line she had been desperately hurt and destroyed.

DOWSING USING A PENDULUM

● *How to do it.* ● *Using it to test for food allergies.* ● *Why we can make the connection.* ● *Catherine's amazing talent.* ● *I visit a retired nurse.* ● *An ill lady is helped by using a pendulum for herself.* ● *The powers must be used responsibly wrong questions must not be asked.* ● *A spiritual healer may be chosen this way.*

Children of a friend, Fiona, suffered from allergies. In an effort to help, I had found a place in London where you could give a blood sample, and it would be mixed with different foods. If the foods damaged the blood then there was an allergy, the seriousness of which was gauged by the amount of harm done to the white cells.

This system was a good one, but if there was a need for checks to be carried out regularly then the exercise became expensive. Nothing is a coincidence, and Fiona met the lady who was to become my psychic guru, Catherine. Catherine showed her how to use a pendulum, and in turn Fiona showed me how to dowse with it.

To establish whether a particular food is good or bad for the patient, all you have to do is put a tiny bit of that food on the palm of the patient's hand, and then let the pendulum swing over it. If the contents of a bottle are to be tested, place a finger against the side of the bottle and let the pendulum swing above it. Packaging appears not to interfere with the findings which is helpful.

The pendulum gives a 'yes' or 'no'. First you have to discover the code which your pendulum will give. For some people it may swing in a clockwise circle for 'yes', and anti-clockwise for 'no', for others the opposite may be true. It may also swing east-west for 'yes', and north-south for 'no' – or the reverse.

So, to discover the 'yes and 'no' which are unique to you, sit quietly on your own with your knees a little apart. Hold the pendulum first above your right knee. Whatever it does, swinging clockwise, from east to west, etc. is your code for 'yes'. Repeat the procedure over the left knee. This will produce a swing in a different direction, and will be your code for 'no'. Once you have established which way it works for you, there is no need to check. The code will remain consistent. The answer yes or no will be given in this way no matter what.

What should a pendulum be like? Try to be sensitive to what feels right for you. I use something small – a shirt button on a piece of thread works perfectly. Some prefer a larger, wooden pendulum, which has more weight. My advice would be not to try to use something fancy. Crystals tend to be unsuitable since they appear to have lives of their own, and you need something inert.

Can everyone use a pendulum? No. But most people can. I have found that more women can than men, but just about everyone who is sensitive in general terms can manage it. Don't expect it to work perfectly immediately, and don't experiment in front of other people. Take yourself off somewhere, quietly, and keep trying. If not much happens the first time, try again later. If there is any movement at all, you will probably get there in the end. I hope it goes without saying that the hand must be held as still as possible!

* * *

For years I used my dowsing skills purely to test for food allergies. Happily I was quite good at it, and I was able to give quite a few people a bit of help. I had vowed never to use the pendulum for anything else, but my medical Guru, Thomas, pointed out that it could have much wider and positive, applications. However, do be aware, while using it, that the energies which make it work are not of our usual day-to-day material world, but are much more subtle, and should be respected.

Anyone who tries to use a pendulum for material gain, or for a dubious purpose, is likely to lose the ability to dowse altogether, and the results will, in any case, be questionable. The energies at work have been given by the power of goodness, and such a gift is not to be abused. Also, there is nothing special about someone who can use a pendulum. The facility should be available to any who might benefit, so, if I have had sessions testing people for food allergies, I generally try to teach them to use the pendulum for themselves. A patient can hold the food in his left hand, and hold the pendulum with his right, if he is right-handed. If left-handed, he should do ever feels comfortable.

How does the pendulum work? We all have psychic abilities whether openly acknowledged or latent. We are all connected to the one all-pervasive spirit. Any connection, a name, photograph, signature, or one of another person's possessions are all one with us. Also, such connections may be made across the divide we call death, if we choose to do so and conditions are right.

Most religions have some terminology to cover this phenomenon. Christians call it the Holy Spirit, in Buddhism there are the countless emanations of the Buddhas filling time and space, and I think the best word of all, is that used by the Aboriginees – 'One-ness'. This leaves no doubt that God is all-pervasive, and that all things are truly inter-related – a Buddhist word.

I do not mean that using a pendulum is a highly spiritual experience – it is not! The use to which we put the available energies determines whether there is anything really beneficial in what we are doing. But it is because we are all connected that we can be given the knowledge that we seek. Psychic power is in itself neutral – it is up to us to employ it responsibly.

* * *

Over the years, I got to know Catherine very well, and naturally, I learned a great deal about her experiences. On one occasion, she took a phone call from a family who were on holiday abroad. Disaster had struck – the father had collapsed with a heart condition and was in hospital. Could anything be done? Catherine asked for time, so his wife agreed ring back the following day.

Try as she might, the only positive indication Catherine found was a remedy for a kidney problem. When the man's wife telephoned Catherine, she explained what had happened. There was a pause. The diagnosis had been wrong and the problem had not been with his heart, but with his kidneys.

Catherine's talent with dowsing is mind-blowing. She has had to put up with much mocking of her 'talents' over the years, but those who sneer and call it hocus-pocus, often run to her for help if things go wrong.

* * *

A naturopath had asked me to go to someone, who had terrible digestive and bowel problems, to see if I could help. Conventional medicine had failed to find a diagnosis.

I rang the bell, and the door was opened by a small but indomitable lady probably in her late sixties. I was greeted with the words in a wonderful Irish brogue, "I have been a professional nurse all my life..." as she gave me a once up-and-down with her extremely critical eye. Oh dear – why had I come! I discovered that she had an allergy to citric acid, a common allergy, especially for migraine sufferers, then we got onto grains. Wheat was a disaster for her, and I explained that I wanted to return at a later date so I could test her with oats – which she did not have in the house – to see whether she was just allergic to wheat, or whether she had the more serious coeliac disease (an allergy to gluten, which is in just about every grain).

At this point she interrupted my questioning. "You ought to know that I have a coeliac condition," she announced. The naturopath had been suspicious that this was the case, but had kept this from me. It was a test.

The poor woman had suffered greatly over the years. Her life had not been easy as she struggled to bring up her family with too little money. All the specialists had dismissed her protests of physical ill-heath telling her that all her problems were caused by the stress of her situation, and were psychosomatic. With justifiable anger she speculated about how much of her pain could have been avoided. The specialists had been stupid indeed, for she was Irish, and people of Irish origin are noted for having a greater incidence of the coeliac condition than most of us.

* * *

The other lady I saw was suffering a terrible strain. She lived with a son who had shown early signs of a brilliant career, and had then become so heavily schizophrenic that he was incapable of doing any sort of work. In fact could do nothing at all. Part of the tragedy was that he was in many ways a caring young man, and was very upset about the course his life had taken.

I visited her twice. (I find it better to visit sufferers since the foods they normally eat are on hand. Sometimes individual brands of things, like margarine, are good or bad.) On each occasion she had masses of allergies – but different ones. Common sense told me that it was more likely that the problem was caused by nervous stress and tension, rather than particular parts of her body malfunctioning consistently.

The poor woman's problem manifested in terrible indigestion and unpredictable and violent diarrhoea so that it was, literally, years since she had dared to go for a walk. I taught her to dowse, which came naturally to her, and suggested that, before eating or preparing any food for eating, she dowse to see if it suited her at that particular time. She really wanted to be well, and following my suggestion kept to the regimen strictly. She was rewarded, and I heard to my delight that she had actually been able to leave the house, and enjoy going for walks.

Interestingly but dangerously the son wanted me to test him. I should have refused since if advising the seriously unbalanced, one is playing with fire. To my amazement all meat was poison to him, yet he was addicted to it, claiming he must have the protein. A few weeks later I saw a newspaper report which said that schizophrenic and violent prisoners in American jails had been deprived of meat, and their personalities had changed dramatically for the better. Was the meat causing toxins to form in the body, I wondered, and poison the brain? I have never met anyone else – not even the most enthusiastic vegetarian – who reacted in that way.

* * *

Once I had been persuaded that I could legitimately use the pendulum for purposes other than detecting food allergy I requested my guides, that if I ever asked a question which I shouldn't, the pendulum was to swing in a neutral (neither yes or no) direction. This has happened a number of times when I have, wrongly, let myself get carried away. I will give you one instance when this happened.

For many years I had parties on Christmas night. All the world and his wife would be invited, if I thought someone might be alone, along with closer friends. Among the regulars was someone who, we guessed, had had mental problems. Other guests were not keen on him, seeing him as a scrounger. Just before one Christmas he arrived on the doorstep, no doubt to ensure his invitation. At a glance I could see his mental condition had deteriorated. Later I felt the need to ask whether it would be all right to have him with other guests, and I got the answer 'yes'. Then I got nosey, and wanted to find out more about his condition. The pendulum, rightly, went neutral, since there was no justification in my trying to find out more details about the poor man's problems.

Obviously 'big' questions, like 'when will I/he/she die?' are also to be avoided.

There are, however, many, many questions which can be answered very beneficially. I and other friends have got good results by selecting spiritual healers through dowsing, for we have discovered that tracking down the right healer for a particular person is vital if the exercise is going to be really worthwhile. Interestingly, one does not need to know personally either the prospective patient or the healer.

MEDICAL MATTERS

● Illnesses, suffering and survival. ● Autopsies of two people who should have been dead for years. ● The determining factors in the time of death. ● People who have cheated death for years. ● Can people live without food or drink? ● Viruses. ● Memories of a sacred place can heal. ● Hepatitus C cured. ● Doctors accept they have no power over life or death. ● Migraines. ● Obsessions with illness increases its chances of manifesting. ● Personal disasters. ● We take health too seriously – the soul is immortal. ● The Vega machine. ● Perception. ● Phantom pains. ● Animals and complementary medicine. ● Autism. ● Helping paralysed children. ● Multiple Sclerosis. ● Cancer. ● Drugs.

One night I felt a wonderful presence with me, but my communicant was anonymous. I wanted to find out about the origin of and reason for disease. This is a huge and complex subject, with many different answers.

Many religions have come up with theories as to why we suffer, or have to suffer. I believe that there is probably some truth in all these theories, but to think there is an easy and glib explanation is to be mistaken.

I was told that genetic conditions could manifest as a result of negative karma created before the present life. This could work either way, one could be physically weak or defective because one had created a bad situation for one's self, or one could have robust health because of a build up of good karma. That's one reason.

Another, was the need for each of us to have a really wide range of experiences over different lifetimes. We need to have different conditions in different incarnations to increase our knowledge and understanding. Without this we would not be able to respond with empathy to the suffering and joy of other people. This aspect is very important since we are not just here for our own benefit but to help and improve the lives of our fellow members of the human race.

I have come across a lot of evidence which leads me to believe that we have to experience opposites, and thus create a balance. Someone, for instance, who is the favoured child of the family in one incarnation may be the unwanted one in another. Sometimes the wheel appears to come full circle, and, as an example, someone who was a bully in one life will have the experience of being the victim of bullies in a subsequent incarnation.

What determines whether we continue to survive? I had been puzzling this for years, having heard about people whose autopsies showed that, physically, they should have died years before they actually did.

* * *

One was a man of about fifty, who had led a very full and active life and who had done things which were physically very challenging right up to the time of his sudden and completely unexpected death. True, he died of a heart attack but the post mortem showed that half his heart had been dead for a long time, and, technically, it should not have been possible for him to live, let alone to have led a normal life.

Similarly, a child of ten who died of cancer should, scientifically speaking, have passed on five years earlier.

I asked how this had been possible, and was told that, in the first case, the man had had spiritual protection which had run out. This had not been inevitable, but someone already dead had wanted him to join him.

So far as the child was concerned the boy had no belief in illness, and this enabled him to survive. Indeed, his condition had gone completely undetected. Not even his father, who was a doctor, guessed that his son was terribly ill. It was only for the last month or two that anyone was aware that there was anything wrong at all, while in fact his whole body was completely riddled with the disease.

I was told that the time of his death was determined by the fact that he had had the experiences which were necessary for him in his life. After he died his parents conceived another son, they already had one older surviving boy, and the dead boy remained with his family, caring for both his brothers.

Apparently there are a lot of people walking around today who are very ill on a physical level but because they have a spirit helper, guardian angel, call it what you will, or people on earth who are petitioning for them, or supporting them strongly, or because they are sufficiently spiritual themselves, their illnesses are overruled.

Over the years I have acquired an unusual hobby. I collect the names of people I know who should be dead, according to the so called medical experts, but who are either still alive or else have lived vastly in excess of their supposed allotted time.

* * *

My first star pupil was Rosemary. She felt ill, went to the doctor, was diagnosed with advanced leukaemia, and was given a maximum of three weeks to live. Coming from a Jewish family she nonetheless became a Christian Scientist, and lived for another nine years. We all have to die sometime, and I know that her time was right for her. Full details about her are given in the Special People, Special Places section.

Mary, who had had breast cancer many years earlier, had a pain in her leg. Bone cancer, unrelated to her earlier illness, was diagnosed. She was expected to die within months. The hospital thought there was little point in offering treatment but grudgingly allowed her one course of radiotherapy. She died twelve years later, an old lady, with her leg intact.

While I was commuting I met Evangeline. Once, while waiting for a post-cancer check at the hospital, I spotted her waiting for a doctor. Neither knew the other had been ill and we exchanged news. She had been given six months to live, but this was eight years before I saw her. I see her still, bright as a button, and it must be at least twelve years later.

Mr Hanson had been given three months with cancer in the lung, stomach, and abdomen. He went to my medical Guru, Thomas, and lived for another three years. However, Thomas was distressed, and convinced he could have lived a lot longer. Tragically just as he was recovering from the trauma of having had cancer, he had to cope with a number of tragedies in his private life and he refused any kind of medical treatment. I saw him just before he died – he was happy, peaceful, and optimistic, and more than ready to go, and he told me both of the sorrows of his life and the blessing he had had in a wonderfully supportive wife.

Margaret, who appeared to be healthy, robust, and extremely active, suddenly collapsed and it was discovered that she had very advanced cancer of the lymph glands. The medicos gave her treatment but expected her to die soon.

Years later, however, she was just as energetic as she had ever been, and had become a mature degree student. She rose at 5.30a.m. to study but told me how, when revising for exams, she had realised she did not have enough time to cover the whole syllabus.

She decided she must make a choice of what subjects to concentrate on, followed her instincts, and when she sat the exam found the questions were exactly what she had prepared for. She has always been a person of faith, being raised as a Roman Catholic before converting to her husband's religion, which was Muslim, and her comment was, "Someone must have been praying for me."

As I talked to her I was aware of feeling happy and revitalised. How was it, I asked myself, that her energy levels were so much stronger than my own? She had been much more ill than I had been with my cancer. As we parted I was aware of a benign presence.

My guides told me this presence had been a female family friend of Margaret's who had become a great healer. I could feel that she wanted to pass on a message. Was it about cancer? Yes. Was it harder to heal someone with cancer than other illnesses? No. For instance, the heart could be strengthened if someone had heart problems and the immune system could be strengthened so it dealt with potential cancer cells.

I asked if this healer's methods were the same as those used by the Harry Edwards Spiritual Healing Sanctuary and was told 'No'. As I had felt fitter after seeing Margaret I asked if her healer helped me and was told she had, as I was a friend of Margaret's. Apparently this healer had not been there at the start of Margaret's illness, but others had.

Many years later, and by a series of coincidences, I again saw Margaret. It was a tonic to me to hear that she was still extremely well and was now a post graduate student studying for the Bar!

At the time I had cancer, this was during the brief time I was with the Political Sect, another in the group had been diagnosed. Apparently just about every organ in her body had been affected, and it was confidently predicted by a medico who was also with the sect that she must die within months. In fact, she died nine years later.

The same medico informed my husband that I would have a maximum of five years to live because of the degree of malignancy the cancer was sure to return. Well, ten years later, as I write this, I am remarkably active for one who was condemned to have been six feet under for the last five years.

* * *

I get quite angry when I hear of doctors 'playing God' by telling people when to die, as I do when I hear people justifying war. A combination of gross arrogance and ignorance rules supreme. These people are not gods, scarcely even tin gods and the psychological damage they do, and the fear they instil, is unforgivable. Of course, people do die. Each and every one of us has a *right* time to die. This may happen to coincide with medical predictions, or it may not. As I write this I have been privileged to have been taught so much about the continuation of life, that the absolute terror which the thought of death once had for me, has melted away. I just want to complete whatever it is that I am supposed to do in this incarnation, and then depart. I suspect that I may 'have never a backward glance'. But who can tell?

The greatest demonstration of someone staying alive when by all scientific reasoning they should be dead must surely be the ability of a few exceptionally spiritual people to survive without food or drink.

Probably the best known example of this was the Roman Catholic nun, Teresa Neumann, about whom quite a bit has been written. She, and Giri Bala are named in *The Autobiography of a Yogi* by Paramahansa Yogananda. Giri used a yogic way of tapping into cosmic energy to stay alive. But can this sort of thing happen in the western world, today?

When I saw a lecture by one of these people advertised I had to go along and find out. The subject was an extremely attractive, fairhaired lady of about fifty. She spoke to a packed hall. At the beginning she enquired how many of the hundreds of people present worked with angels? The response was staggering, at least a third of those present put up their hands. Interestingly, the publicity about her had attracted a wide variety of people, with both sexes, all ages and all classes apparently being well represented.

Jasmuheen, for that was her name, said that she never prepared a lecture since she was always guided in what she must say, and this help had never failed her. She told us about her phenomena, saying that she occasionally would have, perhaps, a cup of tea since friends felt uncomfortable eating a meal in her presence if she had nothing herself. Once in a while she might have a chocolate biscuit, because never experiencing the sense of taste could be boring. However, there was no such thing so far as she was concerned as healthy or unhealthy food. The occasional nibble was simply a harmless luxury.

Some people imagined that, as she did not eat, the organs of her body would shrivel or deteriorate in some way. This was not the case. She asked us to imagine that if we put our cars in the garage and did not run them for a while they would not have deteriorated or lost the ability to be driven again when we went back to using them.

Jasmuheen told us of a programme we could follow towards stopping taking food or drink, and said that there were about five hundred people in the world who needed no conventional sustenance to remain alive. She described herself and these other people as 'lightarians', as they were sustained by light.

She had written a number of books which were on sale, and I bought one. She signed those sold, and I was therefore able to go up to her, and stand within a couple of feet of her. She had an amazing ethereal quality.

Everything she said illustrated that she was outstandingly aware, spiritually, and her aim was to help people and respect our world ecologically. Personally, I feel that very, very few people could forgo food and drink, their spiritual powers would be inadequate.

Later I asked my guides about her. It struck me that while it was amazing that someone could exist without food, as food was readily available I could not see any great virtue in not eating for its own sake. Betty told me that Jasmaheen's lightarian status was a demonstration of what spirituality could achieve. What she had proved was possible was also a reminder that doctors and scientists, tied to what they saw as laws concerning matter, completely failed to take into account much greater powers which were real and available.

I was also told that I must take on board the message which she had given – that each and every one of us should trust the 'I am', accepting the strength within each one of us of our own individual identities.

Jasmuheen spoke about healing. She suggested that one should give a command to one's body, 'Body heal now!' This could be made (it can, I've tried it) with one's tongue between the bottom lip and the teeth, because this provided the right vibration. However, the intensity of the thought was important, I was told.

* * *

In *The Power of Spiritual Healing* Harry Edwards denies the belief held by the medicos that cancers are caused by viruses, and states that such illnesses are caused by an emotional condition. This view was confirmed when I asked about viruses, and their origins.

I was told that viruses were evil things which had previously been in living beings, either alive or dead. While all people have bad thoughts, bad thoughts in basically good people tend to dissipate, rather than building up and hardening. However, people with evil motivation build up a lot of negative psychic power. When they die a residue of this bad energy can be left behind, and it can attach itself to, or enter, someone who is psychically vulnerable. This is not a reflection on the personality of the victim, just an indication that their psychic receptors are unprotected.

It is true to say that a virus is caused by a psychic suggestion. Voodoo could thus be described as a virus. The virus becomes active if circumstances, like being surrounded by people who wish to harm others, are favourable to it in the same way that a hayfever sufferer will manifest symptoms if there is pollen in the air.

There has been publicity about viruses travelling between species. The one particularly mentioned was in a vaccine produced in an animal and then used to immunise humans.

Mervyn told me that viruses could travel between species because the animals involved, human or otherwise, had similar emotions like love, fear, and unhappiness, and were thus psychically vulnerable. However, a virus could never be transferred telepathically.

As a virus is caused by a psychic suggestion it is possible to banish it by another psychic suggestion, though sometimes difficult. But no virus would be strong enough to withstand a true spiritual healing.

Interestingly, this may link in with an account I heard of illness among those working to clear and take wood from rain forests. It was either a radio or television programme that revealed a very high death rate among the teams going into the forest. The workers fell prey to what appeared to be particularly lethal and numerous viruses.

On the whole the group leaders just accepted that they would lose some men, but one started listening to the locals, and respecting their folk lore. The natives said that there were 'bad spirits' in certain parts of the forest, and that if one ventured into these areas one would be ill. If one avoided them, one could stay well. The leader who took their advice and was guided by them about which parts of the forest should be entered or avoided lost no more men.

I was also told that a virus was a buildup of unhappiness. This ties in with the observation, increasingly acknowledged by conventional doctors, that people who have had a very sad or stressful time, are far more likely to be the victims of serious illness than those who have not.

What appears to be a common virus is actually a manifestation of the individual sufferings of the people concerned. Bad motivation can also be seen as a form of suffering though an evil one. Group anguish, in the form of anger, hostility, jealousy, and violence against the spirit can be very powerful in a heavily negative way.

To give another example – I once worked with criminals and I, and others I knew, including a probation officer, found time and time again that if one could isolate a criminal from his peer group and discuss things with him it was possible to get a positive and good response. However, put him back with his peer group, and he reverted to taking on all the negative qualities which were so damaging.

I have been told that a virus which affects many can be the result of group karma, or can be picked up at a psychic level through the state of other people.

This idea is not unreasonable when one considers that it is possible, if one is feeling under the weather, to make the effort to go out and enjoy one's self and socialise, and feel much better as a result. However, this may well be achieved by draining the other people since we have picked up, psychically, the state of those around us.

My medical guru, Thomas, once said that he had noticed that if he was able to clear people of viruses their mental conditions also improved. One patient, a child, that he had cleared of a virus appeared to have also been cleansed of antisocial behaviour.

Thomas discovered that by following Buddhism my whole condition improved and the cancer virus went into decline. I was not the only one finding benefit from our local centre. It became too small, and had to move to larger premises. I was quite upset – all the associations with the old building were such positive ones. Was this a problem and how could I overcome it if it was?

I was told that the memory of such a building gave the opportunity of a mindstate for healing which could last the rest of one's life. It made no difference if the actual room had vanished. Extreme concentration enabled energy, which would flow around me making perfect on the way, to be absorbed at a psychic level. Better than this, because of the nature of the energy it could transcend the psychic and attain the spiritual level and, I was told, in addition to being on a higher plane the spiritual energy reached more subtle levels.

I then heard that a Buddhist was cured of Hepatitis C by doing a long retreat focussing on Vajrasattva, the Buddha of Purification. I have a Buddhist friend who was given the same disease through a contaminated blood transfusion. She works on her condition spiritually and has already lived far longer than the doctors predicted.

Some doctors have come to see that scientific predictions are by no means set in stone. Some years ago my last surviving aunt went into a nursing home. The place was extremely pleasant and well run, but her life was excruciating. She had a constant bad headache, possibly caused by tiny blood clots though no one really knew. All her life she had loved reading but she was completely blind in one eye and the sight in the other was too poor for her to see enough to enjoy a book, or do anything else. She loved classical music, but was too deaf to listen to any, and any attempted conversation involved shouting into her better ear. She was not incontinent, but had to be helped to the loo because she had Ménières disease so her balance was too poor for her to go on her own.

She had always been a very positive character and remained typically stoic. But on one occasion when I visited her, she fixed me with a direct look from her one partially-sighted eye and said, "I have had enough." I knew she meant it. Most people would have, given her circumstances.

Before I left the home I gritted my teeth. I was very fond of her and did not want to lose her. I tracked down a nurse and told her what my aunt had said, and I stressed that I knew she meant it. While I was certainly not asking for any killing to take place if my aunt did get pneumonia, please could treatment aimed at keeping her alive be withheld. I saw my own preference for my aunt's continued existence as selfish. I liked to have her to visit, but I was not the one enduring endless suffering day in and day out.

My aunt eventually got pneumonia, and the home stuffed her full of antibiotics. She survived. I was furious, and wrote an acidic letter to the doctor inviting him to imagine what it was like to lead my aunt's life. There was a woman left with nothing but her intelligence, pain, and frustration. She had had a full life, been a successful businesswoman, and had lots of interests. Old age had robbed her of everything.

Back came the reply. The doctor reported that no note had been made on my aunt's notes, and his tone, I suppose was aimed to placate me!

But the most interesting part of his letter, so far as I was concerned, was that he had, over the years, formed the view that the power of life and death was not in the hands of the medicos. He had treated elderly people who were generally fit in the expectation that their little illnesses would be easily and quickly overcome, but then he had seen them die. Conversely, there were some who had reached a terrible state when they were dying anyway, and treatment was thus given at a 'tender loving care' level only, and they survived.

* * *

Guru Catherine is now an old lady. A medico wanted to check her heart and arranged for her to be wired up for a day to a mobile monitor which would indicate how her circulatory system coped with her routine. But the machine would not work. It was not faulty, and functioned perfectly on the nurse, but not on Catherine.

When she told me of this event, and the poor nurse wailing that this had never happened to her before, I pulled Catherine's leg, telling her that if she was meant to live she would do so even if she had no internal organs but was just stuffed with cotton wool.

She gave me one of her long, hard, profound looks, and told me about a lecture she once attended that was given by a doctor, one of the few enlightened ones. He said that experience had taught him that no body was so riddled with disease that it was incapable of supporting the soul that travelled with it. He firmly believed that we had a time to be born and a time to die.

What then, is the 'reality' of illness?

* * *

Migraine has bugged me throughout my life – almost. Thomas was able to greatly reduce the head pains, but my sessions resulted, routinely, in the loss of half a stone in three days. If I was not sick on a regular basis I felt less fit. My depleted immune system could not cope, I have lost my tonsils, adenoids, appendix, all the lymph nodes under one arm, and have had radiotherapy. Toxins build up therefore, and must be cleared.

However, for two years I did not get them. This was when I was first married, and believed my marriage was one of bliss. What was going on? Did I imagine myself, though wrongly, to be loved and therefore valuable, desirable, and clean? Was I so relaxed that my body could perform smoothly as it never has before or since? My body was the same then as before and after, but one would not have thought so, from the way it functioned.

In those two years I had only one migraine. It followed a brilliant wine and cheese party, when I indulged, wildly. It was scarcely surprising, with my allergies to non-vegetarian cheese, and all wines, that body rebelled!

Only three times has an impending migraine been deflected. I was very aware of the tell-tale signs when I took a friend to a Corinthian church healing session. To my amazement they were able to work their magic even on my migraine. The classic symptoms also vanished once when spirit friend Violet was helping me.

On the third occasion I started panicking as I was due to have a dinner party in a few days' time. I was doing the emanations, and was told to take Echinacea. Luckily I happened to have some, in capsule form, so I took it and the illness did not materialise. I was guided to the Echinacea by Eliza, who had been a gardener in one of her incarnations, and had retained a great understanding of the properties of herbs and other plants.

I once asked my doctor to put me in touch with a hypnotherapist. My monthly migraines were so regular I wondered if I had programmed myself to have them, and might perhaps be able to be re-programmed. He hooted with laughter, saying that I got them just because of the way I was.

However, I had confirmation that a belief in something did indeed make it more likely to manifest. This applied to serious illness and equally to complete recovery. For instance a belief that cancer was sure to return made the unwelcome event more likely. But, equally, a belief that health was restored and would remain good, predisposed the patient to an excellent outcome.

Christian Scientists, who would deny that they had ever been really ill – only went through an erroneous period of belief in poor health – would be most likely to shake off any perceived illness.

Certainly brooding on a bad medical condition, or getting involved mentally with its characteristics, appears to have the potential for harm. I knew of a doctor who specialised in, and knew all there was to know, about liver cancer. He died at a very young age from the disease.

* * *

Most of us have observed that we or our problems appear to contribute to our physical misfortunes. Stresses like divorces, bereavement, redundancy, financial problems etc. have been shown to pre-empt serious illness in many cases. While it is easy, to blame external circumstances for our misfortunes it is actually possible, if we are strong enough, to get through these disasters unscathed. And some people do!

I have a theory that what may be the true cause, is that we have found ourselves faced with rejection, shock, or failure, and our response has been to perceive ourselves as weakened and vulnerable. Others who never question their own strength, be it physical, mental, or spiritual, can be completely unaffected by any misfortune.

I was told that one of our major problems was that we took our illnesses too seriously. The soul is immortal and nothing can harm it – it is the real us. However, in a materialistic world we have started seeing our bodies not as the temple of our souls but as things. Sometimes they are viewed almost as status symbols and people pay fortunes to have face lifts, breast implants etc. even if the surgery involves a lot of unnecessary pain.

* * *

My Guru Thomas uses the Vega machine (described in the chapter *Mother Experience*) with outstanding results. I am aware he uses energies in addition to what is indicated by the machine which is, after all, solely scientific in the conventional sense. To try to determine the degree to which his successes are due to the purely scientific or the spiritual input, can only be a matter for speculation.

However, I wondered whether, if Teresa Neumann had been tested on the machine, it would have indicated that she could indeed survive without sustenance. My guides told me that the machine, working at the mundane level, would have indicated that food and drink were essential. Obviously, it would not be capable of taking paranormal and miraculous influences into account.

* * *

I am convinced that we pay far too little attention to the significance which perception plays in our lives. All kinds of things are going on of which we are completely unaware, in terms of normal consciousness.

There was once a fuss over a television advertisement. Apparently the eye is capable of seeing a certain number of images per second. Fewer than this will result in the jerky appearance one gets in the early films, but what about more?

Today all movement on celluloid is smooth as the number of frames per second is high – greater than the eye can see – and it cannot focus on them individually. The advert in question was sliding in messages by increasing the number of frames and using them to instruct people to buy the product concerned without the viewers realising this. Apparently the brain does receive the message but this bypasses the consciousness of the person being influenced. Such a ploy is, effectively, a subtle form of brainwashing.

People with poor sight have been placed in front of a newspaper which they cannot see well enough to read. Others have been placed in front of it, but given far too little time to read it all. However, under hypnosis both groups have been able to read the paper from memory.

Both phenomena beg the question what might we be seeing and taking on board at a subconscious level of which we are totally unaware? Where do we stand in our relationship to the real world?

Some people who have had their arms or legs amputated may have phantom pains in them, or else can describe in what position they are at present, and whether they are hot or cold. A colleague who had lost an arm could tell me whether he was aware of the elbow being bent.

* * *

Can animals be helped by complementary methods? In my experience cats, the only animals with which I am very familiar, do not respond well to long-term medication. Whenever I have put an elderly cat on a pill-a-day-for-life routine there has been much distress, and the animal has died soon afterwards. Sadly, our relationship has been affected. Pussies simply hate pills!

Believing we were doing the best for our little rescued animal who developed cystitis, we tried first one vet then another. Poor Holly had course after course of antibiotics, which did not work, was forced to eat special, unappetising food and was put through an anaesthetic and an X-ray, all with absolutely no relief, and no further solutions on offer from either vet. Between them their bills came to about £250.

I was becoming desperate, until I mentioned my concern at the Buddhist centre, and was told to go to the local herbalist. A little bottle of a remedy cost all of £1.40, and Holly was cured within a week or so. She has been enjoying a good range of normal food ever since. Could it be that she can relate better to the natural?

Soon after we had her I could tell she was unhappy though not actually ill. The traumas of her earlier life were haunting her. I dowsed, and discovered that she needed a flower remedy to counteract despair and another to help because she was soldiering on in spite of her condition. Spiritual friend Patrick also said I must envisage her as well, and feel determined that a happier state of mind would be restored.

We had another and older cat, Norman, who had suffered during a very hot spell, but who recovered when the weather cooled. "Had any spirits helped him," I asked, but was told, "No". I was also told that there were no spirit vets working either. But animals could benefit from a psychic approach to their healing and not, from the spirit point of view, through conventional medicine.

* * *

I once saw a *Q.E.D.* programme about an autistic child who was taken to the United Stated for two to three weeks of intensive therapy. The people who had started the clinic had themselves had a severely autistic son whom they had completely cured. Their approach appeared unbelievably simple – they imitated everything that the child did, so bridging the gap of understanding. If the child arched its back and screamed so did the therapist. Treatment was carried out in a playroom – a secure area which was designed to be simple and non-threatening.

I had always understood autism to be one of the most tragic and intransigent of conditions – physically perfect children totally failed to relate to their parents or anyone else and were locked in their own little worlds from which they appeared to view everyone else's with hostility and or fear. The programme showed how tremendous progress was made in a very short time. How could such dramatic strides be achieved so relatively easily, and using such a simple principle? I decided to ask a few questions.

Was there a strong spiritual element? 'No'. Apparently it was telepathy which held the key to finding the system. The original parents and their child had achieved success through telepathic communication.

A part of the child's brain had been switched off. This appeared correct. The child about whom the programme was made was normal until he was a toddler – so his condition had been acquired and was not present at birth.

What caused autistic children's brains to switch off? This, I was told by my guides, could arise from, different things – sometimes a feeling of rejection which had been caused by unremarkable and mundane sibling rivalry, or the witnessing of some incident which the child might perceive as a tragedy, disaster, or loss, possibly the breaking of a toy or some other minor event could trigger it. The switching off process tended to be a completely inappropriate response to some very minor incident caused by the child's faulty perception of it. Even an experience while the child was in the womb could cause autism.

So far as the curing of the condition was concerned, a child given 100% attention could not ignore the fact that others were playing his kind of game, and he could thus be weaned back to reality.

Telepathy may have been the key to breaking the child's isolation initially, but while the therapy was taking place the purely practical and persistent approach should be effective. While there should be a high success rate there would not be a successful outcome in every case, my guides informed me.

I had come across newspaper and television accounts of centres in America and the UK where brain damaged children who were paralysed were helped to discover mobility, defying all medical predictions.

The method used was very labour intensive with many helpers handling the patients frequently, and making their bodies move in a way so that normal activity would take place. A child's arms and legs would be manipulated into crawling, for instance.

In answer to questioning I was told that the success was not achieved by purely mechanical means. In fact there was an interaction between the helpers and the patients, and the helpers were willing the patients to perform the movements – a knowledge flowed between them at a subconscious level. Love helped a lot, but the telepathic knowledge effectively educated the child's brain into discovering how to use his or her body. This knowledge encouraged the child's body to start repairing the physical damage, and sometimes apparently miraculous results could be achieved.

* * *

Over the years I have heard various complementary practitioners express the view that helping people with Multiple Sclerosis is extremely difficult. The root cause often appears to be deep and emotional and, sometimes, there seems to be a built-in desire in the patient to wish for disablement in order to get the same care as is received by a dependent child.

Interestingly Catherine, when beaming energies to MS sufferers, has been aware that she has been able to bring about a physical improvement through her work. But she has often found that the patient has denied all knowledge of this.

Thomas, too, feels that there is often little point in getting involved with people suffering from this disease. When I asked questions about this I was told that the patient's mind could become closed, and could not accept an awareness of the improved condition. MS was sometimes the result of someone becoming debilitated through being drained by their own or another's psychic force.

* * *

I don't suppose I am the only person who would prefer to put all references to cancer behind them, but I was told I must ask my guides about it.

I was told that, in my case, the seed of breast cancer was sown before I got the virus (as conventional medicine refers to it) by my mother who hated me and my sexuality. My illness was her subconscious wish for me.

I asked about the effectiveness and lack of effectiveness of anti-cancer drugs – and was told that the drug would, in fact, have a certain effect. However, other factors affecting the patient came into play and these factors were often, wrongly, attributed to the drugs.

Possible influences were numerous but included the placebo effect. This would cover the influence of faith and factors totally unrelated to the drug like mental attitude, support from the living, the family, healers, complementary practitioners, support from the dead, a need to lean on the illness and not to die from it, and predestination to have the disease – though it should be borne in mind that predestined events can be over-ridden.

I was impressed by the words in a Jewish prayer for use during sickness,

> Your (God's) strength and courage are in my spirit and
> Your powers of healing are within my body.

Indeed, yes, we all have God-given powers, even if latent ones, for our own healing.

* * *

People who have psychic or spiritual powers often instinctively know what others need. A very old lady told me how she knew a friend who had cancer must be brought into the sun to get natural radiation treatment years before it was used clinically, and another friend had the insight that cancer cells could be killed by being 'drowned' in oxygen, a treatment described in a paper some time after she had come up with the idea.

* * *

Drugs – I asked how and why one drug might work better than another. Great Auntie Louie told me that if enough people had enough faith in it, it would work well. The faith of the inventor might also play a part. If a company was asked to make a cheap and cheerful drug, possibly for use in a third world country, which they knew to be less pure the employees might well have less confidence in it. This attitude could transmit itself to the drug itself.

There was once a lovely nurse called Rene Caisse. She concocted a herbal drink which had anti-cancer properties, and it had a very good success rate. She called it Essiac Tea – her name spelt backwards. It now sells under the name Flor-Essence.

I asked why this brew was so beneficial and was told that it strengthened the physical receivers in the brain that accept the negative telepathic influences which relate to cancer. The only drawback was that one would be less able to receive positive telepathy, as well.

Apparently those who can receive the relevant telepathic waves easily are very vulnerable to hostile attacks but, of course, they also have the benefit of accepting good influences in the same way that a radio with strong reception can pick up a great number of stations.

I was told that the placebo effect worked well because of a belief in goodness. This belief could be either conscious or subconscious. Even if the patient was a sceptic in this life he would have had belief in some previous lives which would be with him deep in his memory. This ingrained belief explains why some of the most apparently unlikely people have unshakeable religious conviction.

It also explains why some who claim to be atheists – and are in this life – have a built-in confidence when it comes to facing death.

The Power Of Prayer

● *My ten-year-old's prayer.* ● *A family saved.* ● *St. Jude's Norvina.* ● *St. Anthony finds lost objects.* ● *Prayer heals a child.* ● *Lung cancer vanishes.* ● *Healings by my Tibetan Buddhist monk.* ● *A number of prayers answered.* ● *A vicar's prayer.* ● *My mother survives.* ● *Prayer should be for what is best.* ● *Prayers can be answered by a peaceful death.* ● *Auspicious indications.* ● *A cat is rescued.* ● *A lost dog found.* ● *Buddhas, their mantras, and blessings.* ● *Cramp is cured by Christian Science methods.* ● *A car takes an impossibly large load.* ● *Christian Science methods enable me to mend a dress.* ● *A burnt thumb is undamaged.* ● *Catherine guided in the subjects for prayer.*

From my earliest days some instinct made me believe in the power of prayer, and when I was ten years old my first request was answered. It was answered with a bonus, I lay in bed bargaining with God, offering a sacrifice on my own part if a friend could benefit, but that sacrifice was never demanded.

I went to an independent preparatory school which was, for the most part, an 11+ crammer. Many of the parents had no plans to send their offspring to fee-paying secondary schools, and saw the preparatory school as an investment which would enable their sons and daughters to get a good, free education at the local high or grammar school. Other parents planned to send their children to public schools, and saw the preparatory school as an aid to passing entrance examinations.

The headmaster of the preparatory school was thoroughly unpleasant. His greatest delight was to reduce a boy to tears in front of a class of girls and, like many teachers, he had his favourite children and his pet hates. One of the pet hates was Cassandra, a friend whose outgoing personality, huge imagination, and general love of life endeared her to me considerably. She was just the sort of girl the head detested and the spiteful way in which his mind worked manifested very publicly when he deliberately kept her back in a lower class, where she would not be prepared,with her peer group, for her crucial 11+ year.

Cassandra's chances of passing the 11+ had been poor before she was held back, academically she was far from the best in her year although she was not always quite at the bottom, either. But once she was kept down her chances really were nil. I was furious at the treatment she had received, and the complete injustice of it.

While Cassandra's parents had no intention of sending her on to another fee-paying school my parents had decided that, whether or not I passed the 11+ examination, I would go on to public school. In those far off days of good high and grammar schools, there was less demand for the private sector, and it was accepted that I would get the public school entrance exam.

I prayed nightly that Cassandra would, despite all the odds, pass her 11+. I told God that I could fail –I was expected to pass so this was a fair bargain in my eyes – since I would not even take up the high school place if I did pass. The town where I lived had a population of 150,000, but only one girl's school. Overall the pass rate was about 15%, although at my prep. school it was over 50%, taking the children in the top class. No one had ever passed from the lower form. They were usually less bright, and had not been groomed to answer the 11+ questions satisfactorily, or prepared for exam conditions.

Imagine my delight and thankfulness when the results were out, and Cassandra became the first pupil ever to get a good result from a lower form. She herself was ecstatic, and I was convinced that, whatever her academic abilities or lack of them, her sheer personality would carry her through.

The following year I took my 11+ and passed. Perhaps God had a little game with me, for I was aware of doing far below my best when it came to the independent school's exam. I passed but was put in the lower stream. However, at the end of the year I joined the brighter class. If my year spent among the duller girls was my exchange for Cassandra's success then I can confirm that it was well worthwhile.

* * *

I love miracles! I think I was supposed to love them, since I have been privileged over the years to hear about quite a few. Knowledge of the reality of them is something I would like to instil into everyone. It is so encouraging.

One September we all returned to our adult education class. There were the usual pleasantries about the summer holidays, but my friend Katie came up with the shattering news from her holiday, "I nearly lost all of my family."

They had gone to Ireland, where they had a holiday home. The husband and sons loved to go sea fishing, and kept a boat for that purpose. They arrived, unpacked, and as soon as possible launched the boat and set out on an expedition. They did not bother with life jackets or flares.

The weather deteriorated, and a heavy blanket of mist descended. This was not good news, since they had no navigational aids. Then, and far worse, they realised that the boat was leaking. They should have checked it before they set out, when they would have realised it was not seaworthy. They were already quite a distance from the coast, could not be sure in which direction the land lay, and knew themselves to be away from any shipping lane, and thus away from any chance encounter which might have saved them.

Katie had been brought up a Roman Catholic and her boys had attended a Catholic boarding school. The elder one, Toby, had a strong faith. He knelt in the bottom of the boat, and prayed. Out of the mist came another boat. They were taken on board, and their deserted boat sank. "I was so proud of him," my friend said. Her husband had not been in favour of Roman Catholicism, but I should think even he must have been converted.

* * *

When I was a child I was fascinated by what appeared to be an endless list of entries in the Personal column in the *Daily Telegraph* which ended 'Thank you St. Jude.' I later discovered that if one went through a certain procedure one's prayers were sure to be answered. This was to 'say' the following prayer nine times a day and by the eighth day your prayers would be answered. Say it for nine days and it had never been known to fail. So:

> May the Sacred Heart of Jesus be adored, glorified, loved and preserved throughout the world now and forever; Sacred Heart of Jesus pray for us; St. Jude – worker of miracles pray for us; St. Jude helper of the hopeless, pray for us.

The only condition was that the person whose prayer was answered had to publish the fact. Usually this was done almost anonymously, with just the initials being given.

To judge by the frequency of the publishing of positive results a very great many people must have had great faith in St. Jude, and clearly this was wellfounded. St. Jude's *Norvena* was certainly a very much valued part of the lives of a lot of Roman Catholics at that time.

* * *

The power of the Saints can be spectacular. Although not a Roman Catholic my husband has called upon St. Anthony time and time again when he has lost things. They are found almost immediately. I have also benefited from this phenomena, the most appreciated instance involving the finding of a cat, Tabitha.

Friends visited to see a lodger, bringing with them their dog. This was a rescued animal, and while not in the least dangerous he did love a chase – particularly if he could go after a cat. We gave the friends their own room, and trusted that, knowing we had cats, they would keep their dog under control. Unfortunately they did not.

Suddenly all hell broke loose, and there was a tremendous scuffle while our very overweight and elderly Tabitha did what she could to make her escape. Luckily she reached the cat flap, and the dog, which was of a fair size, was unable to pursue her further.

Of course I dashed out after her to see if she was all right. She was nowhere to be found. It was dark, and I went searching for her with a torch. In view of her condition she was not one for jumping up garden walls, and if her fright had given her the strength to achieve this, could she get back again? I called, flashed the torch into the bushes, hunted in odd corners, but found nothing. The fear was that she was lying somewhere, hidden, and possibly having suffered a heart attack.

I called upon St. Anthony. There, on the top of a low wall which formed part of a compost bin was our loved pussy. I had checked the area only minutes earlier, but there sat madam, showing no sign of anxiety, calm and dignified under the dark night sky. Never has an answered prayer been more appreciated, my relief was enormous.

* * *

The year 2002 had two highlights, two healings which I heard about within a few weeks of each other. Elizabeth's grandson had an unusual inherited disease which resulted in tumours growing on nerve endings. These were benign, but had to be checked in case they started pressing on or damaging a vital organ. The condition was little known, and the local hospital ignored one lump for over a year. Then it was realised that it had developed considerably. Doubts that it had remained benign were heightened when a top cancer hospital discovered that it was invading the ribcage and stomach. There were long faces as the surgeon was wary of operating, chemotherapy was mentioned, and radiotherapy too. And there appeared to be a second lump.

Many people heard about the boy. His father helped to run a youth club at a church, and the members all prayed for him, and other groups remembered him in their prayers too. The hospital could not put off taking some form of action any longer. There would be one final round of X-rays, and then treatment must start. The X-rays showed there was one lump, and it was not malignant. It was removed, cleanly, like an apple, and the boy was back home the same night.

* * *

Janie felt unwell with a chest problem, she had been feeling tired for months. Chest X-rays showed she had lung cancer, and it was advanced. A group of cancer experts gathered together to try to agree on the best way to tackle the problem but whichever way they looked at her condition, the prognosis was poor.

But Janie, an extremely spiritual person, told me, "I could feel myself surrounded by a circle of love." Later X-rays showed the cancer had shrunk, and she knew it would continue to diminish.

* * *

I have met two people my Tibetan Buddhist monk Guru has healed. At one festival I sat next to a girl Jacquie who was practically blind. She had Multiple Sclerosis and was in a wheel chair. At one point we were asked to write down a mantra. I volunteered to try to help her, and wrote the four words, luckily all short ones, so that they completely covered an A4 sheet of paper. My friend could just see them.

Possibly a year later, it might have been longer, I saw her at another festival but she was some way off. I could see that she was holding a leaflet of Buddhist prayers, and I lamented to the person beside me, that she would be completely unable to read it. But my neighbour bridled. "My Guru prayed for the Jacquie, and she can now read normal print."

If the weather is fine at the festivals we can laze about on the grass and chat. On one occasion there was a lady in the group who said that something amazing had happened at a previous festival. When she arrived she was suffering from a rodent ulcer, cancer, on the side of her face. She had been due to have an operation shortly after her return home.

As the festival progressed she was aware of the ulcer getting bigger, and of pain shooting up into her head and down into her chest. Then, one day, she realised she had not felt any pain, then the ulcer started shrinking, eventually disappearing. She went to her surgeon, who confirmed that it had vanished.

The next time she was at a festival she mentioned the healing to one of the monks she had seen previously. He started laughing. He had told my Guru about the woman, and the Guru had prayed for her.

Years later I learned that my Guru had been a great healer when he was in Tibet. People would come some distance to be healed. Apparently he got fed up with his patients showing no interest in Buddhism, even though they had been healed through its powers. In a land where there was no electricity or regular services, let alone doctors or hospitals, the sick had to put their trust in Lamas. Their recovery was due to the unshakable faith of these men.

* * *

There is a wonderful little place I go to, a tiny C. of E. church, where there are brilliant healing services. I heard about them through an ex-boyfriend whose father's leg ulcer which he had had for years and the medicos had been unable to cure, vanished after just one of their sessions. At the heart of the services are a team of totally dedicated lay people. They talk to each suppliant individually, employ the laying on of hands, have a healing book to which they refer daily, and will even arrange a prayer chain, where people take it in turns to pray, so that in times of crisis prayer for the sufferer is maintained for many hours.

On one occasion a lady gave an address taking as her subject a Biblical figure who had bargained with God at the point of what would have been death, and He granted her a further fifteen years of life.

Why, we were invited to ask, had this rather obscure reference been selected? The answer was that, when she was at death's door with cancer and was not expected to last the night, a special prayer session had been held for a previous vicar's wife... and she had recovered. Recently, as an elderly lady, she had died – fifteen years after, in medical terms, the time she should have expired.

That lady was not the only one whose cancer was overcome. One of the members of the healing team, hearing that I also had had cancer, said, "I joined this team, and my cancer went away." Yet another member of the congregation who had cancer of the lymph was very much alive years after conventional doctors had expected her to die.

I once took a very ill atheist to the service. He was welcomed warmly, and on declaring that he was without any belief one of the healing team declared, "I don't mind, I shall still pray for you." The poor man did not receive a healing, but he was bowled over by, as someone else put it, "So much love," and he told me that such an experience could only be helpful – the people there were so kind and wonderful.

At one of these healing services the speaker told us that she had always suffered from hay fever. Year after year it was common for her to feel an irritation which would develop into a painful attack of sneezing and watery eyes. Then she found a formula. At the first sign of trouble she would say, "Thank you for healing, Lord," and all the symptoms vanished.

At the beginning of the millennium I decided that I must get a greater direction and purpose in my life if there was to be any point in staying alive. I needed fulfilment but was too exhausted through looking after Timothy. I had too little spare time and no energy. Because I usually know people who are ill, and really need prayers, I generally just petition on their behalf, but at the next service I made a request for myself. I wanted to become spiritually focused and that I should not be so exhausted that I could not be useful.

I was pulled up short when, at the end of the service, one of the lay people thanked God for the healings we had all received, and I realised that I was not expecting to have received any benefit at all. I was rightly disgusted with my lack of faith.

One of my main objectives, in writing this book, was to record my spiritual and psychic experiences, but when I sat at the typewriter I found that either my sight or co-ordination was faulty. I was consistently hitting the wrong keys. Imagine my amazement and delight to discover, after the healing service, that my old speed and fluency at the typewriter had returned to me, after many years.

* * *

An elderly lady was very ill, dying horribly of cancer. I had never met her but I knew her daughter-in-law, so I thought I should try to help. The worst aspect was not the disease, though this was bad enough, but the poor woman's mental and emotional condition. She clung on to her terrible existence instead of just slipping away, which would have been so much gentler.

One night I felt a lovely presence with me, and it was someone who was trying to help. I was told that the lady was not, as the family believed, full of mixed fear and anger, but was ripe for turnaround.

Indications were that the prayer chain organised by the church would be helpful, and this proved to be the case. The poor lady had insisted upon staying at home although her condition made caring for her just about impossible. Her children were beside themselves, and the grandchildren were having a terrible time with such a sick person in the house. The doctors had said she would only survive for a very short time, but weeks dragged into agonizing and exhausting months – the whole situation was terrible.

But once the prayer chain got under way things improved. The lady agreed to go into a hospice, and a former friend from whom she had become estranged healed the rift by insisting upon going there and being with her just about all the time. Healing appeared to be taking place at various levels. When death did come it was much calmer than one would have dared hope for a few weeks earlier.

Of course, prayer certainly does not solve everything, it is not a magic wand. But in some circumstances even the blunting of the agony can be unbelievably welcome.

* * *

I once heard a short sermon from the pulpit which I will never forget. A child was dying of leukaemia. The hospital were trying to control the pain, but they were failing, and the distress felt by the child and parents was terrible.

The family were not churchgoers, but something made the parents decide to call in a priest. When the poor man got to the hospital he realised that he was not being viewed as an ordinary Anglican vicar, but as a follower of Jesus who should be able to perform a miracle healing. Very much aware of his own limitations he approached the room where the dying child lay. As he went in he offered up a desperate prayer, not so much in words but a silent cry for help.

His prayer was, in part, answered. Although the child subsequently died, from the time of his visit there was no pain, and the end came with dignity and peace. The parents, who had been distraught at watching their child in such distress, were much better able to accept their terrible loss because of the gentle nature of the death.

* * *

One night I had a phone call from my mother's sisters to say that she had been taken to hospital with septicaemia, and was not likely to survive the night. It was already late, so I planned to notify the office and travel the one hundred and fifty or so miles to see her the following morning, assuming she was still there to be seen.

I met up with another aunt, who lived much nearer to the hospital and with whom I could stay, and we went to visit. My mother, who was then about sixty-seven, had deteriorated so much that we literally failed to recognize her. We scanned the ward, and were about to settle ourselves by another patient then we realised we had made a mistake. Even so, it took us a few moments to locate the right patient.

If someone had been told that there was a lady of one hundred and five in the ward, and been invited to identify her, my mother was the one that would have been chosen. My aunt, a gentle soul with the gift of understatement, said, "Oh dear, she doesn't look too good."

My mother was too ill to hold any sort of conversation. Her body was so full of poison that I noticed yellow fluid coming out from around her eyes, and the whites of her eyes were no longer white. That day we came and went from the hospital a number of times. Back in those days no one appeared to spend long periods with a patient. Visiting times were pretty rigid and while more flexible if the patient was critical, no one was expected to stay continuously.

We made our last visit at about 8.30 p.m. and as we were about to leave a nurse called us over, and asked me whether I wanted to be called out when my mother died. I saw no point in this, we would only get in the way of the staff, and the body would still be there the next day. We went home, expecting to receive an early phone call in the morning. By 8.30 a.m. we decided that my mother must still be alive, and prepared for our first visit of the day.

Once again, as we made our final evening visit, I was asked if we wished to be notified during the night when my mother died, and once again I declined. Again, the following morning the phone remained strangely silent, and we had another day of short, frequent visits to the hospital.

Clearly, my mother's survival was defying all predictions. As if to emphasize this two other ladies in the ward, who looked infinitely fitter than my mother, although they also had septicaemia, both died. At the time antibiotics were not as good as they are today, and the disease was almost always fatal.

At the end of the third day, a puzzled nurse slightly amended her question to, should I be contacted *if* my mother died? Gradually my mother recovered, or sort of recovered. She was among the early generation of patients given massive and endless doses of steroids for arthritis, and as the drug was withdrawn while she had septicaemia, her whole body collapsed, and she became physically a complete wreck and just about helpless.

When she had been on what appeared to be her deathbed she did at one point manage to be coherent, and said, "I am dying because I want to." I believe she was in great pain. As it became obvious she was having a reprieve she said, "Something has gone wrong. I am still here." She was indeed, and she lived on for a further three years.

Afterwards, we learnt of the only possible explanation for her survival. Her sisters had written to old family friends telling them that my mother was dying. They had already derived great benefit themselves by contacting the Harry Edwards Spiritual Healing Sanctuary at Shere, near Guildford, and they immediately wrote petitioning on my mother's behalf. The tide began to turn for my mother at the time the Sanctuary started to pray for her.

However, this did, with hindsight, raise the question of whether it was kind and merciful for my mother's life to be saved when she was destined to spend the rest of her days a complete invalid and in and out of hospital, which she hated.

My Guru Catherine, before attempting absent healing on anyone, makes it clear that what she is asking for is what is best for them, she does not pre-empt what the outcome should be.

My husband's first wife spent the last three years of her life dying slowly and nastily. She had progressive brain hæmorrhages which robbed her of all mobility, speech, and sight. She eventually almost starved to death, because she was not able to swallow. She was nursed at home, as she wished. Week after week, the congregation in the village church prayed for her survival. She had been a leading light, popular, and no doubt they genuinely wished her well. Her state deteriorated so that no one who loved her would have wished her to continue. Timothy asked that the prayer be altered, so that the request was that she be taken care of in the way that was best for her. Almost immediately, she died.

* * *

Matthew's family got a dog from a rescue centre. They kept him to a ripe old age, but inevitably the end was approaching, and the poor animal lay dying at their feet. Clearly there was not going to be a recovery. Distressed by the animal's condition the mother prayed, 'Please God, help this little dog.' He gave a deep sigh, and died peacefully.

One day, at the Buddhist centre, I saw Francis who was distressed because her cat had died a few days earlier. However, I feel that the cat had an auspicious end. The animal, a beautiful big benevolent black and white moggie, that had arrived as a stray, had been very fit until one morning when it had been apparent that he was obviously very ill, and his breathing, very laboured.

Although she felt the end was in sight Francis decided that she must take her pet to the vet just in case he could be saved. She left him at the surgery, but soon got a phone call to say he had died. She collected the body, doubly upset because she felt that, had she foreseen the outcome, she would have kept him at home quietly, and just stayed with him until he died rather than dragging him off to the vet.

To Buddhists all sentient beings are valuable, and she prayed over him, giving him many blessings. As she finished she looked at her beloved pet, and asked if her prayers had helped him, made any difference... and as she did so there was the sound of a breath as it left his body.

Small and significant indications like this one are experienced quite frequently by practising Buddhists. At one festival I met a middle-aged brother and sister. They had been Anglicans, but had got interested in Buddhism and wanted to investigate it.

The husband's wife who had originally decided to come with them suddenly decided that Buddhism might be wrong, and she pulled out, making the others feel rather uncertain. One night, questioning their wisdom or lack of it, one of them stood looking out of the bedroom window and asked, "Show me a sign – can two religions exist together?" At that moment the moon cast a double reflection on the window.

This couple found the long and profound teachings rather a strain. There is, of course, absolutely no pressure on anyone to attend them, so they decided to give themselves time off. They were standing in the hallway when our Guru returned from giving his session. He smiled at them... but the smile from an enlightened being is unlike an ordinary smile, and they were positively transported into bliss, exclaiming joyfully, "That was better than any teaching could have been!" In a way, the Guru had given them exactly the teaching that they required.

Many owners of cats will empathize with this story. Our beloved cat Norman had been missing for days. He was a home-loving animal, and his disappearance was completely out of character. We paced the streets looking in the gutters in case the poor little fellow had been run over. We posted notices, 'Lost, a tabby cat' on the trees and telegraph poles, but all to no avail.

A house a few doors up from us had been sold to developers who were converting it into flats. Could Norman have got trapped inside? He had disappeared half way through one week and was still missing on the Friday. Hopefully, he might re-appear on Monday when the workman would opened the house. No one was there over the weekend.

Early on I had gone there, calling. At one point I thought I heard a miaow but I could not be sure, and when I returned as I did, a number of times, I was met with silence.

Matthew, our friend who had been staying in the house with us for some years and was also very fond of Norman, was a devout Roman Catholic. It was a Sunday, so he went to church as usual.

That evening there was a clatter at the cat flap. Our other cat was already indoors, but neighbouring cats sometimes made raids on the food bowls. We held our breath. Then, having taken rather a long time about it, in walked Norman. He appeared completely spaced out, and in a very weird mood. I picked him up and immediately smelt the unmistakable aroma, both musty and acid, that told me he had been under floorboards.

Matthew returned home. "Norman's back!" we exclaimed. "When did he come in?" we were asked, "About ten to fifteen minutes ago." "I was praying for him." I was convinced that Norman had been sprung by God and our friend. Again, the power of prayer had been seen to work.

* * *

Violetta told of how her prayer to find her dog was answered. I could not help being amused that such a well-placed and rather superior family had a positive scally-wag of a dog. The animal was allowed to play in their large and well presented garden, but, because his one aim was to escape and get involved in a dust-up with another animal, he had to be chained. Sometimes, however, he still managed to break free. If so, this was his opportunity to make his way to a dog pound, where he could find all the rivals he desired.

On this occasion he went missing, and could not be traced *en route* to, or at, the pound. As time passed the family became more worried. Then Violetta prayed for a happy outcome of the situation, and a picture of a particular area flashed across her consciousness. She went there and found the dog, trapped by his chain which was caught in undergrowth and bushes.

* * *

All religions believe in the power of prayer. One of the strongest powers I have discovered is the energy of Green Tara, the Buddha of active compassion. It is said that because she is a wind element prayers to her are answered very swiftly. My faith in Green Tara is not based on wishful thinking, it is based on hard fact, and I have proof.

Once I had to face a drive of almost three hundred miles with a migraine looming. I was also very tired, and felt I was scarcely safe to drive, but there was no escape. At the beginning of the journey I petitioned Tara, 'Over to you'. I had a dream of a journey. My passenger did not notice, but we reached our destination in a time that was, taking the speed and distance into account, impossible. But with Tara all things are possible.

On one occasion I was aware of a group of boys running across a children's play area. Suddenly there was a terrible screaming. I could not see what had happened but I suspected that one of them had collided with a sandwich board and must have hit his head or some other part of his body very hard indeed. He was not a little boy and no eleven-year-old, or whatever he was, would have lost his street cred among his peer group in this way if he could help it. I called on Tara and the cries of agony ceased. At first I thought, 'Oh no, has he died?' I waited for the sound of an ambulance, but none came.

Another time a girl of about twenty missed her footing on steps and appeared to either break her ankle or twist it very severely. She was almost hysterical. After the mantras, just a minute or so later, she was completely calm.

For a short time there was a man living at the Buddhist centre who had had a rather sad life. When he was eighteen he was told that the woman he had believed to be his mother was actually his grandmother, and he was actually the illegitimate son of the woman he had believed to be his sister. He was told that provided he was prepared to keep up the pretence publicly he could continue as a member of the family, but if he was going to bring dishonour on the family by making their deception public then he must leave.

He married, and for many years had a good relationship. There was one daughter with whom he got on well. Then his marriage collapsed. By this time his daughter was independent and was living in China, he was very alone.

While at the Buddhist centre he developed, as many of us do, a strong connection with Green Tara. She is there for everyone and a very potent force. Eventually he managed to go and visit his daughter and, on his return, told how he had been climbing up one of the local tourist attractions when he looked up to see the vision of Green Tara in front of him.

There is an account of Tara working to help my friend Rosemary given in the chapter *Special People Special Places*.

Some people believe that Tara and the Virgin Mary are of the same essense.

* * *

Mantras work. The Buddhas are there to be called upon. If I see some sort of bad incident, like a motor accident, I try to recite the mantra of Green Tara at least seven times: OM TARE TUTTARE TURE SOHA (pronounced om tar-ray too-tar-ray too-ray so-ha).

The most popular mantra in Tibet was that of the Buddha of compassion, Chenrezig or Avaokiteshvara (one is a Tibetan, one a Sanscrit version of the name) which is OM MANI PAME HUM, (pronounced om man-ee pay-mee hum). This is good for all occasions, and particularly appropriate for animals. Accuracy over the pronunciation of a mantra is not important – if you believe that what you are saying is the mantra then it will be. In Christianity there is the belief that 'God will know what you mean', a similar concept and one based on faith and belief.

* * *

When I was first involved with Buddhism I was amazed but a bit puzzled at how using the image of a Buddha, often a beautifully coloured picture only postcard size, could *work*. Christians are told that one must not worship graven images, and while I knew these images of Buddhas were not graven images, I still marvelled at their power. I am indebted to an Anglican priest who inadvertently gave me the answer when he said, 'Myth points beyond itself to the truth.'

I later learnt that Buddhists believe that an image of a Buddha has the essence of the Buddha. What is intended to be that particular Buddha is. Once our Guru went to a teaching carrying lots of statues of Shakyamuni, the main Buddha for this world age, and the one people are referring to when they just talk about 'Buddha'. Some of the figures were beautifully crafted, some were more rough and ready, and some were by comparison crude. The teaching was that this appearance did not matter. If when the person made the statue it was meant to be Shakyamuni then it was.

I was once discussing Buddhism with someone when my freind Janie heard me explain that, to a Buddhist, the presence of a statue brought blessings. Fascinated by this revelation she said that she and her husband had quite a collection of Buddhas, and that life had become easier since introducing them to their home. A postcard would, of course, also bring blessings on the house. Once when I went to see Thomas he discovered that my thymus gland had been damaged by radiation. This was not good news since that gland was supposed to manufacture cells which killed cancer cells. But a few visits later, he found I was much stronger.

How had this unexpected improvement come about? I had only recently started following Buddhism but was doing a prayer format on Vajrasattva - the Buddha of Purification - on a fairly regular basis. A bit of investigation showed that I was, at a subconscious level, purifying some of the guilt and ghastly memories which had been with me since my mother abused me as a child. My energy channels had been blocked, and this problem was being resolved.

Afterwards I heard of someone who cured himself of Hepititus C by doing a Vajrasattva retreat. It took days and a lot of concentration, but was well worth the effort.

* * *

Suffering from cramp has never been a major problem with me, but once in a while I have woken up, stretched, and within seconds been doubled up in agony over a knotted muscle in my calf. This always appeared to take ages to recover, and my leg would be sore for at least the rest of the that day. Over the years I have tried to devise ways of cheating the problem, either by relaxing, holding, or twisting the affected limb. Nothing worked. Once the thing had manifested to a particular point a full-blown cramp was inevitable.

Until one day. The scenario started, and employing my Christian Science training, I simply said, 'This is not real'. And it wasn't. The pain just went away, for the first time ever. Doubting Thomas that I am, I found myself searching for the condition which was no longer there, almost inviting it back, I realised. I had had my first Christian Science healing.

Within a reasonable space of time I had two more triumphs through using Christian Science techniques, though neither could be described as a 'Healing'.

I had been involved with a sculpture exhibition, and on the day that works had to be dismantled and removed, I took a telephone call from one of the members, Judith. She had just heard that her young cousin had died suddenly, and would not be able to come and collect her things. As I had taken the call, I volunteered to remove her exhibits. Apart from packing unsold pieces this meant taking away the white plinths on which the work had stood. As I finished speaking, I knew that it would almost certainly be impossible to get all the stuff into the car. Although an estate, it had been just about full of my own things on the outward journey.

I collected all the items, hers, mine and that of another sculptor, Davina, to whom I had previously offered a lift, to the side of my car. It was quite obvious from the amount of items, that it would be impossible to pack everything in ... There was no one else to help, and typically, a little group formed to watch, and one of them said, very reasonably, "You just can't do it". The impossible situation was made even worse because while my plinths were made to fit into each other, like Russian Dolls, Judith's would not...I bumbled around insisting that I would get all the stuff into the car. Eventually people drifted away, and I was left alone. I took a grip of the situation. It was right that I should do this, and therefore to do this was possible. Mind was superior to matter. The stuff would, and did, go into the car. Jaws dropped when I told people that I had managed it. I heard someone later refer to the ordinary estate car as 'Alison's removal van'.

My bereaved friend was to pick up her things from my house, quite nearby, when it suited her. Judith came the following day and the amazing events of the packing saga where emphasised when her car, a family-sized hatchback, was loaded with her stuff. The driver and passenger were squashed forward in their front seats, while the rest of the car was filled...

The other Christian Science-inspired solution happened at Glyndebourne. We were to see the world premier of Jonathan Dove's *'Flight'*, which I strongly recommend, by the way. Going to Glyndebourne, not far from home, was one of the treats we allowed ourselves. We do not drink, smoke, or have holidays, so we feel this is well justified. It is even the case that the tickets for the Touring Opera productions, which follow on at the end of the season, are reasonably priced and the productions are as good as those of the summer time.

I popped to the loo before the performance. There were two other ladies washing their hands and combing their hair, but I realised that one had problems. She was young and attractive, and her very pretty dress, new and first-time on I am quite sure, had been stitched with defective cotton. The long zip down the back was parting company from the fabric on both sides, leaving a nine inch strip on either side of it where her slip showed through the gap which was growing longer as she moved. She was quite gung-ho about it. "I don't suppose either of you ladies would have such a thing as a safety pin?" she asked. I did have one. One. "If you don't, I'll have to wear it as it is."

It was ridiculous to try to stitch over half a foot of loose zip with one safety pin. I started trying, and was not successful. Then I changed my approach. I thought, why should this lovely girl's day out be spoilt by anything at all? Of course I could mend the dress. I did. Both sides were together, the join not that visible. The girl was delighted of course. This may seem a trivial event, but it was an excellent example of mind controlling matter.

I was happy that I could achieve this but equally unhappy and annoyed that I could not achieve the more serious issue of curing my beloved friend who was dying! I find it so difficult to accept that matters such as life and death, so huge in one way, are out of my orbit. For a mixture of selfish and caring reasons I want what I perceive as best and right to manifest. But death is not a great thing. It is natural, and we have all died countless times before, just as we may well be born many times in the future.

* * *

I had a dramatic demonstration of Christian Science healing working on one occasion when I inadvertently started a bonfire on my thumb. I was cutting a rope and wanted to seal the end. Previously, and with rope made of different stuff, I do not know what it was, possibly some form of nylon, I had sealed the end by holding it over a flame. The material it was made of melted and fused into itself, making a very neat end.

I repeated the exercise, or thought I would. The new rope ignited fully, and burned fast and strongly. As I was indoors and had been using the gas hob, I needed to get outside quickly. In my state of surprise I temporarily 'lost it', and, waving the rope about and trying to extinguish it, a lump of molten, burning rope fixed itself onto my thumb – and I do mean fixed itself.

For a second images of hours spent in the accident and emergency department of a hospital raced before my eyes, I had never been to one, but the stories one heard were horrendous. Then I told myself firmly that this was not going to happen. As Christian Science instructed, nothing could harm me. I knew that viewing my flaming thumb was unhelpful, so I put it behind my back, and told myself that there would be no damage. And there wasn't.

* * *

Fountain Groups, prayer groups for those of any or no religion, were started decades ago. It was a case of good coming out of evil. The centre of Brighton had been invaded by bikers and others who thoroughly abused the area leaving it disgusting and revolting in every way possible. The area centred on a grassy open space, near the Pavilion, and with beautiful flower gardens and a fountain. After the intruders had left local people got together and felt that they wanted their town centre cleansed.

Prayer meetings with a difference were arranged. All were welcome. They concentrated on beaming love and cleansing first at the area around the fountain, then visualizing it outwards to cover the town, etc. This is just about identical to a Buddhist meditation. One gradually extends one's benevolent visualization outwards, to home, street, town, county, country, continent, and the world.

Guru Catherine was involved with the spread of Fountain Groups, as the popularity of the idea widened and groups formed all over the country. More recently she has dowsed to select a target subject which the members will concentrate on for the month, until the next prayer meeting. She is guided by her guardian angels, as she calls them. Once the subject was coral islands. She has no connection with them, but saw a newspaper article a little later describing how their survival was threatened. Another month they had to concentrate on the silt at the bottom of the sea, the first band in the earth's food chain. The first time the message had to be sustained for a second month was in August and September 2002 when Bush was planning aggression against Iraq, and was 'Peace on Earth; Goodwill toward men.' The next month came 'That no more nuclear weapons be produced.' I then saw in a newspaper that Bush was prepared to be the first to drop nuclear weapons.

Those above often appear to have an overall view which those of us on earth are denied.

HEALING

- *Positive healing energy.* • *Love.* • *Positive belief in healing.* • *Spiritual and conventional remedies.* • *Spirits that help specific people.* • *Healing work is exhausting.* • *Different methods.* • *Invisible third party.* • *Healer is matched.* • *Message at a Buddhist festival.* • *A shoplifter is healed.* • *A child born with a club foot.* • *A Christian Science child.* • *Healings are often temporary.* • *Psychic and spiritual strength.* • *An old wound healed.*

I have been told several times by Betty, Leopold, Veronica, and Rosemary that there is a great cloud of positive power which can be tapped into for healing purposes. The followers of one religion are not favoured over the followers of another, but the organised religions have been extremely unhelpful as they have tried to line up with science, which is just a poor imitation of spiritual healing. Had we retained our link with spiritual consciousness we would have had all the answers we would ever need.

Aspects like the strength of prayer and purity of motivation could influence whether or not we could access the healing energy. Also, the spirits of the dead could join in our requests, and help us.

I asked whether the unloved were more likely to be ill than the well-loved, since they were, in a way, having to accept a form of failure, and possibly saw themselves as weaker. I was told that this was correct.

Conversely, the much loved but very ill could survive against all odds on occasions because they would be aware of their own strength. I have known cases where love and strong prayers have kept the terminally ill alive for ages, but sometimes I have wondered if a swifter end might have been more merciful.

The suggestion that someone is very ill can be generated by

others, and this belief can become a self-fulfilling prophecy. This is how ju-ju works, in the same way that a belief in good health can form the basis for absent healing.

The worst thing you can do for a sick friend is to visualise him or her as seriously ill. See the patient as returned to perfect health, beam the thought that wholeness physical, mental, emotional, and spiritual has been restored.

Mr Skinner and Sarah said it was possible for healing to be the result of a combination of spiritual help and conventional medicine. Sometimes conventional medicine offered the complete solution, but the more serious the illness the greater the importance of spiritual support, generally speaking.

This support can be directly between the patient and God I was told, or by someone, dead or alive, who was petitioning on behalf of the patient.

When I asked whether a dead petitioner could be regarded as a 'guardian angel', I was told they disliked the term. The word angel was too airy-fairy and remote, healing spirits were very down-to-earth, and their feelings were very human.

* * *

I heard of a family who were having a very rough time. I asked whether I should try to get involved psychically and or spiritually to see if I could help but was told 'no'. I asked why. Apparently, when he was a child, the husband's father had had friends who, although not related, he called, 'Uncle and Aunt'. These people maintained a watch on his family, and were now doing their best for the son-in-law of the little boy they had known when they were alive.

I felt the presence of these people a couple of times. They were wonderful, quietly confident, solid, and reliable. I could feel that their powers would be far greater than anything that I could have offered.

Feel free to disagree with me, but I would have no difficulty in calling these people 'Guardian Angels'.

* * *

I knew a man who had to abandon working as a spiritual healer, using the laying on of hands, as he felt he acquired his patients' diseases. It is tremendously important to accept and understand that what we are using is not our own energy. When I first became involved I made all the classical mistakes. Attempting to help a very sad couple who had severe long-term mental problems and a shared life of deep depression I concentrated hard on visualising them, their home, and animals inside a pink cloud, to re-create the love they had felt when first married, and to try to heal the hurt generated by their respective very unhappy childhoods, which I felt were at the heart of their problems.

This process exhausted me! Also involved with them was Mr Skinner who, having had a terrible marriage himself, was anxious about them, and keen to help. While I suppose I must have had some thought that my efforts might be beneficial I was, none-the-less, amazed to hear that the couple did appear to be experiencing a considerable improvement in their conditions, though I would be chary of taking credit for this, Mr Skinner's contribution being vastly superior to my own. Good energy is God's alone!

* * *

Gurus Thomas and Catherine both dowse to see how strong their patients are, and what improvement they have been able to bring about. I was told not to attempt this, particularly because I would get fraught if I found I was failing. I just had to try to do my best.

Again I must stress that no two people will work in the same way. For example, having been given some information by Catherine on how one could embue a substance with particular qualities, I asked if I could pass on the information to another interested party. But I was told 'No' because the potential recipient would have been sceptical. This scepticism would have transmitted, itself, psychically, to the first healer, whose powers would thereby be weakened.

* * *

I heard about an amazing healing event from a man I met at the Buddhist centre. Ed had had severe back pain which did not respond to conventional remedies, so he decided to go to a healer. The lady he found also had medical qualifications.

As he sat for her, Ed felt her twisting his head into all kinds of extraordinary and extreme positions. Had the healer not also been a nurse he would have protested, but he was confident that she knew what she was doing, and he would not suffer further damage.

At the end of the session the amazed healer said she had no idea that anyone would have been able to achieve such incredible positions by twisting the neck. They then realised that neither of them had been manipulating anything – a third party had been responsible.

And Ed had much to thank this manifestation of (divine?) intervention for, as his back trouble was cured.

* * *

Valerie, a wonderful lady who was desperately ill with cancer, was not really open to complementary medicine, but I did eventually persuade her to try a spiritual healer. I sought Catherine's help, as far as I can remember, and we agreed that dowsing indicated one particular man as the ideal practitioner.

To our delight there was immediately very, very good progress. Not only did the physical condition improve, but on a personality level the healer enriched the lives of Valerie and her lovely and very supportive husband.

To my dismay, the healer then went abroad for a considerable time, and Valerie did not even bother to chase him up on his return. Her condition deteriorated.

My response was the obvious and predictable. I was distressed, angry even – far more so than the patient herself. I discovered, through my guides, that the healer had given her great strength by giving her the belief in her own healing powers, not just in this life, but with the conviction that life continues and action continues after death.

On a mundane level he had failed, but in fact he had led her with strength and confidence towards her ultimate healing. I was privileged to see Valerie a few days before she died, and she was peaceful and confident, and she even still managed to look beautiful.

* * *

There came a time when I knew I had to attend a Buddhist festival. I had booked it and got the rail ticket, but a day or two before felt extremely ill. Dare I set out? I rang Thomas for advice. He told me that I would be alright, and also prescribed Merc Sol 50 (a homœopathic remedy), which he had just prescribed for Timothy, so it was readily available. As I put the phone down I felt a great surge of energy and I knew this was no coincidence. (Thank you, Thomas.)

At the festival I received a message which I knew was for me. (The experience of feeling that what is being said is for oneself, as an individual, is by no means unknown and is, I believe, an indication of the state of spiritual advancement of the teacher.) I had to view Timothy as 'not real'. In this state of non-reality, there flashed into my mind the image of a computer screen, and the irregularly shaped stars which manifest when obstacles are knocked out in games. I had to delete the unreal image of Timothy with one of the stars.

* * *

On Wednesday evenings there are Christian Science meetings at which testimonies of healings can be given. 'Healings' can be taken in a broad sense, where anything that was negative or problematic has been turned around and has been healed, resolved, or made good, through the belief that bad and wrong things do not really exist. God made everything. He makes only perfect things, and if we see things as less than perfect this is just our own faulty perception, or 'mortal' as opposed to 'divine' mind as they call it.

Testimonies can be amazing. One that stays with me was given by a lady who clearly did not like speaking in public, but said she just had to let us know what had happened. I for one was so glad that she did!

She had been into her local supermarket to do her weekly shopping and and on the way out remembered that she had to buy a birthday card. She crossed the road to a newsagent's, and asked the lady at the till if she could watch over her bags of shopping while she made her choice. She was away for only a minute or two, but by the time she got back, and much to the dismay and embarrassment of the lady who had been charged with guarding them, the bags had gone.

How did the Christian Scientist who had lost her week's groceries react? She said, "I felt overwhelming love for the person who had taken them. I thought, 'You are not a thief, you do not steal, you are perfect and made in God's image.'" She insisted on leaving her telephone number at the shop and returned home, still feeling great love for the person who had taken her shopping.

It was not long before her 'phone rang. Her shopping had been returned...

There are numerous Christian Science testimonies that I can recall. These are my particular favourites.

One lady described how a baby was born and was immediately seen to have a very deformed foot. Little was said, but for weeks the Christian Scientists did a lot of praying, and denying that the child, made in the image of

God, was anything but perfect. By the end of six weeks the foot was normal. The hospital was amazed, and said that it was unheard of for a club foot to spontaneously heal.

Graham told of how he had been born with extremely poor sight. In fact a part of the eye was missing. The outlook was grim but, to the specialist's amazement, as improvement in the condition was technically impossible, the sight improved.

Graham also recounted how, when he was at school, he had contracted a serious notifiable disease. He was confined to the house, and precautions, a legal necessity, were taken. However, after a few days of Christian Science healing he was completely well. A teacher from his school, concerned for his condition, visited the house, and was amazed to find him up and running about. Stunned by what she had seen, she made no bones about the fact and she wished to learn more about Christian Science, and its methods. She had seen the results! The boy was bright, and she made herself useful by smuggling his lessons in to him so his school work did not suffer.

The family doctor knew the members of the household well – he was bound by the regulations governing the treatment of the disease, and precautions, but knew from past experience that he could stand back, and watch things happen.

* * *

Quite often people who attend healing services get relief from their conditions, but this improvement is not sustained. Leopold told me that there were very few spiritual healers in the world today, most healing took place on a psychic level.

A spiritual healing was instant and absolute, and was permanent, while a psychic healing was almost always impermanent. Spiritual power is God power, while the psychic is dependent upon the inferior energies of a much lesser being.

Attempting to sustain a psychic healing presents problems which is why people trying to heal others can have a good effect initially but are unable to bring about an actual cure.

When Leopold gave me this information he was in a very happy mood as he had just achieved a spiritual healing. He added that telepathy played no part.

It is by no means unknown for healers to be drained by, and sometimes take on the illnesses of, those they try to help. This is because of the psychic energy employed. Anyone who is able to perform a spiritual healing is not using his or her own energy, and will be unaffected. But such spiritual miracle healings are rare today because most of us have fallen victim to scepticism. Science is confusing us and we find it difficult to discount explanations for materialism clouds the issue.

The subject of impermanent healings came up on another occasion, and concerned an old and ill man, and his varicose ulcer. Over the years doctors had tried every possible remedy without success, but following a healing service at a Church of England church there was a gradual but complete healing. The leg remained healthy for a considerable time, then the old man had an accident, giving his leg a hard knock, and the ulcer returned.

It was true that the ulcer had only returned after a new trauma, but why, if the healing had been meant? While still puzzling the logic of the thing I went to a Christian Science testimony meeting. There such an incident would be viewed from a different angle, that we are all perfect as we are in God's image, and that illness is not real, so it had never happened in the first place, or, indeed, ever.

There is no such thing as coincidence, and the subject of problems recurring was raised at another meeting. Graham had trouble with an ankle, which he had healed using Christian Science beliefs. Then someone ran a supermarket trolley into the same ankle, taking a lump out of it. This damage was also denied as unreal, and it healed up again, spontaneously and quickly.

Some time later there was pain, and Graham saw that the wound had opened up again. Again, he firmly denied the reality of the problem, and a quick and complete healing took place.

However, I felt that these two cases showed that there had to be a sustained belief in healing for it to be maintained, and that any expectation of trouble recurring would tend to bring it back.

The Use Of Vizualization

• *All can try to heal.* • *A Jew survived a concentration camp.* • *A sportsman wins.* • *Controlling temperature.* • *Body weight.* • *Finding a parking space.* • *Religious beliefs not needed.* • *Pain can be banished.* • *Cancer and illnesses can be tackled.* • *Negative pictures are to be avoided.* • *Negative view of myself and correction.* • *Dog and an injured woman defy death.* • *Overcoming problems.* • *Never wish for something which will hurt others.* • *Use of an icon.* • *Beam love and healing.* • *Strength through a Buddha.* • *I protect myself and help another.* • *Musicians and artists with a touch of genius.*

Most of us have been in the position of seeing someone we care about suffering enormously through illness, bereavement, or some other personal disaster. Out comes the mantra, 'I wish there was something I could do. I feel so helpless.' There is something we can all do. Visualization can, I feel, come under the general description of absent healing.

Healing should not be regarded as a word relating only to physical illness. *Disease* should be viewed holistically, and disease can apply equally to suffering which is physical, mental, emotional, or spiritual. Labels often do more harm than good. If someone needs help of any sort there is a very simple visualization exercise which a friend or member of the family can do in any place and at any time.

Build up a picture of the one suffering and transform it into his or her perfect state, totally well and completely joyful. Surround the one you are trying to help with light. If you feel comfortable with it, imagine beautiful pure white light, representing all embracing love, blessings like good health, a happy and contented mind, and whatever is particularly appropriate, raining down upon that person, and granting the gift of perfection. This must, of course, be on a spiritual level, we are not talking about winning the lottery!

Petitioning meditations similar to this are found in very many different religions. Over the years they have proved to be very powerful, just beam love and have faith that the good energies flowing into and around your subject, will bring about the desired effect. Anyone who can engage in visualization with total concentration and conviction has a tremendously powerful tool at hand.

During World War II, a Jew held in a concentration camp had the same terrible programme as his peer group – hard labour and almost no food. Most of those incarcerated were men of intellect who had never done manual work and dropped dead, if they were not gassed first. But this particular Jew took himself off at the end of each day and, cutting himself off mentally, visualized himself eating his way through a magnificent meal of many courses – he tasted the fruits and meats – he savoured the wines, and when he was eventually released he was the only one to have retained a normal weight. But vizualization has many applications.

There was an athlete who sustained an injury just when he was supposed to begin training for an important race. He visualized himself training, and also saw himself winning the contest. He did!

I have heard that young Tibetan monks would, for fun, sit in the snow wearing only their robes, and by thinking themselves warm melt the snow on which they sat. The winner was the one surrounded by the biggest pool of water.

In *The Autobiography of a Yogi* by Paramahansa Yogananda there is the description of a young monk whose mother visited him at his monastery. She was horrified to see him, as she considered, emaciated, so overnight he substantially increased his body weight to put her mind at rest.

One of Guru Catherine's relatives was sceptical if not slightly mocking about her work calling it mumbo-jumbo. However, he lived in a congested urban area with too many cars and too few parking spaces. He tried using visualization and discovered that by focusing on imagining an empty parking space, he always found one.

This reminded me of the times when I had taken Rosemary, (my friend with leukaemia referred to in the chapter on Special People, Special Places), shopping. Like magic, we always found a space just where we wanted one. However, Rosemary will not have been using visualization as such, she probably applied her Christian Science belief that absolutely everything is truly perfect. Obstacles do not, cannot exist.

In all prayer, meditation, and visualization remember that the name matters not, and neither does religious belief or lack of belief. For some their faith can be usefully harnessed, but those without any are just as much a part of the whole picture. The positive energies available are just as much there for their use and benefit as they are for everyone else.

* * *

All kinds of illness can be tackled through visualization. I remember someone saying that if one was in pain one should try to give the pain a colour. It was stated that this would be impossible, and therefore the reality of the pain would be denied, and it would vanish.

Cancer makes a very good target for strong and positive visualizations. One can imagine the immune system, either more or less literally as white blood cells or, symbolic men battling with, overcoming, and swallowing up or killing, the malignant cells.

A cancer growth can be envisaged as any sort of lump – a lump which is going to diminish until it has gone. Any extremities which are invading the rest of the body should be seen as withdrawing into themselves, and being sick, so that the affected area of the body becomes strong and healthy.

A big, sore abscess can be seen to reduce in size, and disappear, the skin losing all trace of inflammation, and the poisons cleared.

Someone ill with a fever or infection should be visualized as having regained good health, all trace of the temperature gone, and gently returning to normal life.

The possibilities are endless. Be guided by instinct to do whatever feels right and powerful. Remember that no medical knowledge is necessary. If you envisage something which you intend to represent a trapped nerve it will be a trapped nerve, and the bones or whatever that are trapping it can be viewed literally or, for instance, like the teeth of a shark which suddenly becomes fearful, releasing its grip and edging away.

Optimism is positive, pessimism negative – be positive! I have often caught myself out seeing myself as hopeless and defeated. Once, exhausted, I compared myself to a car struggling up a hill. The engine was inadequate and the radiator boiling dry. That would not do! I changed the picture so I became a toy car being held by a child. I was pushed, with no effort, on flat surfaces, up a hill, and lifted altogether when a vertical surface was encountered. I knew there was no such thing as being under-powered.

Another time, feeling a state of dull depression and an inability to direct my life as I wished, I was sent a picture by Betty, one of my spiritual family. With typical humour, which made the familiar image special, I saw myself as a cork being tossed about on the sea but I always came to the surface. I then had a brief vision of myself lying in a still, beautiful sea. Heaven at last?

As one can be sent a message in a dream, so one can if in a meditative mood. At a Christian-Buddhist retreat we were invited to visualize our hearts. I became aware that I saw mine as an unhealthy object. It had a hole in it, like the hole left by a mouse in a hazelnut, and it was like dead offal, a browny colour.

When I was on my own I asked for guidance about this. I was told by my guides that the hole was where love had drained away and the tissue was struggling to stay alive and function. This was a wrong image. I then had the picture of my heart as a bright red, healthy organ, strong and muscular, pumping away joyfully and to good purpose. Negative pictures can do a lot of damage.

Expectation can become a reality, even if inappropriate, and this is another demonstration of mind over matter. Ignorance of facts which are generally seen as soundly scientific can be a great advantage. A dog once accidentally lost his footing and ran over Beachy Head – and lived. No one had told him he was supposed to die.

Recently a doctor who had worked in an isolated and very under privileged part of Africa recounted how a woman had come to him for treatment for horrendous head injuries. The medical facilities were almost non-existent and he could not understand how she had lived long enough to get to his surgery. She would have had no chance of survival even if she had gone to a well-appointed hospital, but the doctor did what he could, with absolutely no expectation of success. The woman lived, and recovery was miraculously swift. She was totally ignorant of medical matters, and must have had the strong expectation that she would recover from whatever injuries she had.

Bumble bees have long since puzzled scientists, taking the size and weight of their bodies into account and the limited areas of their wings the general opinion is that flight should be impossible – but bumble bees do not know this, so they just grow up expecting that they will fly. However, I was once told by a guide that if the scientists did their research properly they would understand why flight was possible.

Create for yourself a visualization with which you feel comfortable. Make it strong and positive, and hold onto the belief in a good outcome. If life is full of obstacles and you are interested in cricket, you may like to envisage them as cricket stumps and bowl hard, accurate balls at them. If you enjoy football and have goals in life, see yourself kicking them skilfully into a goal mouth. If you are a fisherman see yourself landing fish, each representing peace of mind, good health, or whatever you need.

Remember one thing – you must never wish for something that would damage or be at the expense of anyone else. Even if you did, and the initial result pleased you, the effect in the long term would be counter-productive and you would actually be harming yourself. My visualizations are often based on religious motifs. I freely admit that my interest in religion strengthened after I had cancer. However I have only stuck with it, though very selectively, as I have found it helpful and met some wonderful people who are also interested.

Let me share with you a few of my images. At a time when I was aware of needing protection I visualized one of the most popular icons of three figures representing the Father, Son, and Holy Spirit seated round a table. The fourth space – at the front – is unoccupied to invite the viewer to come in. I pictured this in a tent in the desert. I walked across the desert, and entered the tent. The powers of goodness ensured that nothing unpleasant could enter with me. After a time spent quietly in the presence of such powerful protection I could leave, being indestructible so far as the forces of evil were concerned. I felt this was helpful, and was told that it helped me to link up with my purer, better self.

If one knows friends who need help one can place them, mentally, in a group, then place a powerful image, be it Christ, Buddha, or whoever, above them, with streams of healing light flowing from their bodies onto the people beneath. To send love to the world one can envisage a great umbrella shape covering the globe and sending down a cascade of little drops of, perhaps, golden light, bringing with it love, healing, and cleansing.

I had an amazing experience as a result of doing a Buddhist practice, a cross between a visualisation and a prayer. In these tantric exercises you aim to build up a very strong connection between yourself and the chosen Buddha in the hope that one day you will become an enlightened being and be able to help all people and animals.

Included in a text was, 'I am in the prime of my youth...' There followed a description of the Buddha with which one had to try to identify. I worked on this and, in excess of what is usually done, found I could sit in the full lotus posture for the first time in my life. I also found that when I cycled my legs did not start to ache within the first few yards. It was late that summer, and swimming in the sea between my usual two groynes, I found that I covered the distance not in the one hundred strokes each way, as normal, but in ninety strokes one way and only eighty on the way back.

* * *

Sometimes I feel that I attract people with problems. And people with problems are often damaged and, through being ill at ease with themselves, tend to hit out at others. Those within range can be quite adversely affected by their hostile vibes. To reject the hurt and troubled party would solve nothing. We are all victims in one way or another, and should view other people's misfortunes with compassion.

Today the break up of the family is probably the most common cause of serious personality damage in children. Children get older, and become young disturbed adults. While this condition may manifest in, for instance, overt criminal acts, far more of these people just end up rather odd and maladjusted. It is the latter group that I tend to, inadvertently, gather around me.

In one instance, and the damage to myself will have been magnified because I am so psychic, I found that even my sleep patterns were being destroyed. What could I do?

Previously I had had to contend with a similar problem, and needed to put a barrier between myself and my attacker. I visualized a plastic screen, similar to riot shield, which hovered between us at all times. All hostile thoughts and feelings that were sent towards me were shielded from me. But this was appropriate since the sender of the potential harm was simply malicious, and not damaged.

For the present attacker, hurt and angry, healing was needed. I therefore visualised the person concerned in a pear-shaped bottle, which was open at the top. Neither myself, nor anyone else, could be got at, but I sent, through the open top of the bottle, an awareness of God's love, radiating onto the person concerned. There is a lovely line in a Buddhist prayer:

> From the hearts of all the holy beings streams of light and nectar flow down, granting blessings and purifying.

Bathe the sad and vindictive person in this – love is what is needed.

Ivor suggested that I could visualize myself among a group I was praying for, being aware of the individuals' problems, and apply as a mantra 'God is the only power, we are always whole and well.'

* * *

Some artists with a touch of genius can apparently achieve things which many would regard as scientifically impossible. Their ability to control mind over matter can enter the perceptions of others.

An outstanding pianist has been known to persuade an audience that a note, once struck, can increase in volume. Because the piano is a percussion instrument this is technically impossible, with a note starting to die away as soon as it is struck. How this is achieved, by influencing the note through applying mental energies, or by employing some sort of telepathic communication with the audience, I do not know.

Regular concert goers will know the difference between one musician who can command the undivided and completely rapt attention of, possibly, a couple of thousand people in a hall and those who cannot. Similarly one musician may be able to play a very slow piece of music which incorporates long silences in such a way that the audience stays with him – while with others the cohesion of the piece will just fall apart.

One of the phenomena of the ballet dancer Nijinsky was his ability, when jumping in the air, to increase his speed after he had left the ground – another scientific impossibility.

Beaming Positive Energies

- *Catherine's, Thomas's, and my methods.* • *Different sources of energy are fashionable.* • *People can need energies.* • *Our understanding of these energies.* • *Spirit helpers.* • *Specialist expertise.* • *Malevolent entities.* • *Sources of energy, for me and those helping me.* • *Tracking passages in a book.* • *Light.* • *Use of different colours.* • *Suitable and unsuitable sources.* • *Dowsing a passage in a book.* • *Mantras and homœopathic remedies.* • *Homœopathy and beaming energies.* • *A modern American saint* • *Who should we help?* • *Who will benefit?* • *Such work must be guided by conscience.* • *Lighting a votive candle in a church.*

So far as beaming energies to help people is concerned, Gurus Catherine and Thomas work very differently. Catherine uses some form of identification, possibly a signature given by the patient, or a name and address written on a piece of paper and dowses to see if she can help, and whether she should help. She often finds that she has to use tree or other energies, including images of well-energised places and old artefacts with a power of their own.

Often she can transmit positive energy by just holding her pendulum over the identifying object, or someone's hand. It will swing madly until the patient has been fully re-charged, when it will come to a halt spontaneously.

Thomas, who says little about this aspect of his work, uses, I suspect, religious connections. When I was first involved in Buddhism he was pleased, since he said he did not know any Buddhists. I therefore tried to pass on things I learned. The Buddha Green Tara – the Buddha of active compassion – is called upon particularly at a time of crisis. She is a wind element, and will answer very swiftly. She and her mantra are extremely powerful. Thomas told me that this was the strongest absent healing aid he had discovered.

Both these people are very psychic. The psychic energy is not, in itself, a good or bad power – it is the use to which it is put that makes it beneficial or harmful. With Catherine and Thomas the motivation is wonderful, and I know that the amazing insights they both have are theirs because they are put to such altruistic use. Many, many people have benefited.

But you do not have to be special to try to help people in this way. Having had so much help myself, it was only right that I should try to devise a way in which I, too, could at least attempt to assist people I knew who were in trouble. I set up my system, no two people will work in the same way, and I describe my efforts as doing the emanations.

What do I use for them? All kinds of good, natural things which have in the broadest sense a spiritual content, trees, flowers, prayers, powerful images, symbols from different religions, photographs of sacred places, herbal remedies, beneficial foods, different colours and lights, and radiating patterns which give strength to the weak.

Catherine, Thomas, and myself have all had the experience of finding that some energies appear to go in and out of fashion. A radiating pattern may be used for a number of people for ages then it will not be used at all, and a prayer may become popular.

I was told by my guides that this could be caused by seasonal influence, when the earth's energies are changing. Auras would be affected, and growing plants, remedies, and foods. Religious energies would not change, and if they appeared to, the reason would be that the people to whom they were beamed had shifted to different requirements.

I had noticed that a friend might need the same remedies for months on end and I was concerned that this might indicate that no improvement was taking place. However, Sarah explained that the energies might not be needed by the patient, but by the patient's patient or, for instance a healing centre. Through the connective link of the patient it would be possible, for example, for a healing centre to which the patient was connected to receive the benefit.

A patient can direct an emanation to him or herself, or to anyone, any animal, or any place. The ability to send the energy is one use we can make of the Holy Spirit. The Aborigine's concept of God being One-ness, and the Hindu idea of the all pervading spirit also explain why we are all interrelated – a favourite Buddhist concept.

I was told that when we are choosing the emanations we are drawing on a deeply subconscious knowledge gained in many previous incarnations. They work independently of the patient's belief in his or her condition and may be of benefit even if the patient is believed to be dying.

Had I heard about emanations years ago I would have been very sceptical – but I have benefited from Catherine's and Thomas's talents in this field so greatly that I could not doubt their power even if I wanted to.

One of the beautiful things about doing the emanations is that one is almost sure to have helpers from the spirit world. As a matter of routine I ask whether there is anyone there to help me. There have been times when others have spoken through me, and when I have been told I am on my own, whereupon I always ask if someone can oversee me in case I get things wrong. This has always given a positive. If there is someone there I ask whether that person (spirit) wants me to identify him or her, and go along with the reply. Sometimes one of my spiritual family is there and if we have not been in contact for ages I feel so happy– it is like meeting an old friend in the street!

On one occasion I discovered that Veronica had joined me. She had been a wonderful, colourful, and original family friend, an 'Auntie' and great favourite when I had been a child. Her unique way of looking at things through her life was still with her manifesting in her instructing me to use energies which would never have occurred to me, but which I could see were completely valid.

Eliza, one of my spiritual family, used to work as a gardener in one of her incarnations. Her instinctive knowledge of the properties of plants remains with her, and she provides advice based on wonderful insights.

When I started to collect books which might be useful I came across one listing drugs and a handbook of biochemical remedies. I was told these would not be appropriate. Everything they contained was already accounted for in other books. Modern drugs were physical things which mimic the effect of greater energies. With them we try to overcome and compensate for our lack of spirituality. If we became sufficiently receptive spiritually we would find all our cures through natural God-given energies. In the ultimate state of spirituality I was told we could live, like Teresa Newmann and some others, without food or drink.

It was while I was asking about this that I was aware of a presence with me and discovered it was that of Mr Binay Ranjan Sen, Indian Ambassador to the United Nations, who had met and gave the eulogy at the funeral of Paramahansa Yogananda, author of *Autobiography of a Yogi* on 11 March 1952. Mr Sen was an advanced being and he also showed up among 'all the conquerors of the three times' referred to in a Buddhist prayer.

Another night Mr Binay Sen came to help me. He guided me to a book of saints, and asked me to reinstate a friend, who had died, onto the list of people I was trying to help. He clearly had inside knowledge about these saints, since the information in the book was minimal. One had died praying for the sick, just about nothing else was known – a second was also 'little known , and a photograph which I had taken of a statue was indicated although my attempts to find out who the statue portrayed were unsuccessful.

At times when I have been exhausted, I have been carried along – spiritual friends are wonderful people! Even as I write this, I have a very limited time to put my notes into order, my biographer who is helping me is at my side. He is getting exhausted with the effort, and every hour or couple of hours he tells me to break off for a while, so he can recover. I felt apologetic that my notes were in such a pickle, but was told I should not be sorry as his efforts were worthwhile, from his point of view.

Where there is the good there will also be the bad. Adverse interference is not unknown. One night I was attempting to help someone when I felt a hostile presence arrive. I addressed it directly, saying that what I was doing was between myself, the person concerned, and God. At the word God the malign spirit vanished.

On another occasion I was enquiring to see if the home of one of my Gurus who deals with the paranormal needed protection. Previously this had been necessary, but a little later I was told that while all was well at the time, I should keep checking the house. When I did so the pendulum went all over the place. David was helping me that night, and I knew something had intervened between us. I quietly recited the mantra of a Buddha of protection and when I pendulumed again David was back in control.

Whatever the hostile presence had been it vanished speedily and left no trace. David told me it had been 'unreal' in the same way that Christian Scientists have the belief that since God is the only creator, all must be perfect. The delusion of what they call mortal mind, which embodies a belief in illness, sin, and error, is just that, a delusion with no actual reality, just a figment of mankind's negative imagination.

Interestingly, when the hostile presence arrived I felt a tiny pain, like a little electric shock, just behind my ears. This was a similar sensation to that felt when, my grandfather, who died before I was born, was seen floating above me. I think that in each case the manifestation was using my energy to materialize. The fact that one influence was benign, and one was not, was not, I think, in any way relevant. It was a case of my energy being used as though I was an electric battery.

*   *   *

I dowse to establish which people I should try to help. There can be surprises here. Catherine has also found that sometimes distant acquaintances are indicated. I have often been puzzled that I am told not to help closer friends. I have also been warned not to petition on behalf of my husband as he is unfortunately draining me far too much already.

Having got my list I then dowse to see what is needed. My list of remedy energies are in groups, and it is not too time consuming to establish what is required.

To track down the passage in a book I open it in the centre and ask whether what is needed is in the first or last half, I then keep subdividing on the positive side until the page, sometimes even a sentence, is discovered. To indicate which coloured light I am beaming, I take a small photo album and insert slips of paper stating which colour the page represents, gold, pink, deep pink, etc. When dowsing one often gets a very clear message that, for instance, red is correct and light red is not.

The colours I was told would be useful were silver, bright silver, deep silver, gold, light gold, deep gold, clear light, white light, pink, deep pink, light red, deep red, orange, yellow, pale yellow, deep yellow, pale blue, light blue, deep blue, dark blue, indigo, pale indigo, deep indigo, violet and dark violet.

I was told green and brown had nothing to give.

Apparently the choice of colour was determined by the recipient's state of body, mind, and spirit.

In his book *The Power of Compassion* the Dalai Lama described clear light as the most subtle level of consciousness which appeared to me to make it a sort of super light. Then I was told that it could indeed influence just about any problem which manifested mentally, emotionally, or spiritually. Once I was told to use it for an overweight cat who was suffering the consequences, a reminder that all energies are there to benefit all living beings and not just humans. I was told to add the words 'of bliss' to make the identification 'clear light of bliss'. Some colours can be used either to help the fight against serious disease or in a precautionary way. Predictably, after what I had been told, I noticed a similarity in conditions, both people had blood pressure/circulatory problems, of those needing bright silver. Bright silver could often be used for younger people, while deep silver tended to be for the old who had physical problems, and were probably sicker than someone needing bright silver.

Patrick and Mervyn came to tell me about gold. Gold, light gold, and deep gold were all to heal spiritual problems. No physical conditions would have manifested as a result of this, although the patient may well have other physical problems not connected with those spiritual ones. The spiritual problems were not lack of faith, guilt, etc., but where the subject had been attacked, spiritually, by someone with malevolent motivation, whether at a conscious or subconscious level, for instance, someone who cheated a friend might only see the cheating as a physical thing, but in fact the victim might be deeply damaged, questioning the validity of friendship generally, causing suspicion to the detriment of trust, and a warm and open response to other people.

Gold was used only after damage had taken place, and the deeper the gold the greater the damage which had been done.

Orange was for depression in which the sufferer was putting the blame on other people. This may or may not involve physical damage.

Yellow was also for depression which may or may not be having a physical effect. Pale yellow was for the least affected, and deep yellow for those most damaged.

Colours, I was told, compensated for what the patient did not have, they were healing auras. The actual aura would be a completely different colour.

For instance, I was told that the range of pinks was a colour to give love, and whether pink or deep pink, was determined by the kind of love that was needed. Pink was light and ethereal to compensate for a lack of love, not a failed relationship, which caused tension. Deep pink was more passionate. Anger and frustration had manifested rather than tension, and a failed relationship could be involved.

Deep red gave energy for endurance on a mental and or physical plain, while light red offered endurance on a more physical plain which needed less energy. Someone needing light red was fitter than someone needing deep red.

Blue was calming and to give peace. Pale blue was to give a mental state of calm and light blue, through a calming influence, would heal and neutralize any physical condition. Deep blue was for a spiritual condition which might have influence on the mental and emotional state. This gave a very strengthening influence, and strengthened one's own true self when there may have been the threat of weakening for whatever reason.

Dark blue was similar to deep blue, but was very calming, to help one be true to oneself and not become confused.

Indigo was for mental optimism, when a lack of optimism was having an effect on the physical, and deep indigo was for patience, for the condition where impatience had brought about a physical condition.

Violet was to combat anxiety which could be destructive emotionally, by giving equanimity. Dark violet would induce a sleep state under which conditions bordering on panic could be healed. It could heal a patient's perceptions when those perceptions had become uncontrollable.

* * *

Hunting for more helpful material, I was told that astrological influences would not work as we are utilising things of this world while we are in this world.

While I was told to use the Bible neither the Christian

Science Textbook nor the Hindu's Upanishads or Bhagavad Gita were indicated. The Bible and prayers included ideas in the Textbook while a book on Hindu gods would cover the content of the other books, it was explained.

I realised that I had not investigated whether there was any marine life that would be applicable. Leopold told me to get a book on oceans, although it would be used rarely. I bought one, but when I arrived home I was horrified. There were pictures of hostile fish with big, ugly bodies and vicious teeth. The first time the book was indicated, needed for a very dear friend, Valerie, who was battling against cancer, I opened it with trepidation. Oh ye of little faith! The page required had the most beautiful picture of a delicate coral in the shape of antler seaweed – and its characteristic was that it was able to withstand strong currents and tides in spite of its apparent frailty.

I was told that animal life was not suitable for use in the emanations, as animals existed in their own right, and had their own individual status, unlike growing things, and minerals, etc., which were on the earth partly for our benefit.

* * *

Fascinated to discover how it was possible to dowse for a passage in a book I asked how the process worked, and was told that we can link up with the thought which originally went into the passages when they were written, or the idea, when a photograph was taken.

This would also explain the phenomenon described in a book about Edgar Cayce, the poor white American who worked as a healer. He would go into a trance and come up with a diagnosis and cure for distant patients. During his life he had had to pass exams, and by sleeping with the relevant book by his pillow he would awake with the full knowledge of its contents.

The idea that we have powers to connect up with the

thoughts which someone had many years earlier may sound amazing. It may be amazing, but should we be that surprised? Even in the conventionally scientific world there is much to marvel at.

One scientist who had been an atheist was converted to a belief in there being a God because he found a fish's eye so wonderful, so beautiful, and so complex. I am indebted to Radio 4 for the information that sound travels four times more quickly in water than in air. In answer to my questioning I was told that the speed at which sound travelled in water illustrated its rarefied vibrations.

Homœopathy works only because water retains a memory. No two snowflakes have identical patterns. To me, at least, these things are not mundane.

My Guru Thomas discovered for himself the truth of the Buddhist belief that one could add Buddhist mantras to medicinal remedies. I was once told that if I added a number of mantras to a homœopathic mixture and took four drops every three hours I would not need to take my anti-cancer drug. I did not have the courage to put this to the test!

On another occasion I was told that Buddhist mantras were more effective than Christian prayers would have been when used in this way, because of the Hindu and Buddhist belief that spirits are everywhere, and can inhabit inanimate objects. An acceptance of this is important.

Betty told me that it was one's perception of a particular mantra which made it stronger or weaker than another.

Eliza once advised me to use mantras when envisaging a group of friends, with myself among them. She suggested that I limit the group to four. She was happy for invented mantras to be used, and was happy with, 'God is the only power, we are always whole and well', and 'Divine love is meeting all the needs of all of us all of the time'.

Sometimes when I found that a mantra should be added to a homœopathic remedy I was surprised to discover that the same mantra was not to be used through the emanations. I was curious about this and was told that the homœopathic drops and the emanations work in different ways. The mantras altered the vibrations of the water in the body.

By contrast, emanations work through the body's winds – the creative side of the spirit. It is these winds that permit astral travel – very infrequently among the living and much more commonly in the souls of the dead. The emanations themselves do not travel astrally, they have to be sent, and become effective when they have reached their targets.

Anyone wishing to experiment by making mantra homœopathic remedies might be interested in the following. Water alone retains a memory for a relatively short time. The addition of alchohol – brandy is generally used and is already present in flower remedies for that reason – considerably lengthens the time for which the remedy retains its powers, possibly forever.

Thomas's Vega machine indicated that protective energies were added to the mixture if a mantra was recited into it. One can also use a piece of thread between oneself, so that one's breath goes onto it, and the bottle, or into the fluid, whichever feels right at the time.

When I am doing the emanations I include myself in this exercise. One night I found that a dictionary of Saints was indicated for me. This was a surprise – I am not a Roman Catholic and have little sympathy with the wealth of their church, the position to which they elevate the Pope, and some of the rules and regulations which they lay down and which, so far as I can see, have nothing to do with Christ's teachings whatsoever. However, I know many wonderful people who are Catholics, and I have no doubt that there have been well-motivated and talented people under that umbrella over the centuries.

The lady selected was St Elizabeth Seton, a modern saint from America. When I read about her life I discovered that she had performed miracle healings including helping patients with meningitis. I remembered that my medical

Guru had found that I, in addition to a lifelong tendency towards bad migraines, would be susceptible to meningitis.

Not long after I had, as it were, made contact with St. Elizabeth Seton, I suffered a bad migraine attack. It was made no better by the fact that I had been suffering from some other infection with 'fluey symptoms when it started. I was aware of feeling very under the weather, and thoroughly unhealthy. When I had recovered I asked whether I would have got meningitis had I not had help from St. Elizabeth Seton, and was told it was likely that I would.

I later discovered that my 'flu was actually MRSA, an evil bacteriological infection I had picked up while having a mammogram as a hospital outpatient. This sometimes resulted in septicæmia. No wonder I felt ill!

* * *

It is a wise (or perhaps very foolish) man who claims to understand the full meaning of, and reason, for suffering. There are many explanations – the ripening of karma being but one – and I have sometimes been told that there is some process of suffering which must be worked out by the sufferer who, presumably, is in need of the experience for some predetermined reason. Interference would not be right.

Once, when doing emanations for a terribly sick friend, Margaret, I found she needed a much smaller programme than previously. At first I was concerned in case she might have died, but instead was told that she was much better. This friend was very dear to me, and I wished I could help more. I knew she was very special.

I was guided to a passage which said that one was tested through illness to gain patience if it was pre-ordained that one was to be given great work to do. This passage was from a Muslim script, and Margaret, born a Catholic, had converted to that faith after marrying an Egyptian doctor. I was then told I should do something else – light a candle and offer thanks for her progress in my local church.

There can be reasons why one should not try to help, and one is that the patient, often someone close, is already making great demands and draining energy away from the healer. In other cases a can of worms may be opened from which the healer should be protected. I have found to my cost that a healer should follow 'No – don't get involved' advice scrupulously. I have failed to do so, and have come unstuck, and the patient has not had any real benefit, either. So know your limitations!

The degree to which people benefit from the emanations is dependent upon the subconscious awareness of, and acceptance of, the wind element. Spiritual healing also depends on the wind element, I was told. If the patient is not receptive to the subconscious idea, the deficiency can be overcome by the belief of the healer – but this is very, very hard to achieve. This information was given by an anonymous helper and David confirmed it, saying that a subconscious acceptance of the reality of the winds was necessary for a benefit to be achieved.

Obviously there are times when emanations are not appropriate, and one may be directed to use other things. One of the most beautiful messages I received was that the only thing I should do for a dear, dying friend Valerie, was to bathe her in love... and the worse her situation, the greater the love should be.

There is one moral dilemma faced by those wishing to heal. Is it right to try to do so without getting the patient's prior permission? This is exactly the same dilemma a hospital may find itself in, if the parents of a very sick child refuse treatment on the child's behalf. I have known people with wonderful motivation take different sides on this one.

All I can say is that each one of us can only be guided by our own conscience. I almost always opt out of taking the decision by penduluming and asking the 'should I or shouldn't I?' question, and abide by whatever my guides are instructing me.

This will have sounded very strange – even spooky – to quite a few people. Stand back a minute. What are we doing when we enter a church and light a candle to help someone who is about to have a serious operation, or wear a cross? There is symbolism, and presumably a belief in or acknowledgement of the availability of some sort of power when we do this, and it is seen as unremarkable.

THE FLUIDITY OF MATTER

● *Missing passport.* ● *An ornament disappears then rematerializes.* ● *Lost fragment appears in an impossible place.* ● *Toys from my childhood reappear.*

Today 'ordinary' science sees matter as solid. More advanced and enlightened science knows it to be made up of the most microscopic particles and tends to see it as far more fluid. The only explanation I have found of how miracle healings, and the miraculous materialization and dematerialization of matter is possible – and can and does happen – is in *The Autobiography of a Yogi*. I am not going to try to elaborate here, but rest assured that his reason is convincing.

I can give a few examples of matter materializing. Some years ago friends from Canada, who had met Timothy and his first wife when they were on holiday, re-visited London and we had a meal together. Conversation was a bit laboured, but the husband suddenly turned to me and said, "I don't suppose you'll believe this." He then told me how a family, friends of his, had been going on holiday. The husband needed a new passport, and applied in lots of time. However, the document did not arrive, and endless telephone calls produced nothing. On the very day when the flight was to go, the family were assured that the passport would be at a desk in the airport, waiting for them. It was not. They queued to get on the plane, almost certain that the husband would be turned back. As the queue moved along they glanced down. The husband's passport lay at their feet.

Rebecca's mother had given her two little ornaments before she died so they had sentimental value. They were in a room used by students whom my friend used to care for and teach. After one of the students left Rebecca saw that one of the ornaments had vanished. A thorough search revealed nothing, and in the months that followed many students came and went, and the room was frequently cleared and emptied without the ornament being found. Then, out of the blue, Rebecca went into the room to see the ornament back in place, as though it had never been lost.

On one occasion we had a little sculpture exhibition. It remained open for some months so, from time to time, we changed the pieces exhibited. Once I went in and saw a broken piece of sculpture had been placed on a plinth. It did not match anything on display, but I put it in a pocket to see if I could trace the owner. I did. But the piece of sculpture it had come off had never been near the exhibition – this fragment, the size of a thumb, had been broken off by her grandson at home.

My childhood was not, as you have read, particularly happy, but my most contented moments were probably spent alone playing with what I called my farm things. These were little metal models of animals, a couple of farmers, a house, and pony and cart, and fencing. The fencing could be linked to make fields of different shapes. It kept me quiet and happy for hours.

One day – I think it must have been just before I left school – my mother announced that some charity had come round to collect things to sell, and she had given them my farm things. I felt sad. At that point in my life, and for many years after, I had a need to hang onto things that had mattered to me. When I cleared the house after her death, I had hoped to find them, but as the saying is, they had gone. However, years later, possibly during a house move, they reappeared and I have to confess that, along with my teddy bear, I still have them!

Astrology

• *An astrologer accurately forecasts the unlikely details of my marriage*

When I was about thirty, I met an extremely accomplished astrologer. He created my unique birth chart and over the years made many extremely accurate predictions. I was surprised to receive with these items, a copied letter which acknowledged the power and might of God. His customers were made aware that they should call upon the spirit of goodness for guidance and protection. He was not just a good astrologer: he seemed a wise man too.

One prediction, that of my eventual marriage, made a great impression. The odds against this made his skill look all the more impressive as I did not marry until I was forty. He correctly predicted the time of my marriage to within a few months, and that my future spouse would have had experience of a previous marriage and that he would be free to remarry.

Timothy was younger that his first wife. For most of their married life he thought she was seven years older, but in fact she was ten. She was a bright and an active person and, until the last few terrible years, carried her age well. About three years before she died she started having strokes. The progression of small but devastating brain hæmorrhages did their worst and she ended up blind, unable to speak, and she more or less starved to death as she could not swallow. It was a very difficult time for both Timothy and the team of home nurses who cared for her until she died.

The result was that when I married Timothy, not many months after his wife's death, he was exhausted and in a pretty poor physical shape. I wrote to my astrologer hoping for advice on how to do the best I could for him, but my letter was returned marked 'Gone away'. Whether he had actually gone away I shall never know. For, as you have read earlier, it was not Timothy who was destined to be ill but myself. Could it be that he did not want to impart bad news? Based on his past predictions, he would almost certainly have 'seen' the horrors that awaited me in my married life. I shall never know.

But I must stress again that all the nasty things that have happened to me have had a profound purpose. While I have hated going through the experiences I would not have avoided or escaped them even if I had had the choice.

Earlier in my life, when I had been working, it was by no means unusual for my stars in one of the national papers to be quite accurate in their predictions. A colleague in the office used to take delight in telling each of us what sort of a day we would have. But once I had started on my real life's experiences, my communication with my spiritual guides, I found that no astrological prediction had any relevance at all.

Could it be that different people came under different influences? Veronica came to me to explain how different people relate to different truths. Astrology, she said, was never spiritual. Clairvoyance might or might not be, and this depended on the state of mind and spirituality of the clairvoyant. It could be spiritual or positively evil.

As the moon can influence the tides, so astrological factors can influence the body. If there were 'guardian angels' helping whoever was likely to be influenced adversely, this problem could be overcome. Any person, if sufficiently strong spiritually, could counteract these influences.

In retrospect, when I had my back to the wall and was, as it were, if not forced then at least strongly encouraged, to seek help from spiritual quarters, I ceased to be influenced by the stars. I had moved on. Many other people, whether they are aware of it or not, must have had the same experience.

Crystal Energies

● *A protective stone appears to be protected by one protected by a Buddhist deity or was the second just stronger than the first?* ● *A blue stone protects a friend from a psychic attack*

My knowledge of different sorts of rock energies is far from great, but I did witness one interesting manifestation. I had been directed to protect myself using moldavite, a green stone which, originating outside our planet and found in meteorites, had the ability to judge between right and wrong, and give protection accordingly.

I had heard that most crystals needed cleaning from time to time, and, as it were, feeding with sunlight, though in moderation. I found that my piece of moldavite needed cleaning regularly, and bathing in sunlight every few days.

Then, at a Buddhist event, I was given a clear piece to crystal which had been imbued with the essence of a darma protector. These are deities which try to protect the teachings given in their particular lineage of Tibetan Buddhism. I added it to my piece of moldavite. To my amazement the piece of moldavite changed so that it needed cleaning and feeding far less frequently.

For quite a while I thought that the two stones must have been interreacting, then I realised that there was another interpretation, that the darma protector was helping me so that the moldavite had less work to do, and its energies got used up less quickly.

My friend Elizabeth was aware that she was being attacked psychically. I was directed to get a piece of blue stone which would help her. A complete ignoramus in these matters I went to the appropriate shop where the people selling the crystals were rather surprised at my choice.

However, I dowsed and one little rock was immediately very positive. To my delight Elizabeth found it did help with her problem as described in the chapter on Psychic Attacks.

Thomas discovered, at one time, that a lot of people benefited from wearing crystal necklaces, but he had his doubts about quartz, and wondered if people would be better off not wearing quartz watches. However, the findings were inconclusive.

A word of warning, crystals can be powerful things. The fact one may look attractive does not necessarily mean it will be compatible with someone attracted to it. I once visited a lady with severe health problems. She had a magnificent crystal but both of us discovered that it pendulumed very negatively for her.

Death And Dying

● *Viewing my first corpse – a deeply religious experience.* ● *After death experiences of three people.* ● *A horrible death may bode well.* ● *Some bodies look beautiful.* ● *Our spirits are the same.* ● *Our spirits are immortal.* ● *The distress of mutilated bodies.* ● *Face death with optimism.* ● *Animals accept death.*

It was Christmas Eve many years ago. I was a commuter, and had a live-in boyfriend. Expecting a group of friends round the next day I had, fortunately as it turned out, got up early to ensure we had the turkey. I had returned home – my boy friend had gone out to do some last minute shopping.

The phone rang. 'This is Gloria. Simon has just died and Elise is at the flat waiting for the undertakers. She is on her own, and I can't go.' I did the decent thing and immediately offered to go round.

As I put the phone down I questioned my own wisdom. I had never really seen a body before, if one discounted people lying at the side of the road as one drove by accidents. How would I react?

Whatever happened, I must not be weak. I rang Simon's flat to tell Elise I was on my way, then grabbed a piece of toast, and jumped into the car.

What I beheld was, as I told many people over that Christmas in a fit of youthful enthusiasm, one of the most religious experiences of my life. Simon had been such a lovely, twinkly man, with a good brain, and an even better sense of humour. While in his mid eighties he had the gift of being interested in whatever topics interested other people – an attribute so rare in any age group, particularly the old.

I was once on the beach with him, and we spotted something cheeky, I forget what it was, a bursting bikini, something of that sort.

We made silly comment after silly comment after silly comment, and ended up both in tears of laughter on the pebbles. How many people can you share that with?

But the 'it' I beheld when I got to the flat was nothing of Simon. I would not even have recognized him. The features, though perfectly pleasant, there was nothing nasty about the body, held no likeness whatsoever. I had indeed seen that the soul had flown, and I knew that the soul was the real Simon. Later I wrote to Joanna who is deeply religious, and she reported that my experience was a common one. Perhaps if, when viewing bodies, people had it explained to them that what they are looking at is just the husk, not the fruit itself, they could be more detached about anything they may see that distresses them.

* * *

There have, over the years, been a number of books citing the after-death experiences of people who have technically died, and then been resuscitated – often following heart attacks. The general pattern appears to be the sensation of travelling along a tunnel towards a light, and then being greeted by those who have already died. I remember reading of one instance where someone recalled seeing in the next world a distant friend who was still believed to be alive, but subsequent enquiries showed that the person had indeed died. The news had simply not been passed on.

I am going to give only a few instances, of those I have heard directly from the people concerned.

A prominent local Jew was giving a talk on his religion. At the end questions were invited. As I had never been able to get a clear answer out of my Jewish friends about what they believed happened after death, I popped the question. The speaker said that they simply did not know. The audience shuffled a bit, I was not the only one interested in the subject.

Then the man's attitude completely changed. Waving his

religion aside he said that, speaking as an individual, he had had the most wonderful after-death experience which had completely removed his fear of dying, and that he was looking forward to the event as he knew it would be so joyful. I think his experience followed more or less the most common experience, but I must admit the thing that I remember most was his sheer pleasure at remembering his experience.

At another talk a lady revealed how, at the age of about nineteen or twenty, she had been knocked down. She floated above her body, watching the concern and distress in the street, that such a young woman should have been killed. She thought how silly it was that her body, rather than she herself, was attracting all the attention.

Then the scene changed. She was, as it were, being shown an account of her life so far.

Looking back from the perspective of her middle-aged self she said that she had been a typically selfish teenager who had achieved little towards being a really good and caring human being. Her faults were shown to her, but in a kindly fashion.

However, she had, while at school, befriended a handicapped girl, and this very positive act of compassion was emphasised, and she was given much credit for it.

Then she had to return, and get on with her life.

A very good friend of mine, Martha, the soul of kindness and generosity, had been treated very badly by her mother and sister. The sister had set the mother against Martha, presumably to ensure that she herself got the lion's share of the estate when her mother died. Ultimately the ploy worked, but before dying the mother had a near-death experience. Coming out of unconsciousness the mother told my friend, "I was told I must go back, and say how sorry I am for all the trouble I have caused you, and the way I have treated you."

* * *

While most near-death, or after-death, experiences are

pleasant and positive this does not apply to all. I once visited a friend in hospital and got chatting to another patient. This man had been admitted following a very mild heart attack. However, he was absolutely terrified as he had previously had a very bad heart attack and had technically died. His experience had been of going through a tunnel and the absolute silence filled him with fear.

He was a very nice man, and I could not understand why he should have had such a bad experience. However, I subsequently heard that it was not unknown for this to happen, but a far more pleasant experience followed quickly.

* * *

My guides told me that someone who dies an agonizing death might go straight to a state of bliss as all bad karma would have been paid back. For instance martyrs who were burned at the stake would have had no time to fall from grace between suffering the pain and dying.

There is one myth I would like to dispel. Not all bodies look terrible after death, some look wonderful – death becomes them. When my grandfather, Thomas Cordingley, died in hospital following a stroke, it was not his wife or favourite older daughter who went to collect his possessions, but the middle daughter, the one who most resembled his side of the family. One of the nurses stopped her and asked her if she was going to view the body. She said she was not, but the nurse insisted, "You must. He is the most handsome man who has ever come into this hospital." My aunt did go to see him, and he did, indeed, look wonderful.

Kenneth reported that his father, laid out after his death, also looked wonderful – the word repeatedly used in both cases. His mother was so impressed she wanted a photograph, but he felt that would be inappropriate. Both men had one thing in common – they had been married to women who could be absolute bitches, dictating how all the members of the family lived their lives... but the marriages lasted in spite of everything.

* * *

We wrongly perceive that there is a great divide between a spirit attached to a body – one of us – and a spirit that has shed his or her body after death. When a distant but greatly-valued relative died, I discovered what had made her so special. It was her faith. She had the passage about death being 'nothing at all' at her funeral, and we were all told to talk about her as we always had, not so much 'as if' she were still there, but accepting that she really was 'still there'. With her I find it a particularly easy thing to do.

We should all beam in to this concept. It would make both life and death so much easier. I once read in a Hindu text – it must have been either in the *Bhagavad Gita* or the *Upanishas* – a pearl of wisdom about the stupidity of trying to kill one's enemies. There was a relatively throw-away comment that of course one could not dispose of the opposition in this way. One may cause them to throw away their bodies but the real them, their spirit, was unkillable. The indestructibility of the spirit was taken as read.

Of course not all corpses are a pretty sight. People who have had heart attacks are often curled up and tensed with the pain they have felt. A bit of dirt clinging to the side of a face where the last fall took place can be felt as distressing.

We should remember we are the ones distressed, not the one who has died.

Most of us would hate to do the job of the emergency services, who sometimes have to collect bits of human bodies off the road, or gather human fragments of a suicide who chose to walk in front of a train. It is easy to be glib and say that what we are looking at is not the real person. Such scenes are bound to be very upsetting, but we must accept the truth that, again, ours is the sorrow, and the deceased is away from such distress.

All children should be taught to accept this truth – the soul is not confined in the body. Almost every page of this book is evidence that we have continuation of our consciousness and retain our individuality after death. Even more amazing is the fact that, mystically, we are all linked together, in a one great spirit. We are all interconnected, and are there, for, and with, each other.

We should face death, whether ours or someone else's, with optimism. This book also demonstrates the mercy of God. The dead are welcomed to their new home and offered good and constructive things to do, and learn.

Animals cope with death, on the whole, better than we do. Many will go away, aware of their own mortal illness, and die quietly on their own. It is as though they accept easily that the time has come for them to return to their maker.

When I was a child our cat Topper used to bring in birds. We rescued them as best we could. Many were damaged, and several, all twisted and mangled, died in my hands. Almost without exception at the moment of death their frail little bodies would straighten up and they would look perfect. "It is over," we used to say. Yes, it was over, but it had also just begun.

Helping Those Who Have Died

● *What we should do for a friend's dead friend.* ● *Prayers for Jack.* ● *Spiritual uplift.* ● *Trapped after death.* ● *Catherine finds a spook.* ● *The Church of England step in.*

My friend Elizabeth was upset as a friend of hers, Gwendoline, was dying. David gave me the message that an old school friend of Gwendoline's was preparing to receive her – this lady had also died of cancer. She and Gwendoline had not kept in touch since their schooldays, but she was there for her as she faced death.

Between Gwendoline dying and my hearing about it I had a dream. We were in an undefined area and I knew that Gwendoline was among a group of about ten people, all in old fashioned clothes, including grey mackintoshes. The crowd obscured her although the few people who were near me did not get in the way. I knew I must have eye-contact with her. Eventually the people parted, and our eyes met.

I then received the message that I must recite a Buddhist mantra, which I did in the dream, and I also had to ask Elizabeth to recite the same mantra for Gwendoline twenty-one times, which she did, every day, for a while. This, I was told, was to enable Gwendoline to regain strength quickly. She also needed help in coming to terms with being dead. After death she was destined to experience great happiness and peace. Lots of people would be there to greet her particularly the friends who had predeceased her.

An account of my doing some Buddhist prayers for my friend Jack whose funeral I was unable to attend, and the fact that Jack's presence, together with his irrepressible humour, pervaded the house, is given in the chapter on my Spiritual Family and Spiritual Friends.

My husband came home and said that an elderly lady who had been a member of the Political Sect had died. Apparently a relative of Ivy's was keen for me to know. I intended cutting off all connections with them but wondered if I was supposed to 'do something' for the recently departed.

I asked about this, and was told that I must. I must play a Buddhist chant and follow the words in the sadana, to try to compensate for the lack of spirituality in the group.

Ivy had lived too long by most of our standards. Few would elect to spend years completely incapacitated and in a nursing home, rarely recognising anyone and unable to move about without help. However, I was told that death had come at the right time, when she was at peace with all those living on earth, and when her husband and others who had predeceased her were there to give her a warm welcome.

My helper with this had been Leopold, the member of my spiritual family with a Jewish background. He said he had been particularly impressed with the lady's war record. Hers had not been an easy life, her husband dying young and forcing her to become the breadwinner at a time when women were not expected to take that role. She had had some pretty robust jobs, at one time being a driver.

I was also told that the experience she had gained in this life, of having to accept big responsibilities in hard circumstances, would be used in the next, when she would have a much easier time as a male Muslim. However, she was not going to rush into reincarnation and, probably for two or three years and perhaps longer, she would be keeping an eye on the least capable member of her family.

It was quite a long time after his death that I heard that Frederick had died. He was the father of an ex-boyfriend, and a less than favourite member of his family. To me he was always extremely pleasant, which was generous of him, since I lived with but would not marry his favourite son.

There was a history to Fred's attitude. He had been the less favoured offspring, and was small in stature. His brother, I understood, was larger and more outgoing. Fred had had a hell of a life. He was extremely lucky in meeting and marrying a lovely, caring lady, and they had three children. But money represented for him security and his strength. He had had a good job and been held in high regard at his workplace, but he was not going to part with his cash.

They could easily have bought a good family house, but instead he insisted that they rented a small terraced house in a less-than-wonderful area. His wife made it into a good home for my memories of it are extremely happy ones, but it must have been a squash for the five of them to live there.

A grand-daughter, Alice, had a dream in which Fred appeared as a young man, wretched and tied down, trapped by his own condition. My guides told me that this was correct. Obviously we could pray, but indications were that this was not enough – it would take a priest to sort things out.

At that time I was going to a meditation group which was mostly made up of Roman Catholics. Fred had been Church of England as much as he was anything, and was, or claimed to be, against Roman Catholicism. However, his daughter married a Catholic and became a convert and, at her wedding, his younger son met a Catholic relative of the in-laws, and eventually they married. All the grandchildren had been Roman Catholics, of varying degrees. Indications were that a Catholic priest was needed to help the soul of Fred, and I asked a wonderful person, a nun who worked with the homeless and whom I met at the meditation group, if she could help. She accepted my account of what had happened, and arranged for a priest to say a Mass for Fred. Indications were that this had healed his troubled soul.

When I was relatively new to penduluming, it was the day that we had lunch with Catherine, and Timothy saw my grand-father floating above me, she asked if she could dowse to see if there were hostile spirits in our house. I drew her a plan and she checked the rooms. To my surprise she found a bad area – under the stairs and including a bit of the dining room. The cats have never shunned this part so I did not think we had been living with anything too terrible. Catherine said she would deal with it.

When I got home I thought about our spook, and decided that as I had been coping, albeit inadequately, with my mother's hostile spirit it was unlikely that I would encounter anything worse. I was on the spot and should have a go to see if I could do anything.

Where to begin? I stood dangling the pendulum over the kitchen units (near to the stairs). Then I remembered that computers work solely on a yes/no system, and I started asking questions. I asked whether, whoever it was, was there, and got a 'Yes'. Was the problem anything to do with the house that was built about 1882? 'No'. Had the event happened in the 1800s? 'No'. The 1700s? 'No'. The 1600s? 'yes'.

I discovered that two people had been trapped and died in a barn where hay had been stored. One had gone to his rest, but the other was planning to marry a girl he had got pregnant. He resented the ground on which this had happened and had been doing bad things in the house because of this. I asked, if I tried to help him, whether he would stop his activities, and he said 'Yes'.

The Lord's prayer and the *Twenty-third Psalm* showed as positive so I recited them for him, the girl, and the baby.

A little later we went to an *All Souls Day Requiem* service to try to help sort out the trouble with my mother. We wrote her name on a paper placed at the back of the church – to be read out during the service. As soon as I sat down I fancied I could feel the man who had burnt to death wanting to be included, too. He had previously told me he was a farm labourer, but had refused to give his name. I got up and added 'a farm worker' to the list on the paper. I just hope he and his family found peace.

On one occasion Pauline told me in hushed tones that they were living in a haunted house. They had bought it with the knowledge a lady who was apparently very sociable and well-liked had died from a drugs overdose in her bedroom.

The poor woman had had cancer and, initially, thought she had made a recovery. When she was told the disease had returned she killed herself. She was probably in her fifties.

Pauline and her family did not expect any problems as I was told, 'There would be a lot of praying in the house.' However, the bedroom where the sad event had happened was definitely not a restful place, and the teenager who was supposed to sleep in it was, predictably, anything but happy.

I managed to persuade Pauline to let me contact the Church of England, and ask for help from one of their experts. This I did, and the selected priest said he would carry out the relevant service in his church. He stressed that if there were further problems he should be contacted at once, and he would visit the house.

His visit was not necessary. After the prayers in the church the bedroom became peaceful.

One should never put off seeking help in these cases. There are two sides to the story. From our side there will be a house with problems which we would prefer not to live with while, on the other side, there is a distressed soul who needs help. Dying and waking up on the other side can be a traumatic and difficult time for some souls, particularly if they have, during their lifetimes, denied any possibility of their consciousness continuing after death. Then there are others who feel they have unfinished business, a great need to say or do something, and fail to leave the earthly plain as they should. Whatever the cause, these spirits do need help.

Accept that these dead people are people just like us, but without their bodies. If you saw someone lost, or distressed, by worrying thoughts, wouldn't you want to try to help?

Special People, Special Places

- *Rosemary who was psychic.* • *Two people without any desire for vengeance.* • *My local Buddhist centre.* • *A friend enlightens me.* • *A sponsored child.* • *My guru in the aspect of a Buddha.* • *The lady who enabled me to save my life.* • *Messages at the Corinthian church.* • *A man who could have been dead twice over.* • *Quiet little angel on earth.*

At times I feel I have been fantastically lucky with people I have met, and places where I have been. I have even let myself feel guilty because others do not appear to have had such wonderful privileges. However, I do believe that there is a great law which decrees, *Seek and ye shall find*. But you do have to seek. If seeking is confined to 'where do I get the money for a new status symbol' then forget it. My innate belief in the existence of some form of benevolent and powerful God, and in the power of prayer, gave me a great advantage. If the most doubting agnostics could keep their minds open, even just a chink, they might gain an insight.

Many widely differing people have crossed my path. Some have taught me much, others one fact which I particularly needed to know at that time. I have walked into places which people, who are far more spiritually advanced than I am, have embued with an atmosphere which has been a mixture of bliss and balm. When inside these places, I have been able to soak up their feelings, and their gift of the knowledge that the power and existence of Good, even in today's world, is alive, well, and available to all.

First I would like to tell you about Rosemary. Initially there was no great rapport. While I have never been good-looking, and am scruffy rather than smart, she was acutely aware of being attractive, and very much minded how she dressed, and spent time seeing that she presented herself well. Apart from this, we had two things in common, sculpture and cats.

When I heard she was very ill I decided to visit her in hospital. I discovered that, eight years previously, she had been diagnosed with leukaemia, and was given three weeks to live. She came from a Jewish family, some members being more orthodox than others, but she responded to her illness by investigating the beliefs of the Christian Science religion.

Rosemary embraced the idea that her body was not diseased, and proved her so-called medical specialists very wrong indeed. We all have to die some time, however, and I have no doubt that the timing of her death, which must have been nine years later, was right for her.

In addition to the mundane, Rosemary and I had another thing in common, we were psychic. She, I think, more so than I am. We were able to share this, and it was extremely meaningful. I learned a great deal from her. She illustrated that those who have faith, and accept that the spirits of those who have died can be actively helping us, make it relatively easy for positive paranormal happenings to manifest.

While she was still well, and many years earlier, a friend of Rosemary's had asked her if she would accompany her to see a fortune-teller. The friend explained that the woman lived on a rough housing estate, and she was nervous of going there on her own. They made their journey, and while the friend and the fortune-teller sat together, Rosemary was in another room. There were the usual pleasantries as they left, and the fortune-teller told Rosemary that she had a brother and sister. As Rosemary only had a brother, she corrected this announcement, but was told that, in the spirit world, she had a sister whose name was Heather.

Later, Rosemary was telling her mother about this episode, and said that her friend must have been conned. Unexpectedly her mother turned quite pale and after a short pause, explained matters in detail. She had become pregnant for the third time after Rosemary and her brother had been born, but Rosemary's father did not want more children, and insisted that she had an abortion. But, before the abortion, they decided, if the child was a girl, they would call her Heather.

As Rosemary drew towards death she was strongly aware of her mother and Heather waiting for her.

Rosemary took a turn for the worse, and ended up in a dismal old hospital. There are times when over twenty-four hours, a patient's appearance can change dramatically. This obvious and devastating deterioration had taken place, and when I left, I did not expect to see her alive again.

That night, with no expectation that she would survive, I decided to do Buddhist prayers. Green Tara, the Buddha of Active Compassion, is a wind element, and responds quickly to a call for help. However, while I felt I could ask her on Rosemary's behalf, I went through the motions in a routine and humdrum manner. I was paying lip-service, but nothing more.

I returned to the hospital the next day. Rosemary was sitting up in bed, alert and full of life. "Something happened last night," she said, "a crisis was averted." She described how she had suddenly broken out into an enormous sweat, so that she was soaking wet all over, including her hair. She had, she said, never experienced perspiration like it, but, she invited me to see the obvious, "Look how much fitter I am today. A crisis has been averted," she repeated. I know not whether it was the power of Green Tara, the most potent and swiftest power I have ever come across or whether, possibly, the mother and sister had used their influence. I only know that something little short of miraculous had happened.

Rosemary, in her new lease of life, went back home for a while, before having a spell in a much nicer private nursing home. Like me, Rosemary loved to be out in the open. The people at the nursing home told her that she could be allowed out for a little while, if someone with a car could take her ... of course, I volunteered, though not without some misgivings. To be responsible for such an ill person is quite daunting.

No sooner had Rosemary got into the car than she announced that she must go back to her flat, to track down private medical insurance papers. This was definitely outside doctor's orders, and I was concerned, but we made light of the risk, and said that if she did collapse, I would simply have to make her comfortable, and run for help. Two intelligent people should be capable of coping with this, I thought.

After greeting and being greeted by her cat Rosemary disappeared into her bedroom to hunt among her papers. I played with Tibby, a 'rescued' cat, then waited, and waited, and waited.

* * *

Rosemary had told me about her previous pet, Bridie, and I saw photographs of a huge, fat, black and white cat. It was not the size that struck me, though, but the animal's eyes. They were almost human. I had never seen any feline which had such an un-catlike expression. It was quite unnerving.

Rosemary was convinced that, since Bridie's death, she had been with her. Bridie knew that Rosemary loved cut flowers, making much of the vase in the main living room. After Bridie died, people going to visit Rosemary often found individual cut flowers lying on the pavement, picked them up, and brought them in as an offering.

This phenomenon once happened to me. I was walking to the hospice cutting across the car park of a church, and saw a pink carnation on the ground. I left it there – it must have been out of a wreath or a wedding bouquet. But when it was still there on the way back I thought I could at least rescue it, and put it in water and, of course, the next day I took it to Rosemary. How lucky that it was a carnation, no other flower would have lasted so well.

* * *

As time dragged on I began to curse myself for being party to this. I could not help Rosemary, and was only aware that a very ill friend was using up more energy than she had to spare, and I was a collaborator. Depressed and useless, I started silently using the Tara mantra. After a minute or two I was aware of a wonderful atmosphere. It was as though a cone of pink light (though I saw no colour) descended around me, giving love and peace.

Eventually Rosemary reappeared with the news that she could not find the papers, and the insurance company would simply have to track down her policy on their computer. Far from looking at death's door, she was bright, and when I suggested that I had better rush her back to the nursing home she announced that she wanted to have a drive to the sea, and breathe in some fresh air on the promenade. We went there, and she even had a short walk without any sign of being tired!

Time passed and once again poor Rosemary was back in hospital, though this time in a more attractive private ward. The medicos had got hold of her. They had found her stomach stuck out, and were going to investigate. It was obvious that they expected to find a tumour. Rosemary was indignant – her stomach had been that shape all her life, and she did not want to be pulled about any more. It was Rosemary and myself against the intrusive doctors, with their nasty little ways and instruments! Rosemary formulated a plan. The first words in the preface of *Science and Health*, the Christian Science textbook are, 'To those leaning on the sustaining infinite, today is big with blessings'. "Today," said Rosemary, "not yesterday, or tomorrow. Today." She intended to repeat that, over and over. I learned the quote, and also recalled it during the day. When I next saw Rosemary she was delighted. The medicos had been very disappointed – they had been unable to find anything wrong. There was no cancerous lump.

Eventually Rosemary's condition deteriorated so that she moved into a hospice. Considering that, nine years ago, she had been given three weeks to live, she approached her stay with confidence. She treated the hospice more like a hotel, being remarkably active, and playing host to relatives who came to visit her by taking them out for meals. She was there for months, not weeks, and made the most of every day.

Completely unafraid of death, and aware of the presence of her mother and aborted sister-in-spirit waiting for her, she viewed the end very positively. I knew it was not right to pray for her recovery or the prolongation of her life. Her time had come, and it was right for her.

Then, one night, I had a psychic tap on the shoulder that I must, again, repeat the Green Tara prayers for her. I argued with whoever was guiding me, but the message remained firm. I told whoever it was that I would do the Tara prayers, but took no responsibility if I was doing the wrong thing.

I later learned that the day after I had gone through the prayers, Rosemary, defying her condition entirely, had summoned a taxi, returned to her flat, collected her cat, and they had driven to a town about ten miles away where a kind friend was waiting to give Tibby a home. I can only think that the injection of power which, hopefully, Green Tara had given her, had been right, and utilised for that trip. She delivered Tibby on a Tuesday, and died the following Friday night. I saw her on the Friday morning, and as I left she gave me a radiant smile and a wave.

* * *

She left a legacy of memories. Occasionally, while Rosemary was relatively fit and active, we would take her out in the car. Once we went to a large old house in a village some distance out of town. We had to go round with a guide rather than just prowl round and explore the place for ourselves.

Rosemary was at the front of the group as the guide opened a door. "Oh look, did you see that? A cat!" She had seen a cat streak round the door and into the room. There was no cat in the room which did not surprise Rosemary, as she knew it to be a ghost cat. Neither I, nor anyone else, saw anything, but I know that, at some level, it will have been there.

I have a humorously-carved wooden cat, stripey, with his head down and his bottom up, which Rosemary gave me. She had insisted that I have a keepsake, and at first wanted me to take something more valuable. I won her round, however, by arguing that I genuinely liked the cat – she admitted she did too – and that it would be a good connection between us. During her illness she was very generous, beautiful packets of smoked salmon used to come through the letter box, with her love and thanks.

There were many sequels to Rosemary's story. The hospice had a charity shop in a road I rarely visited, but Rosemary told me I must patronise it if I was ever nearby. One day I found myself there and went into the shop. One of Rosemary's friends, possibly envious of her figure, had been in the habit of telling her off for dressing in a tarty fashion. Her skirts were short, but she carried them off well.

As I searched for something to buy I came across a dress which was size ten. I am a twelve, but because of the elasticated waist, and the fact that I am flat-busted, I poured myself into it, and it fitted exactly. I was a perfect example of mutton dressed as lamb. It was a positive mid-blue in colour, and was exactly what I would never buy, but what Rosemary would have dressed me in. I bought it!

Some time later I saw a free Christian Science lecture advertised. Thinking that Rosemary would have advised me to go along I did so, and this triggered my visits to their Wednesday night testimony meetings. I found the people wonderful, welcoming and sincere, and I heard many accounts of what most would have describe as miracle healings. After a while I was able to testify myself, though I had nothing very dramatic to report. However I did once save my burning hand and, on a different note, manage to rescue a girl whose dress had given way, amazingly controlling a twelve inch fault with a safety pin. (Read a fuller account in *The Power of Prayer*.)

All one has to do is to accept the truth that all is in the mind – Divine mind – and that matter does not exist. All perceived sickness and every other kind of distress or evil is simply an erroneous invention of mortal mind. Perceive everything as perfect, and perfect it will be.

* * *

I have known some very spiritually advanced but apparently very ordinary people. There is the rather smug and prim phrase, 'teaching by example', but when this enters real life powerfully and unselfconsciously it is really impressive.

One man was born with genetic problems, and he did well to work. His first marriage collapsed, but he met and married a bright and vivacious woman and they had two delightful children. They went away for a weekend. During this time they met another couple, and the man's wife and the other lady's husband decided to ditch their current partners and make their life together. This they did. Friends of the handicapped husband were horrified and extremely worried, his sight had deteriorated and he could no longer work. He lost everything. The house was sold and he had to move into a tiny flat. He saw his adored children only occasionally.

Would he be suicidal? He coped magnificently. His response to the news that his wife and children were to leave him was simply, "What can I do but wish them well and hope they are happy." Wow! When you think of the vindictive way most people, with far less reason, set out to spite partners they believe to have failed them...

Being free of wishing for retribution is a great gift. I was discussing a current issue – there had been a nasty racially – motivated attack – with a Jewish friend. As the victims were Jewish she might well have felt inclined to wish harm on the attackers, but not so. I told her that someone had suggested a particularly nasty death would be appropriate as a punishment and she said, "What a terrible thing to wish. You should wish that they would change, and become nice people..."

* * *

My two years with the Political Sect with its lack of spirituality resulted in my seeking meditation and discovering Tibetan Buddhism. I thus started going to the centre, and soon found I loved their prayers and chants. Here is a favourite:

> From the hearts of all the Holy beings streams of light and nectar flow down, granting blessings and purifying.

From my initial visit to the local centre I progressed to major festivals, and received teachings from one of my four Gurus, a man who has performed many miracle healings, and whose teachings hold the thousands who attend them spellbound. I found both the local and headquarters centres absolutely magical, and I still marvel at my good luck in having found them.

Had I stayed with the Church of England rather than finding something as unsatisfactory as the sect, I might never have been driven to seek meditation, and would therefore never have met the Buddhists. It could even be argued that the Political Sect was, for me, the right place at the right time. When I joined it I was comfortably-placed, financially speaking. I was certainly shown some of the evils of materialism, into which I now realise I was steadily sinking.

My local Buddhist centre closes for some weeks during the summer. I have tried different Buddhist groups but have found their teachings woolly by comparison, less focused, and less powerful. (I love miracles, and my Buddhist Guru actually performs them!)

However, one of the other groups offered an excellent piece of advice which I will pass on – it sounds obvious but is not as easy to follow as you might think.

We all see things that annoy us. A loutish football player may have a vast income while someone who is wholly decent and does something far more worthwhile (like a nurse or a really good teacher of handicapped children) may earn relatively little. Examples that are equally annoying include criminals who have committed evil deeds walking free from a court on a legal technicality and people who injure themselves through their own stupidity but manage to pin the blame on their employers. So many injustices get to us, and we develop a state of prolonged irritation.

This state of mind helps no-one and solves nothing. We are damaging ourselves. The Buddhists' advice? 'Drop it!'

* * *

Carol was someone I knew for only short time. I felt no immediate empathy, although I could tell that she was extremely caring and well-motivated. She also had total faith, which manifested in her coping with her fatal illness extremely well and positively. In some ways we were diametrically opposed. While I loved what I regarded as tearjerkingly beautiful sacred music she liked Christian pop songs, and while I believed that illness in this world could be overcome by spiritual solutions she took the view that we were put in this world to be of this world, and to suffer the physical consequences.

No matter, we got on well. She did not have children, and her good job and family circumstances meant that she was, like myself, financially comfortable. Because Timothy was a lot older than I was, and had elected not to have a pension which was transferable to his wife, a decision taken when his first wife was alive, I insisted that quite a bit of the money he got from selling his house when he moved into mine should be invested in lieu of my pension. I was therefore sitting on a sum of money which I may or may not need. In fairness, it was not unknown for us to, occasionally, bail out a friend in need, but I felt uneasy. I was torn between risking future poverty by reducing the investment and giving more of it away and holding on to it. I also noted the high sums charities pay their senior employees ... and the money wasted...

One day Carol opened the subject of money, saying that she had been lucky financially, and had, 'Tried to do good works.' They had got involved with the scheme whereby someone can sponsor a child in the Third World, and had good personal contact. Then she uttered the line which I needed to hear. "We own nothing in this life. We are merely the custodians of it." Indeed. To some extent my conscience was salved. I would not stand by and watch friends starve, neither would I waste money on silly status symbols. Hopefully, mine were a steady pair of hands, as a custodian. A big 'thank you', Carol.

Carol's influence was, even after her death, very positive for me. She had given me the prod I needed to sponsor a child in the third world. I have never been child-minded. It was no accident that I married late and did not procreate. I regard childlessness as one of the successes of my life. However, I always have been very concerned about poor little children growing up in desperately sad and deprived conditions.

For years I had toyed with the idea of sponsoring a child but did nothing.

As we do not drink alcohol we rarely go into pubs, but my friend Rebecca had often, after our sessions with the healing group, taken me for a coffee at a pub-restaurant in the town. One day when the weather was poor Timothy and I took our exercise by way of shopping in the same area, and we went in for a coffee.

We went to the 'no smoking' area. On the table was a copy of the *Times*, out of which had fallen, but was still on the table, an application form for sponsoring a child. I picked it up, and put it in my pocket.

When I got it home it was very scruffy. The rain had got to it. However, I would fill it in. One was given options over sex, age, and the part of the world. Hoping to get a less obviously popular choice I supposed I would ask for a girl... then I decided to dowse. I was told to ask for a boy, aged about eleven, and from South America.

When I had done this I had a few moments of excitement. Somewhere, already, was a boy to whom I would become connected. He was about to have a sponsor. Somehow, I felt the thing as special. What was going on? I asked whether I had found the child through my own psychic powers and was told, 'No'. Had someone else, one of the spiritual family for instance, helped? 'No'. But I had been told that I had been guided. In a humorous moment I suggested, 'Did a Buddha find him for me?' The pendulum went madly to 'Yes'. A second later I had rumbled it, my Guru Tibetan monk had, at some spiritual level, been instrumental in it.

It may sound like wishful thinking, saying that my Guru is a Buddha, but I am sure he is. When he was in Tibet he carried out many miracle healings. I have met one lady he cured of cancer and another of blindness, both in England.

During one of his teachings I was amazed to see that his hair – kept very short as monks do – had formed the shape of the Buddha Amitabha on the top of his head. It remained there for a while. What I saw did not appear on the closed circuit television screen, I observed, but I could see it clearly. Many Buddhas have 'Amitabha in his top-knot, eternally radiating light,' and so had my Guru.

Almost by return came news about my little boy. His middle name was the same as mine in my last incarnation. To my amazement he was born on exactly the same day, was precisely the same age as my friend Elizabeth's grandson about whom we were all so concerned. A lump had been found on his ribcage almost a year earlier, and one hospital, apart from looking at a scan, had done nothing. A second hospital expressed great concern...

There was another coincidence. My husband is old enough to be my father, and this boy's father was very much older than his mother... Certainly this little boy was the right one for me.

* * *

People can sometimes enter and leave our lives swiftly but give vital information. Evaline was the lady I met at my Brighton Buddhist centre at the time I knew my mother was trying to kill me. If things are meant to happen, they will. For no obvious reason she told me of her work with the paranormal, so I was able to tell her about my mother, and she was then able to tell me of the existence of my wonderful Guru, Julian.

Talking to her I also heard her gainsay my belief that it was wrong to try to contact the dead. She corrected me, saying that if the dead wished to contact us they should be allowed to. If they wished to help they should not be denied the opportunity – it was beneficial for their karma.

This brief chance meeting saved my life and predisposed me to listen to the spirits and write this book.

* * *

Special places offer special experiences. One Christian church has among its members a number of spiritualists, who are seriously into the healing ministry. I and Rebecca went there regularly – Rebecca, who suffers from a longstanding health condition, found the sessions particularly helpful.

On one occasion, after she had had a session, Rebecca was in a particularly thoughtful mood. One of the healers had said that he felt someone with her, and it turned out to be her brother who had died when he was two. She had just about no memory of him, and he was never referred to in family circles, but clearly he was still concerned for his sister's welfare.

On another occasion I was told that I had a nun, though I was told the spirit was no longer a nun and had moved on to greater spiritual realizations, walking with me. On questioning my guides when I got home I discovered that it was my wonderful Angela manifesting as she had been in one of her many previous incarnations.

I was given the message that, 'Everything is going to be all right.' This was accompanied by an awareness of a beautiful sea washing in and out. The healer who had received the message was delighted when I told him that I am a keen all-the-year-round sea swimmer, so the visualization did indeed have significance. On another occasion a healer had a lovely vision of clouds drifting by as he worked on me.

Once when I was there I met a most amazing man. He was of good average height, had longish grey hair, and a dent in his throat which advertised the fact he had had a very serious cancer operation. He was lame, hence he carried a splendid walking stick with him. It looked very strong, and its length bedecked with beads and feathers.

We got into conversation. He had no religion, but a belief in some form of great consciousness to which we were all joined. His stick looked so much like an artefact of the Red Indians that I asked if there was any connection, but he said simply that a friend gave him the feathers that his parrot shed.

In some ways, discounting his huge misfortunes, he had had a charmed life. Not only had he survived cancer, but the damaged leg was as the result of a fall sustained while climbing. He crashed down sixty feet, and lived to tell the tale!

As he fell the first twenty feet the whole of his life flashed before him. During the next twenty he felt sorry for the family and friends he was leaving behind, and for the last twenty he had a sense of absolute freedom.

* * *

One of my aunts had a friend and the two of them used to come and stay with me. Sadly my aunt died suddenly, and her friend, although younger, discovered she had cancer shortly after. At the time there was no hospice in the area, and the poor woman remained living alone at home. Just doing everyday tasks became difficult for the growth was around her shoulders, preventing her from using her hands. She became more and more helpless.

A neighbour and friend from her church rallied round. She visited her morning and night, and took on the intimate and difficult jobs of helping the poor woman by literally – wiping her bottom. I keep in touch with Joanna – she is an inspiration.

It's quite amazing how quiet and ordinary people, can have such wonderful hidden depths.

More Examples Of Serendipity

● *A Buddhist with a Burrswood connection.* ● *Burrswood again and again* ● *Angels – all over the place.* ● *Advice regarding my experience as an abused child.* ● *Others with mother problems.* ● *Chance meetings.* ● *Elizabeth transmits a humorous message.* ● *Neighbour divorces and Asperger's syndrome.* ● *Wrong things turn out to be right ones.* ● *My guru gives messages.* ● *I find what I am seeking.* ● *Appropriate flowers at funerals.* ● *Silent retreats.* ● *One-ness embraces all.*

Guru Catherine says I have a *thing* with Burrswood. She is right! On one occasion I was at the Buddhist centre for a special weekend event. I was also using it to chill out and was avoiding any involvement in conversations, as much as possible. I happened to be looking at leaflets of future events and found myself standing next to a very pleasant young man.

I have no idea how it happened, but he volunteered that his father was a Christian priest who had been given a job at – he need not have told me, I already knew – Burrswood. He gave me his father's name and told me he was reading all he could about its founder Dorothy Kerin. The man sounded perfect for his job. He was, however, concerned about his son's interest in Buddhism, knowing little about it. I took the liberty of writing to him, telling him how wonderful it was, and hoping to put his mind at rest.

Within weeks I had to collect a folder from the parish office at a local church, and leave a note for the vicar, who was out. I was shown his in-tray. As it was pointed out to me my helper tapped the letter which was uppermost. "This was urgent yesterday!" she exclaimed. On the letterhead was the name of the Buddhist's father. I blinked, and saw 'Burrswood'.

Back home I realised that there was a message for me. Indeed there was. My guides told me to go there to petition on behalf of a little boy who had to have tumours removed, and a friend who was suffering from angina. I was also told to pray for me. I went, and put all the names in the petitions box. At the alter rail I held a card with just my friends' names on it. But the priest, having read them, added, "And yourself." When I was in the grounds I saw people talking. There, on the chest of one of the men, a priest, was the identifying badge giving the name of my Buddhist's father.

* * *

Once I went there, and it appeared I was destined to come away with a particular book. While it is relatively easy to control one's actions, one's thoughts are a different matter. I cannot think of anything more spontaneous than a thought! To control one's thoughts usually means, at least in my case, that I have a bad original thought and then a second, correcting thought. (Actually, this is a third thought, the second being a recognition that the first left much to be desired.)

I was extremely unpleasant for the first part of my life, and I have been conscious of the need to reform. This is not easy. I have known myself to go through stages when I thought I was making progress and then backsliding, and being in angry states of mind when I have felt critical and full of hatred.

At this time I was browsing in the Burrswood bookshop because I had heard about an author who had sounded interesting, and wanted to investigate. I found nothing that attracted me. Then my eye fell on a book which was on one of the poems of St. John of the Cross. Dipping into it I saw a highly relevant passage about temptations without and within. Clearly, St. John appreciated that the rocky path was not just rocky externally. Far from being a 'holier than thou' individual he appeared to have had great humour and be very, very human indeed. He admitted to feeling himself in need of spiritual improvement, which I found most encouraging.

Then, still engaged in my personal battle, I went to a Buddhist teaching. There the idea was put forward that one should be able to be happy with each thought one had – so happy that one would be content if one dropped dead just after having it. What a challenge! I wish...

But the Christian Scientists believe that we are all, actually, perfect since God made us, and He makes nothing imperfect. Our faults, sins, and failings are not 'real', just the products of our faulty perception. . . Clearly, while I was meant to work on my failings, I was also to be reassured that no-one could be beyond the pale. After all, one is taught that God has infinite mercy, and Christ died for the sins of all men and, as Julian of Norwich says "All will be well."

* * *

Angels! Suddenly people around me started talking about them. Three people, one of Jewish origin, one of a Christian and rather 'godly' background, and the third who had had a rough and varied life, were all into angels, either seeing them, wishing to find them, having a gut feeling about them, or simply wanting to find out more about them thus showing a belief in their possible reality.

There are many definitions of angels, from conventionally portrayed images with wings, to relatively ordinary figures who manifest, perform some altruistic act, and then vanish, to 'angel thoughts' which light upon us and we can feel that they come from a very positive force.

Timothy was away so I was free to enjoy myself as I wished. I went to a healing service at Burrswood as Catherine is of the opinion that I should go there from time to time. Just as I was leaving a friend rang to say they had heard there was to be a talk about angels, she would send me details.

There is a good bookshop at Burrswood. I love the early Christian mystics. Julian of Norwich is my favourite, and when I saw a little display about *Hildegard of Bingen* my curiosity was aroused. Unfortunately it was mostly audio, talking books. All I wanted was a small and inexpensive book. Those that I could see were all rather superior volumes. However I loitered, flicking through the pages of one of the hardbacks. I glanced down. Another book had appeared, also about Hildegard, in paperback, and inexpensive... This sort of manifestation is not uncommon since I have been with Buddhism and Christian Science, where mind is regarded as so much stronger than material things.

I bought the little volume and that night had a long bath – the bath is one of the few places where I can get on with a bit of quiet reading.

Later I went into the little church for the service. A lady gave an address. Her subject was 'Angels!'

She had a tremendous knowledge on the subject and I learned that many people had seen angels, in various forms, while staying at Burrswood. I later wrote and asked the lady for a transcript of her talk. She kindly obliged. I have the notes to this day and they remain inspirational.

There was another reason why I went there that day. I had to (again) hear the message that if petitioning for other people one should neither anticipate what would be right for them, nor try to force recovery or whatever upon them. One's own energies should not come into it. One should just hold them up to God and let them rest in God.

* * *

Memories of being abused as a child had been thoroughly pushed under the surface until my mother's troubled soul made its presence known. Then I felt I must try to dredge them up to make sense of what was happening to me. I have always known that counselling is definitely not for me. I feel I should be able to sort myself out. This has been the case, one does not have to court help, serendipity means that one will come across messages and advice which present themselves in the normal course of one's life.

On another trip to Burrswood the priest had been recounting an incident at home – it was obvious he had a lovely happy family life with his children – when he suddenly pulled up short, and in hushed tones expressed his sadness for those whose early life had not been happy and whose parents had not been loving. The same acknowledgement also came up in a Buddhist teaching.

Buddhists are encouraged to believe that, because we have had thousands of previous incarnations, all other living beings were, at one time, our mothers. The idea behind this is that one should have the same feelings for all sentient beings as one does for a loving mother. However, the teacher broke off, and said in some cases it was not possible to accept that one's mother had been kind and loving, some were not. One should then substitute another person who had shown affection.

Then the Christian Scientists happened to raise the subject of unloved children, and said that the problems from this experience could be healed if one accepted that the love of father-mother God had been, and always would be, there. No one had ever been unloved.

I view with great concern, and considerable anger, the effects of today's disfunctional families on their children. The mantra of the selfish adult is, 'Children are resilient'. They are not. Whether they conceal their hurt or not, and the more they conceal it the greater the damage is likely to be, they will have been devastatingly traumatized. This response, mixed with inappropriate guilt and confusion, is bound to manifest in personality defects, serious illness, criminal behaviour, addictions or whatever, either in the short or longterm future. Gerald's father had been harsh with him. Gerald realised that the panic attacks he had when he was sixty had their origins in his childhood experiences.

* * *

However, if one has had nasty experiences as a child one does have the advantage of understanding what others with similar backgrounds have been through. I recall two women I met whose mothers, like mine, were well-practised in the art of emotional blackmail. Pat was a fellow commuter. She was small, and appeared neurotic. The day came when the train journey took far longer than it should have done, and we got into conversation.

It was not long before Pat started talking about the terrible time she was having with her mother – and she gave a full description of the woman. I exclaimed, "That is a perfect description of my mother." We compared our experiences, and the similarities were enormous! Sharing them was as helpful to me as it must have been for her, as at the time neither of us had anyone in whom we could confide. It was just as well that our friends could not hear us criticizing our mothers, for we would have been criticized ourselves. Mothers tend to be put on pedestals!

The other lady, Sherry, was a complete contrast to the first and I met her at work. Big, blousy, jolly, carefree – until she mentioned her mother, whereupon she sat trembling in her shoes. Sherry, as I had previously, felt very alone with this problem, and I think I helped by letting her know that I understood her situation perfectly, and she could be absolutely honest with me. I knew I could believe her every word.

Meetings between people with something that they need to share but who otherwise may have little common ground do not happen by accident. We are meant to be put in a position where we can support each other.

* * *

So called chance meetings can bring great pleasure. I love animals and have had many conversations with cats and dogs along the way. Out walking one day, a friendly 'woof' came from a dog that bounded over to me and I fell into conversation with his owner. He was no ordinary dog, but a hero. His mistress had to use two sticks to walk and had been walking along a towpath of a canal. Her dog, once let off his lead, had raced ahead. Suddenly, a man jumped on her and tried to drag her into the bushes. The dog turned round, saw what was happening, raced back, and took a large lump out of the attacker's leg. The offender fled in fear.

Little positive encounters like this are, I find, very pleasant and encouraging.

* * *

Serendipity often takes the form of little bits of encouragement. I suspect many are arranged by benevolent spirits. One day I wanted to take advantage of Timothy's absence to get on typing this book, but I was tired and restless. I could feel I was functioning ineffectively. I was frustrated and felt useless.

The phone went and I cursed, but became pleased when the caller wanted details of guru Thomas. I have made notes about his work and photocopied them, as I want other people to have the advantage that I had. At least I could be useful by delivering these – the lady who made the request lived quite near me. It would only be a short walk.

It was drizzling but I did not mind for I had something positive to do. On the return journey I decided to make a detour. I had planned to do a squirrel in my sculpture class but had had difficulty finding photographs to use for reference. As I walked through a churchyard I found myself surrounded by what must have been the most tame squirrels in the town. I was able to study them thoroughly, taking a mental note of their shape, positions and proportions.

There was an added bonus, I met a lady with a bright little dog. The path was narrow, and the animal was hesitant about passing me. The pooch had been rescued after being treated badly, and I had a pleasant little chat with the owner.

One day Timothy had been particularly hard going and

miserable – his sister's description as *heavy* is superb. So I had gone to the beach on my own. As I walked along the front I spotted a man I knew. "How is my favourite ex-boy friend?" I asked, a smiling face came as a relief. "Not ex", came the reply, "I'm still a boy and we are still friends." We celebrated with a big, harmless hug. More encouragement, and just at the right time!

Anyone who has been having a tough time will know how comforting it is to find a fellow sufferer in similar circumstances. I hope it was no coincidence that both Gwendoline and myself knew Elizabeth – our go-between.

Gwendoline and her husband had a long running disagreement on whether or not they should have double glazing installed in their house. Gwendoline was against it, her husband in favour. Things took a nasty turn when Gwendoline was obviously dying of cancer, and he remarked that when she was dead the first thing he would do would be to order double glazing. Understandably she was hurt. The eager anticipation of a spouse's demise is quite common, and I told Elizabeth to tell Gwendoline of my experience.

Timothy, well over eighty, had, in an unguarded moment, said that when I was dead he was going to have fertility treatment and sire a child. Elizabeth could not believe her ears, but I insisted she pass on the message.

Timothy's comment had not disturbed me. I had been aware of him trying to line up Mrs X as his third wife, and my only feeling towards the woman he appeared to be considering was one of pity as I knew she hated him.

A 'For Sale' board went up on a neighbour's house, and when I saw her I said I was sorry she was leaving. This was not a particularly happy move in one way. There was to be a divorce. I could see her struggle in trying not to be too dramatic or disloyal, but she said she could not watch her husband, who was so unpleasant, destroy her daughter. We had a chat and a coffee and compared notes.

We had both imagined each other's respective marriages

were happy. The similarity between our husbands was very marked – neither appeared to care for anyone except himself. I was greatly indebted to her for telling me that her sister, a nurse, believed that an actual illness was to blame Asperger's syndrome, a lesser form of autism. If people cannot help their condition they are not really to be blamed.

Angela had once told me Timothy could not help being the way he was, but that makes no difference to the fact that his unpleasantness has to be endured. However, a spirit guide told me that Timothy's endless acts of spite were deliberate and calculated, and were not caused by his condition.

* * *

Very often 'right' things happen by a circuitous route and mistakes are often not mistakes at all. I was once discussing with a Christian Science friend how sometimes I mis-read a passage but what I saw was what I needed to hear. She reported that this often happened to her, and she accepted the phenomenon as quite normal.

* * *

Sometimes messages manifest in a very special way. My Buddhist Guru gives teachings at festivals where there may be well over a thousand people. Devotees often sit there, notebooks in hand and pens poised.

While the teachings given remain firm quite often followers hear messages which are unique to them, and which other people, including those taking notes verbatim, do not hear. One boy had heard someone denigrating the teacher, and insulting him by saying he looked like a monkey... and at the next teaching the boy heard the Guru laughingly remark that people said he looked like a monkey. The boy told me he knew that message was particularly for him.

I had a similar experience. At the festival I managed to get to when Timothy was recovering from his pneumonia and when I had been living in a world of cleaning out commodes, and coping with terrible problems, I heard the words, "Your life may be horrible, really horrible – but Buddhism has the answers. I know, I have done it. Leave your family, leave your homes leave your country for Dharma.". He knew I had had to move heaven and earth to get there, getting Timothy into a home, cat sitters for the cat... he also knew the future was uncertain. "If you cannot get to places then your own wisdom may have to be your spiritual guide." Even as I heard it I wondered at its relevance to me but how, in the context of the rest of the teaching, it would probably have made nonsense to the other thousand or so people there.

* * *

Seek and ye shall find. Over and over again I have found this to be true.

I had wanted to discover a prayer which would represent the Hindu religion, and circumstances drew me to it. 'Let our meditation be on the glorious light of Savitri. May this light illumine our minds.' This, I read, was what millions of Hindus had recited over hundreds of years.

But who was Savitri? The Hindus have many gods, and I had two books with quite a few of them, though not Savitri. I patronize my favourite bookshop regularly so while I was visiting to buy one book I flipped through a few others to see if I could find a reference to the illusive god. No luck. Then, just as I was leaving the shop, I saw a little book about India on a rotating stand. On the back of it was a coloured illustration of Savitri – he was the god of action.

* * *

Things can assume a symbolic aspect. For a few years when I attended funerals I noticed that the choice, and arrangement of, flowers echoed the essence of the deceased. Veronica's main display was a case in point – a wonderful, rich, abundant, generous, and varied collection of flowers which described exactly her hugely and widely caring personality.

When my paternal aunt died the flowers showed a delicate and restrained refinement, a sort of purity. I realised that this her been at her inner core, though the aspect of her which I saw was much more robust. We got along very well, and I viewed her more as a friend than a relative, and I was shattered when she died, without warning, of a heart attack, as a very active seventy-five year old.

* * *

For a time a very nice Scottish family ran a grocer's shop in my locality. The son knew I was interested in Buddhist meditation and, when the Buddhist centre closed for the summer, he suggested that I might like to try a meditation group which he went to. This casual suggestion turned out to be a king pin in my spiritual development.

It had occurred to me for some time that, while into interfaith matters, I had had no interest in Roman Catholicism. I felt it would scarcely be worthwhile since the Christian message would be the same, and I thoroughly disapproved of the Vatican's wealth, and their views on birth control.

On arrival at the new group I discovered I was the only Protestant there, though Carol arrived later. Through this group I heard about the silent Buddhist Christian retreats which I was later to attend, and which remain an unforgettable and wonderful part of my life. And through those retreats I also met one of my closest friends, Teresa.

First I must tell you about these retreats. They were organized by two wonderful people, a lady who had, for a while, been a nun, but eventually, after giving up her robes, decided that her spiritual path lay with Tibetan Buddhism, and an elderly Benedictine monk, an adorable man who radiated benevolence.

Anyone who is horrified at the idea of a silent retreat should think again. They really are heaven on earth. Because the group was there to celebrate both Buddhism and Christianity there were no fundamentalists, just open-minded, enquiring people.

If one finds oneself with a group of strangers with whom one is going to spend a few days one would, in the normal way, be obliged to indulge in polite conversation and formalities. With speech barred the usual banalities were replaced with a silent empathy, and an awareness of a deeply-shared love and compassion for mankind. At mealtimes we sat down together, each allowed to have his or her uninterrupted thoughts.

Also at these retreats, more serendipity, I met Teresa, who soon became a very important person in my life. She is a devout Roman Catholic, but is very open-minded and critical of her church. She is one of the tiny handful of people with whom I can say exactly what I think or feel about spiritual matters. I hope that I am also able to offer her something, too.

In our mutual spiritual support partnership we share, compare, and contrast ideas, and exchange books. In some ways we are very different. While I spend my life dashing about, waiting on my husband, doing sculpture and what feels like a million other things she 'waits on the Lord'. Our contrasting backgrounds must be eye-openers for both of us. I have read quite a few books with a Catholic flavour, which I would otherwise not have read and, eventually after much effort – I got her to read my favourite-of-all-book, *Autobiography of a Yogi*.

I awaited her response with interest, but had never expected the reaction I got. After wading half way though it she felt it had taught her nothing she did not know, but the second part she greeted with delight. It had made her understand Christ's resurrection more fully. She observed that the writer knew the Bible better than we did. She was also fascinated with the Eastern yogis' ability to die without illness or trauma – to just sit there, and decide to die naturally and calmly.

All this because I had gone to a meditation group, and the group itself, what did it do for me?

Their method was to follow the teaching of the late John Main, a Benedictine monk. First there was a tape about meditation or a suitable subject, then a short piece of music or a chant, and this was followed by half an hour in which one silently repeated the word 'Maranatha'which meant 'Come Lord'. He considered that with this formula one would need no other prayer. One was also told to meditate on Maranatha at home, morning and night.

Because I was not a Catholic, I did not feel bound to obey the monk's instructions blindly or to the letter. But I felt that if, occasionally during the day, I could just bring Maranatha to mind, I would find it beneficial. In Buddhism I had been taught that the 'meditation break', the vast majority of life which is lived in between meditation sessions, was actually more important than the meditation sessions themselves. (In Christian terms it is not much good to behave well on a Sunday and badly for the rest of the week.) I went to bed feeling I had had a spiritually good experience, and slept well.

In the morning, contrary to my usual pattern, I had the strong feeling that I must sort out the place I had reached on my spiritual journey. I was aware that the previous night had changed me.

I had a Buddhist commitment to recite a prayer and mantra a set number of times. Many others with the same commitment found this a trial, and I had wondered how this could really be helpful. Could this instruction be right when I felt that the monk's dictum, which was identical in all but the label of a different religion, had been flawed for some people? I took the pendulum to ask whether, if I used a spiritual formula which was just taking place in my mind, I needed to do the daily recitation. Surely my formula would embody all prayers and all mantras – and I was told that it would.

My formula was a combination of Maranatha and the Christian Science belief, which dispels all kinds of sickness, that 'God is in charge' or 'The only Power is God'. This also embodied all the qualities of all the Buddhas, and settled comfortably under the concept of One-ness of which the Aboriginees spoke, and which I had come to see was the only complete and right way to view the one great and absolute creative and sustaining force, *love*.

> Everything is God and is of God. This acknowledgement covers everything. I therefore ask that God/Oneness/Love should come to all living beings, particularly sick friends, that we should all be aware of Him within us, that we should feel and understand His (or His/Her) control over our lives, and be open to receive the limitless blessings which this Oneness wants to give us.

This prayer and acceptance surely covered everything. One could ask for nothing more, but just grow deeper into the belief and feel absolute gratitude that The Creator had become more accessible.

As I contemplated on this I felt that I was having a moment of true revelation. Words cannot describe it, but they must try to. If embued with total Love and total Faith the ability to have a belief in the reality of wrong, pain, guilt and doubt, must vanish, for these, in the presence of the others – the Love and the Faith – could not exist. A dark room cannot remain dark when a light has been lit. Darkness is banished.

My awareness of the truth of this was so strong that I momentarily recalled the prayer 'Lord Jesus Christ, Son of the living God, have mercy on me, a sinner,' and found it almost repugnant. People repeated it over and over again, day in and day out. I felt as the Christian Scientists believed that God created me and I am perfect. I have sinned horribly, but if I believe I should also accept forgiveness – and for which Christians believe Christ paid with His life. And Buddhists, of course, believe that there is Buddha nature in us all, and that bad karma can be purified.

All this felt like a blissful revelation. The prayers and mantras, which I had laboured long and hard to use in an attempt to achieve a higher level of spirituality, became irrelevant. However good, they were merely fragments of this Whole.

I had an overview of my Buddhist master and Benedictine monk devising means through which the spirituality of those greatly wishing for spiritual enlightenment could be led towards it...

I saw also how with the great religious figures, Christ, Mohammed, Buddha and all the rest, their message was of love – it always had been and always would be. But they were merely the Holy vehicles for that message, in the way that a body is just a temporary sheath for the eternal soul it housed. Their message, their whole eternal spirit and essence, will never die, but their bodies given for the convenience of conveying the message had no real relevance, even if the Resurrection was so necessary to convince people of the Truth and Strength of God.

I could only look to the time when the One-ness – the total all-pervasiveness of God – would be accepted by all as the ultimate Truth, when we have all stopped learning, and just 'Know'.

Having seen the mountain I was trying to climb by struggling up by different bits of different paths I suddenly viewed the whole in its. . . no words can be adequate, but in that moment there were many aspects which mingled into the one Absolute, Perfect Whole, and they included Love, Beauty, Glory, Truth, Givingness, Acceptance, Forgiveness, Protection, Certainty, and a huge Coming Home in spirit to the Maker of All, Unifying One-ness.

And so, what about all the different Holy men, and the different religions? Each and every one, the genuine, inspired teacher with his message of Love, was encircled by the mantle of this One-ness, doing His work, and trying to help us to bring our innate spirituality to fruition.

And at the end of all this, the many roads I had explored and walked down, came the Absolute Simplicity of the message of the One-ness. I knew that my petition for all living beings, and especially for friends with special needs, and not forgetting myself either, was that we should all ask to have more of God's being in us, and that we should know that God is the Power over all.

Let all living beings know that God is inside them, and with them, and let them live with a faith which knows that God is in absolute control. There cannot, ever, be anything to fear.

Over the next few days I modified this slightly, 'us' meaning myself and all for whom I was praying. 'Cannot' implies that there might have been, a pure positive would be better. Thus:

Let us know that One-ness/God/Buddha/Immaculate-Spiritual-Love is in us, with us, and in absolute control of all things, all is well, there is nothing to fear.

As though to endorse this, the next time I went to the Christian Science meeting the thought for the week was displayed on their board: 'Nothing can thwart God's purpose for me"... Beautifully put!

DREAMS

• *Foxes represent the I.R.A.* • *Future work, for a fortune-teller.* • *Messages.* • *Jennifer.* • *A man's first visit but had dreamed about it often.* • *Dreams may portend an unhappy event.* • *Reconciliation.* • *Air crashes, survivor and predictions.* • *I dig for my cancer virus.* • *A faulty lift.* • *Blue hands restrain my mother.* • *God making all things perfect.* • *Two friends appear in the aspect of Buddhas.* • *My path.* • *One dream assures me.* • *Another warns me.* • *My mother tries to kill my father, then arranges my funeral.* • *I am warned.* • *I sleep with a boy friend and we both dream of death.* • *Spiritual progress is hard and dangerous.* • *Preferring the spiritual to the mundane.*

Messages can be sent through dreams. They often are. My Guru Thomas heard of a case where, during the Irish troubles, a man would dream about a certain place and a group of the people there would be portrayed as foxes. He came to realise that this indicated the place was being used as an I.R.A. cell. He convinced the police about the accuracy of his information, and they found his tip-offs very useful.

Thomas himself had a dream in which his wife told him about a dream she had had. A lady who had worked at the hospital where Thomas had been employed returned to say that since her death she had become a 'lifer' – someone who helped people who were still on earth. She did not have to do this, and could move on elsewhere if she chose. But she also said that her husband was dead – which he wasn't.

* * *

I cannot tell you about the actual dream itself in the next case, but its message also deals with how we might spend our time after we have completed our present lives.

A lady who was a fortune-teller went to a Buddhist festival. She was concerned that her work might, in some way, be damaging people, although her motive was to help them. She made an appointment with my Buddhist Guru who was able to put her mind at rest on this point.

She then asked him about a dream she had had, which she felt was significant. He was able to interpret it and say that, after her death, the fortune-teller would spend her time welcoming the newly-dead into the next world, explaining their altered state to them, and helping them to cope with their changed circumstances. She was delighted to think she would still have a useful job!

* * *

I was very fond of Jennifer, who was a kind and caring mother-figure. l was told she had been a valued aunt to me in my incarnation when Valerie and I were fishermen brothers and Great Auntie Louie was our mother.

When this sort of connection is made it has profound roots, and coincidences happen. They are meant. Jennifer died and at her funeral I learned that one card I had sent her was received the day she went into a hospice, and another the day she actually died. When I heard she had died, I sent the family the Bishop Brent passage, likening someone's death to a ship going over the horizon, to be met with joy by people who were out of sight. At the funeral one speaker likened death to a ship being launched and coming home. I thought that his idea had been based on the Bishop Brent card, but in fact he did not see it until after the funeral.

Jennifer's family knew that I had had psychic and paranormal experiences and were able to share with me news of auspicious dreams she had had before her passing. In one her mother had come to her, and said, "Your house is broken", which they knew meant that her body, which housed her soul, was finished. Then, very comfortingly, in another dream, her late husband featured in a state of great happiness. This was wonderful, since he had been a difficult and demanding man, and had at times caused the family unhappiness. But now, both he and her mother showed great joy at the prospect of Jennifer joining them.

As you can imagine, this revelation gave great comfort to the family.

* * *

A friend, Rufus, returned from his summer holiday. He and his wife had been to Italy, a country they had never visited before. "Something amazing happened," he told me. "We went to one town and it was a place I had been to often, in my dreams." He had known it as well as if he had lived there.

* * *

Sometimes a particular message will be interpreted correctly by the recipient although the content may be obscure to anyone else.

I once worked with an extremely attractive girl, Penelope, who had a steady boy friend she had met at university. I am sure she would have married him, but his parents had had a bad marriage, he had suffered a lot as a result, and had decided that he was never going to marry anyone.

She once told me that she had watched her dog gave birth, and the first poor little puppy was a breeches birth, and had died. Penelope was still upset about this experience years later, when she discovered she was pregnant.

Her boyfriend refused to marry her, and she had an abortion. She said she had had a dream about dancing women, I believe it was something similar to a wild tarantella and she 'knew what it meant'. For her it had portended the dead baby. She remembered the puppy. 'The first thing I saw born was born dead'.

* * *

A friend who later became a Buddhist monk had suffered the trauma of his parents splitting up. He had always been his mother's favourite and was upset when she deserted the family, finding that he could not bring himself to communicate with her. However, he had a dream showing that only through contact with her could right things happen. The imagery of the dream involved fish, one of which became huge and magnificent as a result of the good relationship being restored. He obeyed his dream.

* * *

Rebecca frequently dreams about accidents or misfortunes which are about to happen or, once or twice, appear to have happened simultaneously. Air crashes are foreseen, and once she had a nightmare involving rabbits just before her friend's domestic pet was killed.

* * *

My earliest indication that I had any kind of psychic ability came when I was quite a young child. I predicted a plane crash. I was with my parents in an aeroplane (which was not at all like a real plane) and I was trying to persuade them to climb out, and sit on the wings, as it was going to crash. They were dismissive of the idea, but I got them out of it, and onto the top. The plane then crashed, turning into what I believed to be a bread basket, but which was more like a cane or wicker laundry basket or hamper, and burst into flames. Everyone inside must have been trapped, and people around where the plane crashed fell to their knees and prayed, knowing that so many lives had been lost.

From then on I dreamed of just about every air crash that happened. I always got the circumstances right, for instance if a plane went into the sea I dreamt that, while if it came down in the countryside, or into a built-up area, I was accurate. The business was horrible. I would wake up, be very aware of the dream, and know that almost certainly many people had died or would die. At one time I was so aware that I knew about the smallest crashes, even when only two people were aboard, and got killed. I accurately predicted literally hundreds of crashes. Why? I still have no answer. The thing was unpleasant and pointless, since I could do nothing to prevent them happening.

The greatest coincidence of my life involved an interview at work. A young American came before me, for questioning. He was very pleasant, but I found something eerie about him. It transpired that as a tiny baby, and landing in a snowdrift, he had been the only survivor of a midair collision in America, which I had predicted. I cannot stress too much what a very agreeable man he was but there was some sort of weird connection with me, as I could not cope with the vibes I picked up... I once heard that if a lorry drove across a bridge, and the bridge had not been built properly, and the lorry set off the wrong velocity, the bridge could disintegrate. I felt that his vibes had me on the brink of disintegration. It was very strange feeling. I gripped my desk, to keep myself focused.

My terrible ability to foresee these crashes went on for many years. Then, one night, I woke up dreaming that I had turned into a plane, my arms having become wings, and saying, "I am flying, and I love it." But instinctively I knew that this would be a really terrible crash. It was. A Russian plane had come down, and, at the time, it was the world's worst air disaster, with the greatest number of people having been killed. But this dream experience just about put an end to my predictive powers, thank goodness. It was as though the last had been so traumatic that future crashes were blanked out. Just once in a while I would foresee one, or else had a sleepless night instead.

Many people predict plane crashes. but I have no idea what it is about a future air crash which appears to make it so accessible to so many. In my dreams death has always been represented by flying.

* * *

I was walking along a crowded pavement. There were too many people for me to make good progress comfortably, and the cars which should have been travelling along the road were stuck in traffic jams. I remembered that I had left my dream-world take-to-bits aeroplane at the kerbside a little way away so, believing that I would be able to escape the crowded pavement and the road, I went and collected it.

The plane, in the dream, was not like a real plane. It consisted of a couple of box-shaped parts, a small beam which went from front to back, and two bars which went from side to side. I started putting it together and realised that I did not know which end of the beam was at the front, and I could not risk constructing it the wrong way round. Then I realised that there should have been a skin, which would have covered the frame of the plane, and it was missing. I simply could not put the plane together.

I would have liked to fly (in a sense, to die) to escape from the hassle, but I was not able to, and had to go back to battling my way along the pavement.

Interestingly, the evening before I had this dream I had been to a Buddhist meeting at which we were invited to see that however unpleasant our present lives may be we should view them as if they were a few nights in a bad holiday hotel. We have already had many incarnations, and will have more, and each life was really just a transitory experience.

When I had a lovely, happy dream about getting onto a plane to go on holiday I awoke to wonder if I was going to die. For at the time, I had been ill for ages, initially as a result of a bug I picked up during a hospital visit.

I would willingly have moved on elsewhere, but I felt the cats needed me. Norman was old and was given pills daily. My husband never took a turn at administering them, treated the process as a joke, and occasionally lost the tablets. Poor rescued Holly trusted very few people, and I soldiered on, but life was a joyless exercise.

However, I was destined not to escape. I was told that I must have faith my life did have purpose and it was Sarah who gave me the message. This was further endorsed in another dream.

I was on a grubby underground train. The only other people in the carriage were an elderly couple who were both depressed and depressing. The train was going to an airport terminal and when it arrived the couple got off – they were going for a lovely holiday. I had the chance to go, too, but I stayed on the dreary tube train – opting to continue with my life.

* * *

One night, after attending a healing session, I was told that I should try to eliminate my cancer virus. While I slept I dreamt that I was digging into my body with a spade. This sounds macabre, but I had a great feeling of determination and satisfaction. My body was made of field-like constituents, and part of it was covered with a sheet, beneath which was an evil spirit. As I dug to eliminate it, it sometimes moved, protesting at my work. Only when it was dead, and still, could I stop my digging. I awoke the next morning with a great sense of peace.

* * *

In another dream, I was offered a length of material from a tightly-folded bale, from which I understood that I could make all the clothing I would ever want. Even taking into account the fact that it was folded I did not think there would be much width to it, or much material.

Then I looked again. The material had been opened, and I could see that it was immensely wide, far in excess of what I could possibly ever want. Instead of being folded the material, which was of a sort of dull green-grey colour, lay in gentle, welcoming curves as far as the eye could see.

There was a break, and confusion. The material had gone to an in-between size and was harshly crumpled. The night before I had had this dream I had been talking to Betty and Anthony, and they had been advising me about religion. The dream was to be understood thus:

The first bale had the look of something being stored rather than used, and was my faulty and pessimistic view of God's offering to me, the second, endless and welcoming, was the true offering, and the third represented my erroneous perception, a falsely restricted picture of God's gift.

Something else had happened during the night. For months I had suspected I was suffering from a kidney problem. I appeared to be retaining fluid and had back pains. I hate doctors and was less prepared to visit a surgery than ever because the last time I had been (I just wanted something for a 'flu bug which had left me chesty for three weeks) I got an aggressive female locum who looked at my records and desperately wanted to prove that my wheezing was no mere bug and that I should have a scan. She then had to backtrack when she remembered that I was still being checked regularly by the hospital.

When I awoke my back had returned to normal, as everything else, I was being given wonderful encouragement – and I knew that my beloved Anthony and Betty were bathing me with their love.

While I always believed, intellectually, that God did help all of us, including myself, I had great difficulty in feeling the faith necessary to take a confident view of life. I had a dream to help me with this.

I was going up in a lift. It stopped, and a man got into it. It started to go up again, but then went faster and faster, terrifyingly obviously it was going to crash and we would be killed. I thought, 'It won't do any good, but I'll call on God to help.' I did, and could scarcely believe it when the lift slowed down, and we were saved.

* * *

In another dream I had to leave the house at a particular time. I was waiting for the appointed hour and, when I was sure it was right, I glanced at the clock. To my amazement the time was earlier than I had expected.

Then I saw that the numbers on the clock had changed so that there was more time to go before the 12. The 10 was positioned where the 9 should have been, so at 10 o'clock there would still be three hours before it was midday.

This was a message that I would be given time to do the things I needed to do before I died. It was a reminder that time is unreal, fluid, and something we have invented.

* * *

In another dream I had actually died, and was moving among people walking along a pavement. I was taller than I am at my present height, and I was gliding, no longer having or using feet, and my sight and hearing were perfect. At present my sight and hearing are not good.

I had no body but felt no loss because of this, in fact I was joyful, and woke with the thought that I could help people much better in my 'dead' state than I had when I was alive. There was a great sense of freedom and a calm happiness.

* * *

I had a dream in which good, eventually, overcame evil. The

symbolism took the form of a series of pictures. The first showed a black entity, which was amœba-shaped, towering over and threatening a much smaller white one, also amœba-shaped. At first the white one felt totally defeated. Its natural space had been completely invaded, and it had no way to defend itself, or did it? It suddenly found within itself a little living flame, representing God-strength.

The following images showed, progressively, how the flame increased, and with it how the white image grew in size while the black one diminished. Eventually the two entities were in their own spaces, the black one cringing, although not actually being challenged, while the white one, having found its true self and strength, assumed a regular and peaceful shape, blossoming into its own reality.

At the time I wrote: 'From dying alone I find God within me and am able to resist that which is against me. No longer succoured by my distress, it diminishes...'

* * *

Before my mother's soul was laid to rest, and while she was still intent on damaging me, I had a dream in which she was trying to come down to attack me, but many pairs of disembodied hands held and restrained her.

While the idea of disembodied hands may sound unpleasant, these appeared as very beautiful. They were bluish, and radiated calm. In no way did they harm my mother, who had assumed an angular appearance, they were just preventing her from doing harm.

* * *

Another night I was shown a computer screen. On it were portrayed images of animals in their environment. They were not harmonious, there was discord. They were represented as in stained glass images, broken down into areas, but instead of the areas being defined by lead strips there were just thin lines, which were rounded and regular.

At I watched the lines and the areas within them they were constantly moving. It was as if the imperfections were being drawn into the middle of the screen so that what I saw became more and more perfect. Eventually complete harmony and perfection were achieved. The last thing to be adjusted was the colour. At all times the speed of this wonderful transition had been just too fast for me to focus on.

I had seen ordinary things become immaculate, and the force that made them so, showed a speed and a power in excess of anything I could achieve.

Excited by this revelation, and half awake, I tried to repeat this transformation with other, similar images, which I tried to feed onto the screen. It was impossible. I could not bring about a change in either form or colour. However, I had seen the wonderful ability of what I call God-energy to restructure existing things and make them perfect. As Julian of Norwich observed, 'All will be well'.

* * *

Twice I have had dreams which gave me an insight into just how lucky I have been with my friends. On separate occasions I saw Guru Thomas and Elizabeth in the aspect of Buddhas. This came as no surprise. Anyone who has brought back as many people from the brink of death as Thomas has, and anyone who can charm terrified animals the way Elizabeth can, has something very super-special.

* * *

Years ago, when I had given up work, had cancer, and was living on my husband's pension, I wanted to make more of my life. Then I had a dream about roads.

There was a junction with about four or five roads off it,

and all of them appeared to be sealed off by cones. Although a potentially busy spot in a town it was deserted with no traffic, pedestrians, or workmen. The surrounding area was also deserted. I was at the centre of the junction and thought how nice and quiet it was.

Then I realised that being there was no good as I could not move on, and I saw that there was one road along which I could pass. I asked my guides about the meaning of this and was told that there would always be a right way to progress, that I need not stagnate, and that my life would be a lonely path. (This would never worry me, I have always liked my own company and needed a lot of space.)

There were no indications that I should get a job, though a job could be part of the whole picture. While I would be happy on my own, whatever I could do would only come to fruition if I got involved with people, though this could be through communication rather than by being surrounded by family and friends. Symbolically, the one exit will always be adequate. I was told that the whole dream was to give guidance.

* * *

I had an amazing dream which told me that I had come to terms with the disillusionment of my marriage, and that I was no longer being harmed by it. It was so vivid! At the beginning it was unimaginably beautiful. I was in a perfect Cornish village, with a bay. I looked into the water, and saw perfect rock pools, the water pristine, with beautiful fresh seaweed, and shrimps and small fish swimming in them.

I realised they were deep, with the sea covering them, and I could swim in them, so I went in and started swimming. But I soon found, to my disappointment, that the pools suddenly became shallow, so my legs grazed against the rocks as I swam. The tide went out in seconds, leaving me stranded on a pebbly beach. I walked back.

Then, in a pool by a jetty, I saw two rats, a big white one, and a smaller brown one clinging together in a rock pool. They were both obviously dead. I thought I could not leave them as they would contaminate the water.

I expected them to smell as I pulled them out, and I gingerly took the white rat by the end of its tail, and they both came out together. However, as soon as I put them on the jetty, to my amazement, they started to revive, and drew apart. The white rat dived straight back into the pool, and I knew that this was right, as I realised it was a water rat.

The brown rat, which had a swollen right eye, started to move along the jetty, and I thought that the poor thing would not have much protection, and would be vulnerable.

I then drove homewards, away from the village. I remembered the perfection of the first sight of the village and water, and how the beauty was lost, but I did not resent it. I just accepted the whole thing as an experience, and was glad of the memory of the (very short-lived) happiness....

In the morning I found my right eye was sore and bloodshot but by the next day it had completely recovered.

* * *

Although cars have given me pleasure they have twice featured in warning dreams. I was trying to park on a hill but neither the hand- nor foot-brake, would hold. The car slid back, colliding with cars parked behind me. In the passenger seat was my husband, a very familiar look in his eyes. He was applying his psychic powers and knew he was winning the battle to harm and control me.

When I was a child we had a very old car, a 1935 Renault. It was a sporty-looking job, with a softtop, narrow windscreen, and two very wide doors. The starter motor packed up, and it was sent to a specialist garage, for them to produce a new one. They lost it, and from then on the car could only be started on the crank handle. The danger of the car being in gear when the handle was being turned was greatly impressed upon me. I often travelled on my mother's lap, in the front seat, and it was very easy to move the gear stick. If the car were to be put into gear accidentally, my father could run himself over as he tried to start it!

In my dream my father went to start the car. It was in gear, and the engine started, so the car ran into my father, then bounced back. My mother then put her foot on the accelerator so that it again struck my father, then it again bounced back, and again, and again, my mother pressed down the accelerator, and I awoke to the image of my father, having assumed the likeness of a rag doll, being tossed fatally backwards and forwards – while my mother's joy and signs of liberation, and triumph, completed the impression.

Years later, when I first saw my mother after my father's sudden death, and feeling traumatised, I said to her, "Isn't it terrible?" "No," she replied firmly. "It is not." She had had to wait a long time, but her wish came true.

* * *

While I was at school I dreamt that my mother had arranged my funeral. I was going along with the idea completely, even trying out the coffin for size – it fitted well. The date for the funeral had been fixed and was getting nearer but I wasn't even ill. I began to panic. Would I die in time? Then I had the thought, 'But do I really want to die?' I awoke thinking that I should decide to remain alive.

* * *

For a few years, in my mid twenties, I had a wild life. I was in a job with set hours which left me lots of time to enjoy myself, and I had boundless energy. I was also compensating for what had up to then been a poor social life. At this otherwise pleasant time my father died.

One of the boy friends was shown, in a dream, reacting very oddly to my father's death. He was leering and mocking in a manner which was not nice. I knew that, while we would remain friends, I would never get involved.

I was not particular about the men I associated with, the more the merrier. This led me to get involved, for a short time, with Jason who, though older than myself, had never been capable of having sex with a woman, despite numerous attempts. He managed it with me, then immediately resented the fact I did not look like his mother. Having gone from job to job he pursued me because he felt my parents were sufficiently well off to make it worth while. I had no intention of settling down with him. When we slept together I dreamt of warfare, bloodshed, and death, thoughts which I banished on waking.

Imagine my surprise when Jason asked me if I had been dreaming of death, because he had. I seem to remember that I lied through my teeth, and denied it.

Interestingly, although he was in many ways extremely unpleasant I now see that there were indications that he could have been quite advanced, spiritually. Like many brought up as Roman Catholics he had turned against that religion to an extreme degree, but he had the advanced conception of time spent in the afterlife making new worlds which he believed would be wonderful.

* * *

Over the years I have had bad dreams with a recurring theme. I am always trying to climb up, often inside a building, using stairs of one sort or another which are damaged, missing, or at the side of a sheer drop. I have never actually fallen, but what I have been trying to achieve has been frightening and dangerous. Often I have been on my own but if other people have been with me they have always had a much easier route for their ascent.

I once got into conversation with a Buddhist monk about these dreams. What I perceived as bad dreams he chose to see as auspicious. I was very sceptical, until, having understood that my uncomfortable attempts at getting higher were symbolic of my wish to progress spiritually, I had a dream where I had the conviction that however hazardous was the climb which presented itself to me, I would survive, and not fall as I feared.

After many years of this sort of dream I had, as it were, a reverse message. Disaster had struck. I had invited friends to a dinner party but had no food to offer them. I stalled, giving the impression I was going to complete arrangements in the kitchen but wandered into the street, finding myself in a strange town, and initially searching in vain for any shop selling food. Eventually I saw a delicatessen, but I was unable to reach it. I was on a pavement at first floor height, and there was no way of getting down to the door. Another lady was having the same problem.

This dream confirmed what I knew. As I got more involved in accepting, as right and preferable, more spiritual and less materialistic standards, the ordinary things of life became harder to tolerate. Necessary shopping expeditions were perceived as an irritation because, while necessary, they had no obvious spiritual content. Very inconvenient!

THE BARDO – LIFE BETWEEN LIVES

● We can see many kind spirits devoting their energies to helping. ● Shortly after his death, Steve is shown his possible future activities. ● Anthony makes use of latent talents. ● We reap what we sow. ● Some spirits leave the earth behind and go to work on different, distant worlds.

'So what happens to us in the time spent between lives – known as the Bardo? Different people have different experiences. Some, while not actually being earth bound, choose to remain helping or working with those still alive.

This exercise enables the dead to progress along their own spiritual paths. Helping, encouraging, and healing one's fellowmen is the simplest way to achieve this.

If you refer to the chapters on Visitations after Death; Messages from Spirit Helpers etc., you can see how busy members of my spiritual family are in the Bardo. In the chapter on My Spiritual Family and Spiritual Friends you can see how they benefit from their good work. Mr Skinner grew in stature, Leopold became a happier being as he was healed of his traumatic experiences, My Frances found the message of Christian Science which was right for her. Each found the unique and appropriate path.

Very many people are aware of the presence of a loved one soon after that person has died. When Angela appeared at her own funeral it will have been to reassure those present, and when she visited me it was to give me the great gift of her mother's love that I had not had in this incarnation.

Thomas's father once came to visit me, and wished me to give Thomas a message. He still regretted that he had been killed and so had been unable to provide the services of an ordinary father in the traditional way. However, he had been around since. I asked if there was anything in particular that he had helped Thomas and his family with, and he said he had guided them to find their house – a home in the country with space for their animals.

If a friend dies I offer Buddhist prayers if the indications are right. These appear to be very strong. Twice I have felt that those to whom they have been dedicated have been with me.

Steve was a distant relative who had had a less than happy life. His father had died when he was child and his mother had told him, on her deathbed, that the 'old aunt' who lived with them was actually her mother, his grandmother, and that she herself had been illegitimate, a condition seen as shameful in those days. The family had lived their life in a state of guilt and anxiety lest their secret be revealed.

Steve's natural grandfather came from a well-placed family and while he did not marry his mistress he did ensure her family did not starve, and Steve also realised, retrospectively, that he was the man who came to visit them occasionally.

After Steve's father's death his mother remarried. I was given to understand her second husband had two daughters, older than Steve, who were not very kind to him. He was almost certainly homosexual and would not have coped well at defending himself. He grew up to enjoy large powerful motorbikes, was heavily into the Church of England, and had a steady job. But he was not a good home-maker and was very lucky that towards the end of his life a very kind lady gave him a home and cared for him. The poor man had cancer which recurred over a period of over twenty years.

Shortly after his death I offered Buddhist prayers for Steve, and he came to visit me. I gathered that he was, as it were, being shown around to decide how he would spend his time. He was interested in the way I was beaming energies for absent healing but I suggested that he see all the options as there might be something even better for him to do. When I had given this advice I tried to extinguish the candle I had lit, but it did not want to go out and I had to blow on it several times.

Steve never returned, and I am sure he found a worthwhile activity which would enable him to make use of his kind and well-motivated nature.

One night Anthony, my loved husband of a previous incarnation who is a member of my spiritual family and is referred to in the section on Reincarnation, came to me to help me do the emanations.

I took the opportunity to ask him about his present life. He had people around him whom he had known in his immediate past life including some homosexual friends. Sexual orientation was irrelevant spiritually speaking, it was whether or not one hurt people that counted, he told me.

While he had had psychic perceptions in his last life he had not used them, or known of their healing potential. He was now using them for this purpose. Later he had other work to do, as described in the chapter on Reincarnation.

What about people who have been badly motivated while on earth? Those who have delighted in hurting their fellow human beings, or been totally selfish?

Such entities have to be re-educated and healed of their conceptions of how to view and treat people and all living things. There is no escaping the fact that they will have to pay, in one form or another, for their misdeeds. Some will have to return to earth and cope with difficult lives while some will stay in the Bardo and have to face their destiny there.

This idea is not a million miles away from the concept of the evil suffering in hell. Heaven and hell, I was told on many occasions, were the states of mind we created for ourselves. Any suffering we endure as a result of our lives on earth was self-generated. No one else can be blamed.

Inescapably and inevitably we really do reap what we sow. One idea which I have come across at different times and from different people, is that they will spend their time after death creating new worlds, or involved in other work involving movement between planets. This sounds as if I am getting caught up in the world of science fiction, but I assure you I am not.

Once I was visiting a dear old man, Hugh, in hospital. We all, including himself, believed he was dying although he recovered and lived on for a number of years. Although he had always declared himself to be against religion, saying that the followers were a lot of hypocrites, he started expounding his beliefs.

He had a strong conviction that the soul survived, and he was sure that he was going to be busy working in an interplanetary system. Hugh could not countenance any other reality.

Jason, the ex-boyfriend with whom I was the only woman he had been physically capable, had a poor education and a series of tedious clerical jobs. He was also against religion, blaming the Roman Catholic Church for the fact he had very bad problems relating to people sexually. His church's condemnation of masturbation had done a lot of damage.

However, he looked forward to the time when he would love his work. He had the belief that, after death, his employment would be the wonderful making of new worlds. I wondered if either or both of these men had any residual memories of being engaged in such activities before.

I was once told that spirits in the work of creating new worlds were very advanced, and would have a choice of how they employed their energies.

Interestingly, Eastbourne Christian Spiritualists gave me a book entitled *Entwining Lives* which documented messages through mediums. Included in the information are facts about the smallness of our world compared with the infinitely greater whole to which spirits may have access.

Reincarnation

● *The logic.* ● *People remember fragments of past lives.* ● *Each incarnation is meaningful.* ● *My immediate past life .* ● *Attitudes and desires created in previous ones.* ● *My Tibetan monk's mother is reincarnated.* ● *Newly-born child.* ● *We meet the same people.* ● *Inexplicable love.* ● *Once a woman.* ● *Members of my Spiritual Family and Spiritual Friends.* ● *Flashbacks.* ● *Personalities.* ● *Close feeling.* ● *Unnaturally knowing children.* ● *The right circumstances.* ● *The acceptance and non-acceptance.*

As a child, and I have no idea why I considered the subject, I saw reincarnation as the only logical way that our learning process could evolve, and our lives could be meaningful in a long-term sense. Throughout all of nature there are seasons and cycles which are absolutely vital for just about any kind of life as we know it to be sustained.

If we only had one life the experience of each would be terribly limited – one can only have the thoughts, feelings, and awareness of one individual and can only live surrounded by one set of circumstances in one home, one country, and with one set of friends and relations.

Also, I believed in a loving and just God, and what would be fair about having one's one and only life spent severely handicapped, in great pain, or experiencing nothing but a series of disasters?

There was also the fact that, during one long and active life, one could learn quite a lot. What would be the sense in acquiring all that knowledge if when one died, none of it could ever again be put to any sort of use?

Over the years I have come to see another aspect, that we are a meant to experience opposites. In one life one might be a spoilt only child who sneers at less favoured members of the peer group, while in the next life one might have a much rougher ride, and be deprived, and suffer in the same way as one of one's own previous victims, the wheel having come full circle. This can also be interpreted as *you reap what you sow*, or karma.

Many people are having little bits of memory or awareness which points them towards some knowledge of a previous life or lives. It took me years to realize that some of the characteristics, attitudes, and talents which I know have come through from previous incarnations.

There is often an all important reason for a particular incarnation. I know that, during this life, I had to learn to feel compassion for other people and all living things which are capable of suffering. This is one of the reasons I discovered Tibetan Mahayana Buddhism, for an awareness of the feelings of all sentient beings is at the core of their teachings.

I used to kill snails in their thousands – now I collect them and deposit them on a lush piece of waste land which in completely uncultivated and where the grass and weeds are never cut. It is a truth that if we kill anything – even a greenfly – what is an inconsequential action to most people is actually the ending of a God-given life.

As a child I had a 'thing' about a proper Tibetan Buddhist monk. There was no logical reason why, at that time, such a mythical figure should have captured my imagination so completely, but he had. A short time after I started going to a Buddhist Centre I heard that a festival had been arranged, and I could actually see the Guru who had founded my group of Buddhists in the flesh, and receive teachings from him. I booked a place for the festival, viewing the activities slightly humorously initially, but soon realizing that here, was one of the most marvellous men of God who was alive and working in the world today. Surely, all this must have been in the blue print of my present life. My genuine Tibetan Buddhist monk has exceeded all expectation.

It took me a long time to realize who I had been in my

immediate past life. In fact I was given quite a few clues. There were many things about me which had no obvious origin in my present life.

When I was three years old a pair of elderly sisters, who were very distant relations, came to visit us. As they lived in Scotland and had no car, and we were in the south of England, we met very seldom. During the whole of the day we spent together I behaved perfectly. I was a happy and contented child and, even at that tender age, said and did all the right things. My mother, who spent much of her time finding fault with me, had nothing to criticize.

I would not have known about this but the sisters took photographs of me, and sent them round the family. Ours was known as the snapshot taken on the one and only day of my life when I had behaved perfectly. There I stand, in my little coat, in the park which was near to where we used to live, happy, smiling, and still for the ladies – I was never goodlooking, but all children have some sweetness and charm. Fancy a child of three behaving well for a whole day!

My father had a very severe stroke just after I had entered the sixth form and the following summer, suffering from depression, he could not cope with going on holiday. One of the two elderly sisters had died, but the other invited me, along with one of my aunts, to stay with her, and she would show me something of Scotland.

On entering her house I spotted a very good water colour and pencil drawing of sea shells in the hall. I was struck that, whoever had painted it, had exactly the same colour sense that I had. We both used the same 'warm grey' colours, though the artist was much better than I was as an A Level student. I also did English and history at A level – we did political history involving almost unknown figures. I hated it, and preferred doodling architectural sketches of houses, caravans, and boats to doing history essays.

After a polite delay I asked about the painting. "Alexander did that for us." Alexander was the youngest of the family of three girls and one boy. The apple of everyone's eye he became an architect, working on the Singapore docks, and then, I believe, volunteered for the first World War. He died in the Battle of the Somme.

The elderly sister lived in Glasgow, but she had organized a very good itinerary. She and her elder sister – they were the ones who had visited us – had both been teachers, and the family had not been poor in the first place. We had a boat trip on Loch Katrine and investigated the Trossacks. Her niece, who had a car, was commandeered to give us another day out. On another occasion we went to Edinburgh, and she bought tickets for the Tattoo which was a part of the festival.

When the commentator announced, "The Argyll and Southerland Highlanders" the old lady sat on the edge of her seat, and said with reverence, "Alexander's regiment." I was less impressed. I hated war and did not find men in skirts, albeit rather splendid kilts, a turn on.

Some years later a female work colleague, with whom I was friendly, asked if I ever had a dream in which I was a member of the opposite sex, and I replied, "No – yes! No one would ever have to tell me what it was like in the trenches during the first World War. I had been there, and this knowledge was nothing you could get from a book or film." I had a dream of standing, totally vulnerable, on a ridge, young and full of promise, fearless, but surprised at what I found around me... Then there were other dreams, after I had been shot. In one I did not feel too bad, but I knew that while the second bullet might not be fatal, the first definitely would be. My colleague had had similar dreams.

I have only been abroad once. I was not a bit frightened by the coach or ferry journey to and around Europe, and I did enjoy the holiday, but I found myself thinking continuously, "I don't want to die abroad, I must get home before I die..." I was born at the end of 1945 when wartime experiences were on everyone's lips. My father had been in a reserved occupation which was lucky as I could not see him, ever, trying to kill anyone.

My mother, on the other hand, loved to hate, and I could feel she would have preferred it if my father had been conscripted, to kill or be killed. The war was just up her street. I was dragged off to see all the main war films and I remember, when I was quite tiny, her describing with a thrill of delight (I could see she was getting a sort of mental orgasm) the saturation bombings of Dresden and other cities.

I found this all totally repellent, and, had I known the word, would have labelled all wars and the saturation bombings as obscene, a view which I hold to this day. I am not a pacifist, however. One could not let Hitler exterminate the Jews, though if it had just been land that he was after I do not think that the terrible killings would have been justified.

I must have been almost fifty before the realization dawned that I had been Alexander – Alexander McNidder. My Christian name initials were also 'A.M. and Margaret, my middle name, was the same as one of the sisters. My father had insisted on my being called Alison, although other people in the family did not like it.

With the logic of hindsight I realised that, on the day when I behaved perfectly, I found myself suddenly being removed from being the only child of a mother who did not want me to being the little sibling of the two sisters who had adored me. Of course, nothing was understood at a conscious level, but at a much deeper level of perception a lot must have been going on.

My hatred of war is innate. I react to Remembrance Day with distaste, as it invites people to glorify war. I was once more or less forced to watch a service on television – I also saw the thing as ridiculous. Down went a poppy for me but here I was, middle aged in my next life. No one 'died' in the war, they simply lost their bodies. In Hindu scriptures I once read that it was silly to think you could kill your enemy – the part that really mattered would remain very much alive what ever you did. How true, and how wise.

A desire for holidays abroad is something which has passed me by. If I were to choose one country to visit, in fact the only country which holds any appeal at all, it is India. No, I don't want to see the *Taj Mahal*, wonderful though it may be, but from my earliest times I have wanted to be in a poor Indian village, surrounded by people who had scarcely seen a motor car, and whose level of spirituality would be unimpaired by technological progress. To them animals were sacred, and the care of family and friends in what we in the civilized world would call deprived conditions would be all important.

Why should I have this 'thing', this desire to live in so-called poverty? I was given the answer. The wish to be in India has been with me a lot longer than the fifty-plus years I have lived in my present incarnation.

Before being Alexander McNidder I was conceived in India, but at four months was miscarried. I asked why and was told that life would have been too harsh. My parents already had too many children, and they struggled to feed and clothe them. Their response to my conception had been adverse.

Apparently I had also been a seven months' miscarriage, again in India, in the 1300s, but this almost-incarnation was in a busy and prosperous place, not in a poor village.

I was told that babies who are miscarried learn a lot while in the womb, but forget this afterwards, so they can start a new life with a clean slate. However, these memories continue to exist at a very deep subconscious level.

Of course, the acquisition of knowledge applies to all babies still in the womb. It would appear that their awareness is very considerable. Even at a lighter level I remember a heavily pregnant friend being able to tell me, at the end of a concert of classical music, which pieces the baby had responded to most favourably.

My Buddhist Guru has been aware of a most wonderful manifestation of a reincarnation. When his mother died in Tibet he prayed that she should be re-born in England, so that he could look after her. Some time later young friends of his had a baby girl. The first time the Guru saw her he recognised her as his mother. Like many Tibetans her favourite mantra had been that of the Buddha of Compassion, OM MANI PAME HUM. The young couple found that if their baby was distressed she was soothed by hearing the words of the mantra. As the child grew up she started attending major festivals, where her son was teaching.

A friend who had been present at the birth of his daughter told me of his surprise that, on first looking into his child's eyes, he did not see the equivalent of a blank sheet of paper, as if awaiting the story of her life to be written on it, but an all knowing expression which had him, the father, weighed up and judged completely and absolutely in that first second. Understandably, he found this quite daunting!

I was interested to hear that quite a few doctors have reported a similar phenomenon. They too have seen knowledge already present in the eyes of the newly-born, though this has then vanished as the child starts his or her new life.

It is normal to meet, in one's present life, people one knew in previous incarnations. Sometimes one of the parties feels a closeness, but not the other, while at other times there is a great mutual feeling of linking up. I am sure that there must be many times when we fail to recognize any connection, although it is there.

I met Pauline at a Buddhist centre, she was very good looking and younger than I was, and I was flattered that she should bother to have me as a friend. She practised Reiki, and I had seen her working on a girl who had back problems. I could feel a wonderful peace around them. I have never seen an aura, but I could feel that if I had been able to on this occasion it would have been very beautiful.

Pauline once said to me that she thought we had been together in a previous life, but although I wished this were true, I felt it unlikely. However, I was wrong. Feeling under the weather, I decided to go to Pauline for help. I lay as any other Reiki patient, silent, relaxed, emptying my mind...

Suddenly I had the vision of a lovely big orange sun. It completely filled my consciousness, and was strong, but gentle and positive. I continued to lie quietly, but made a note that I must tell Pauline about the experience when she had finished the treatment. But as soon as she stopped Pauline exclaimed, "Did you feel that – the orange...?" I said, "Yes wasn't it beautiful?" "No, she replied. "It was like a pair of meteors!" When she had been in the area of my ovaries she had felt two orange balls, like a pair of meteors, flying by. This had felt quite violent, and was followed by an awareness of red.

We puzzled over the possible significance, and when I got home I started asking my guides about this. It took ages, since I did not know where to start. However, I rumbled it in the end. In fact, we had been together in the 12th Century. At that time there were four in our family. Pauline was the father, there was her wife, their son, and a younger daughter – myself. When I was sixteen and my brother eighteen, the mother (Pauline's wife) and the son died. It was believed they had been victims of the plague, but in fact they had contacted another, similar, illness.

Pauline felt that it was the position of the surviving daughter – myself – to look after him, as the widowed father. However, I married and had a child, and my father was not pleased. What I perceived as the completion of my family, – a father, husband, and child – my father felt as a threat. The two meteors that had been fired from my ovaries showed his attitude, while the warm all-embracing sun, which I had experienced, was very different. I was told that the red which followed the two meteors meant a coming together, a healing between us. I had been twenty-four when my father had died, aged fifty-one, and I died when I was thirty-three. Interestingly, in our present lives, there was something a little akin to a reversal of situations. I was childless and married to a much older man while Pauline was married for the second time, and had a beautiful little daughter, in addition to her first family.

When I told her of my findings she said, "I wasn't very nice, was I?" She then said how her present father had been rather as she had been then. He was very difficult when daughters or other girls in the family wanted to marry, finding all sorts of objections. So far as Pauline was concerned, karma had come full circle.

When I was in the Sixth form, I fell in love with a neighbour. Unlike the boy friends of my peer group, he was a man in his thirties, and homosexual. I did not deny his homosexuality, but somehow I also saw him as completely male. (In fact he appeared to be the feminine half of his relationship.) Anthony was the distant passion of my life.

What was equally amazing was that he appeared to feel something for me, too. My mother having indoctrinated me with the idea that I was so hideous that no man would ever want me, coupled with being rendered totally inarticulate by my overwhelming passion, I was completely unable to respond. In any case, the thing would have been hopeless. A middleaged, established homosexual suddenly chasing after a kid in school uniform... And I always knew that it would be impossible to marry while my mother was alive. One way or another she would have destroyed the relationship.

My meetings with him were brief. In those days people often took buses, rather than cars, to work, and we met at the bus stop as I made my way to school. These encounters lasted for only a short time, since I was destined to leave home once I had my A levels, and go into my first job as a trainee newspaper reporter.

When I heard that he planned to move I seriously contemplated suicide. Although I was away from home, the fact he was a neighbour of my parents, whom I visited about every six weeks, meant that all hope had not quite died.

In fact, we were to be together in a completely different way, about thirty years later...

At a lunch party I found myself opposite a very agreeable man and his wife. We chatted, and I discovered that the husband was a design engineer. Anthony had been chief designer for a big local company. Then the name of a place was mentioned – it was the same place name which had been Anthony's surname... There is no such thing as coincidence – or is there?

That night I asked questions. Yes, Anthony was there, and our mutual love and happiness at being together again was truly indescribable. Perhaps you have guessed it. Anthony had been my husband in what was probably the happiest incarnation I have ever had. We had a great and enduring love for each other, and produced a number of children.

There was another reason why I felt such a closeness to Anthony, he had been my teacher when we were between lives, immediately before my incarnation as Alexander NcNidder.

Despite his homosexuality he felt a closeness because of what had gone before – a recognition at a very deep level, a feeling of kinship totally unconnected with anything to do with our current lives.

When I knew Anthony he was about 17 years older than I was. I had not been aware of his death as I lost all contact with the town where I was brought up once my mother had died, but I learnt that when he had made his presence known to me, he had been dead for about three years. He had had a fatal heart attack in his early sixties, following exactly the pattern of his mother's death. He had spent the years immediately after his death caring for his friends on earth – the ones he had made during his immediate past incarnation. But he was now making himself more mobile.

A long time after Anthony made contact with me, and we

were blissfully happy, I was disconcerted to feel him manifesting uncharacteristic angry vibes. Had I caused some huge offence in some way? Betty told me that he had moved on to a different kind of work, and had forgotten about me. He needed to experience anger after being so benevolent for so long, and was now entering other people's bodies to stir them up in a scenario where there was domestic abuse which needed to be sorted out and not tolerated. The people concerned needed to be given a prod to do something about it.

In addition to Anthony making himself available to me after his death, another major role-player in our previous shared incarnation has made contact with me, and is one of the most important members of the group of people I call 'My spiritual family and friends'. She is Betty, who was then my mother.

I have been told that we lived in South East Ireland, and enjoyed a good standard of living compared to many. My husband, now Anthony, was a farmer. It was stressed that he grew crops rather than keeping animals. I was then called Sarah, and Betty was Catherine. I was born in 1725 and died in 1781, of cancer. My mother predeceased me by six weeks. She is now working to try to stop history repeating itself, to see that I do not get a recurrence of my cancer. In my Irish incarnation it had taken a little under six months to kill me, I was told. I had been selfish in that life, but as I genuinely loved my family no great harm was done. I also had psychic powers which I never used. When I tried to find out our surname I felt a response of consternation, and I realised that we had been illiterate. However, the nearest I could get to it, phonetically, was *Yoorgrow*.

David is another member of my spiritual family. Over the years he has given me a lot of healing and advice. During my Irish incarnation he was my uncle. David also featured during my lifetime in Italy, as a fresco painter. I had been born in 1804, and died in 1859 of 'stomach flu'. My maternal grandfather had been a doctor, and David had been a young medical friend of his who was a great hero of mine, and a big influence in my life. Apparently I had psychic powers during this incarnation, but made no use of them.

Another person from this life who manifested in my present one was a onetime live-in boyfriend Gerald. We had both been fresco painters, and friends. In this life Gerald was a very good classical pianist. Although he had managed to reach forty without marrying when he saw me he apparently thought, 'That is the sort of girl I could spend the rest of my life with'. I am not good-looking, but I think there must have been a recognition at a deep level so his perception went beyond the obvious. We were not destined to stay together, but I am convinced we were stepping stones in each other's lives. We married other people within weeks of each other.

During our years together I got to know his family well, and they were very good about the fact that although we were free to marry we did not do so. I realised early on that a permanent, legal arrangement would not be a good idea. However, I had my common-law nephews and nieces.

One of these girls, Alice, was a pretty child with fair hair, pleasant features, and blue eyes. I did not particularly like her, however, as she always appeared to be moody and aloof. There were a number of occasions when she was self-centred. My affair with her uncle came to an end, and my contact with his family waned to some extent, though we never lost touch.

Alice claimed she was forced into a marriage she did not want by her mother and a Roman Catholic priest. It was true she had had a relationship with her boyfriend, but she was not pregnant by him and to me it was disgraceful if she had been pressurized into marriage. Predictably, the marriage failed. She then had a couple of other boyfriends, and she produced an unplanned child by one of them.

In all this confusion she started contacting me again. I was not a little surprised. Somehow this girl, to whom I had never given any encouragement, saw me as someone who would lend a sympathetic ear. She and her siblings had been given little guidance as they grew up and while I saw the production of the child as irresponsible I knew Alice to be basically a decent person and when I got to know her better I knew she had many good points. However, eventually events indicated that many of her problems she had brought on herself.

Why had Alice come to me? And why did we have such a strong telepathic link? We would not be in touch for months, then our letters would cross in the post. I would buy the child a little present and, Oh dear – particularly as there was not much money – Alice would have bought her exactly the same thing. We discovered that Alice had been my daughter in the happy incarnation when Betty was my mother, and Anthony my husband. Such memories are very, very deep, but also very, very strong.

Spirit lives are very inter-woven. Alice told me about friends with whom she felt a deep bond. When I inquired, I discovered that one of them had been one of my children in another incarnation, as Alice had herself, while two others were not, but had known Alice in two previous incarnations. I was told that a maternal aunt, Auntie Winifred, was giving these facts, and that she had been Betty's sister.

For me 'coincidence' means 'it was meant to happen'. To the question, 'Why?' there is always an answer, though it can be veiled. I was about to return home from a holiday, and had a choice of routes. There was one that I had favoured for years – it was shorter although it involved driving over miles of very narrow winding roads – while the other was longer and while the roads were capable of carrying heavier traffic, and a bit faster, there was, again, almost no opportunity to overtake. I felt I should dowse, though puzzled by my own enquiry.

The longer route was indicated, although there could be no advantage to me unless there had been something very remarkable on the more minor roads, which was very unlikely. However, I was guided by the indications. What was going to happen? Would an explanation be forthcoming?

As I drove along I saw a dead cat lying on the opposite side of the road. I recited some Buddhist mantras as I passed by, and, when I was close to it, felt a strong impression of a beautiful soft, cuddly, gentle, family-loving little animal – the way the poor little thing had been while it was alive. I kept going but, a mile or two on, I thought I should check that the animal was dead and not just unconscious, and I should at least move the body to the side of the road so it should not be flattened by the passing traffic. I turned the car around.

I pulled up just past the cat, then walked back. The accident had happened outside an isolated country cottage, and I heard what I first took to be the sound of an argument taking place. Then I realised that the hapless owner had just opened her bedroom curtains and seen the beloved pet lying in the road. The sound had been her grieving.

I eased the poor little cat off the road, and laid it away from the traffic. I heard her, 'Thank you.' I drove on to my but soon I stopped again, as the early sun was catching traffic haze on the windscreen, and I needed to wipe it. While I was parked in the layby two cars drove past on what had been the cat's side of the road. Would they have squashed it further?

A couple of days after getting home I had a question and answer session. The owner of the cat and I had been close in about 1725, when she, a girl of ten, had lost her mother and I, a neighbour, did my best to be there for her and her siblings. I had represented comfort and security for her, and that was why we had made contact over the cat. Someone up there must have had quite a job synchronizing our movements... I had to overshoot the area, to use up time until I would appear at the exact moment the woman looked through her window.

My informant was Anthony, and I discovered that in my 1725 incarnation we had both been women, and he and I had been close friends. It was stupid of me to be so taken aback by beholding Anthony in a female incarnation – possibly this was to show me that I had become inappropriately attached to him in his role as my loved husband and partner, in a sexual as well as a non-sexual relationship.

He, or she, also felt it necessary to give me a sharp rebuke. I was failing to get down to it and write this account of what I had been told, which was certainly not for my benefit only. I should be making it available to a lot of people.

This was totally justified for I was failing, but for there to be any form of criticism or rejection from Anthony hurt!

As if to help me on my way one of my spiritual friends, the discreet homosexual Christian Scientist, made a rare appearance, to offer support. It was very sweet of him, and I felt the homosexual aspect was to confirm for me that erotic matters should not be allowed to sidetrack important spiritual things.

There are many accounts of people retaining fears and phobias from past lives. Someone who is terrified of birds, seeing them quite inappropriately as flying threateningly towards him, is discovered to have died in the desert in an earlier incarnation, where his last memories were of carrion birds descending to feed off his dying body.

But sometimes there is a flashback of a different kind – a sudden, positive, and otherwise unexplained need. Some years ago there was a splendid exhibition in London of the art of Pompei, the city which in 79AD was wiped out by first a pyroclastic flow and then buried under lava from the volcanic eruption of Mount Vesuvius. A courtyard had been reconstructed. Seeing it with its wonderful murals, I was completely overwhelmed, and thought, 'I would sacrifice everything I have today, family, friends, and possessions if I could live in these surroundings.' A few seconds later I marvelled at just how strong my feelings had been for I really had meant what I thought. The experience lived with me, and when I enquired of my guides I was told that I had been a fresco painter. Interestingly, in this life I have dabbled in sculpture and am aware that I have a built in awareness of the qualities of plasters, which is greater than some of my fellow sculptors.

I feel it is likely that child prodigies – of which I am definitely not one! – are displaying talents learnt in past lives – and a good thing, too. A child who can play the piano brilliantly at a precocious age can give pleasure to many people.

A friend, Peggy, told me that her little grandson, not yet even of school age, was showing a great interest in the guitar. While, predictably, he got quite a few things wrong as he played, Peggy was amazed at how much he managed to get right. The little boy said that he had been a guitarist last time, and he would be a guitarist this time, too. Once someone asked him whether he would marry, and he said he would not, as he had married last time and didn't think much of it.

People who make a study of such things have often come upon instances where, for example, recurring extremely bad headaches without any apparent medical origin are traced to a remembered experience in a past life. By remembered I mean at a deep level, which may be uncovered by hypnosis. In fact there have been instances of doctors who started off with no belief in an after-life changing their minds after encountering such patients, and curing them by bringing the memory to the surface, and providing an explanation.

I was extremely curious about one case involving a young man, normally gentle and caring, who had killed his mother. The story was told in a television programme, and the main thing that came across was the tragedy of the event. The killer was devastated, and unable to account for what had happened. Other members of the family gave him their support – his actions had been totally out of character.

The killer was interviewed, and his eyes held only feelings of huge remorse, love, and kindness. Everything has an explanation, and one night I got down to work with the pendulum, to see if I could unearth the reason why this tragedy had happened.

I was told that the young man had been an abused child in his immediate past life. He had been at the receiving end of great cruelty. A doctor who had tried to find a mental reason for the murder discovered that the man had a moment-to-moment memory disorder. This was partly to blame for the fact that he believed that there were conversations in his present life which indicated he was threatened. He claimed to hear voices coming from the television set, but I was told that this was irrelevant, the important fact was that he heard, again, the threats he had suffered in his last life.

In an attempt to survive in his past life he had fought back, physically, as hard as he was able. Even so, he had died at the age of five. In his present incarnation, with his moment-to-moment memory disorder, he had responded to conversations he heard – re-lived – as he had when a child, in his previous life but, being a grown man now attacking an unsuspecting adult, he won his battle, with tragic and fatal results.

Why is he or she like that? In one family there can be a complete range of totally different characters and personalities. While brothers and sisters have their parents, friends, and homes in common, there may be little or no similarity between them. But why should we be so surprised? Should we be amazed that present physical genetic factors and a home, family, and friends in common should completely mask the result of thousands of years of evolving, spiritually, along our own individual paths with all our unique experiences?

In a family of three there was a girl and two boys, all very different. But while both the boys were easy to get on with, and manageable, Karen presented her parents with big problems. Although quite bright she was very disruptive at school, setting herself up as the leader of the troublemaking squad, while at home she constantly opposed her parents who were by nature very loving, caring, and supportive. It was lucky they had the boys, as a comfort! The parents went to the school and jointly they tried to sort out the girl, but just about everything had been tried, and nothing worked.

Was the girl just naturally unpleasant? Then I heard a little more about her, and wondered if something was going on at a more subtle level. Karen, had always been a great worrier. This struck me as at odds with her brash and challenging attitude. Her brothers, who had a genetic problem which, while not serious or lifethreatening, needed watching, had regular hospital checks. Karen was heard to say that she wished she was ill, too, so that she could die. It was pointed out to her that her brothers were not in any danger of this. But I saw this reaction as a possible clue. The girl was clearly confused and unhappy. People who are nasty to others are almost always unhappy in themselves – but why?

I asked a few questions, and was told that in her immediate past incarnation the girl had had a very unhappy childhood. Her father had been extremely cruel, and she had not survived. In the life before this one she had been a boy, but again her early life had been very unhappy, though she at least lived to adulthood. After these experiences I suspected that she had no expectation that parents could be kind – they were to be viewed with suspicion. She was programmed to believe that life would be hard, and she maintained this faulty perception into her present life. Her death when a child had been a great relief, and the idea one she hung onto. I was told that anyone wishing to help should try to beam a happy mind at Karen.

On my first day of receiving radiotherapy a wonderful lady came out of the treatment room ahead of me, and smiled a warm, friendly, positive smile. As our appointment slots were only five minutes apart, and as we both arrived early, I got to know Valerie as we chatted easily and enjoyed each other's company. Apparently one of the radiographers remarked to her that it was lovely when the patients got on so well, and made their time at the hospital so pleasant.

I felt a great attachment to Valerie but I knew that, while we became friends, we met only infrequently, and I meant much less to her than she did to me. Why? And why had I instantly felt this closeness? On investigation I was told that we had been brothers together in the 11th century and both fishermen. Valerie had been a nicer and better person than I was (this situation had not changed!) but we were good brothers who enjoyed an excellent relationship, and cared for each other. I was told that time was irrelevant where these contacts were concerned, it was the intensity of the feeling that counted. They transcended time and space.

Sadly, Valerie's cancer returned. She put up a magnificent battle, surviving much longer than was expected. I visited her a few days before she died. She was at home, with her lovely, caring husband, and back-up nurses. The doctor and nurses were just going as I arrived, and, just too late, Valerie's husband realised that the doctor had forgotten to sign the vital prescription for Diamorphine, to keep her out of pain. I was so pleased that I could be a little bit useful, sitting with Valerie while her husband went chasing after the doctor, and then made a round of chemists until the prescription could be met.

Valerie was very sleepy for most of the time, and we just held hands. She did have a couple of little drinks of water, and I proved incompetent in administering the first, not realizing how much help was needed. A little water spilled onto the pretty nightdress, and I was rather pleased to see that Valerie immediately mopped it up, her pride in her very nice appearance remained with her until the end. She asked me if I was still free of cancer, and I said that I was. It was typical of her to be caring for others even though she was at death's door, literally, herself. She asked for her daughter, and I said that she would be visiting as soon as she finished work. As her husband had told me, there were brief moments when Valerie showed the sparkle of her old self. But for the most part I just tried to will love to her, and felt very privileged to share these precious moments.

The lady who had been our mother when we were fishermen brothers was to become a great aunt by marriage to me in my present incarnation.

I think I only met Great Auntie Louie once, but I felt greatly attracted to her. She was jolly and kind, and lived in a little country cottage at the bottom of a steep lane which was only just suitable for cars. It must have been about 1949, 1 think, and civilization had not quite reached that part of the world – the loo was a chemical commode by the bed! My mother was suitably scathing, but I was not in the least disposed to be critical. The loo seat was the most beautifully polished piece of wood I had ever seen in my life. One Christmas Great Auntie Louie (her proper name was Louisa, but no one ever called her that) gave me a book, one of those for small children with cardboard pages, lots of pictures, and not much writing. The little story about ducks was told in verse. I was enchanted, and thought how kind Great Auntie Louie was to give me a present when she did not really know me.

I discovered that, once she had died, Great Auntie Louie had tried to help and protect me when my mother tried to harm me. As far as Auntie Louie was concerned it must have been the case of, 'Once a mother, always a mother'. Bless her.

"She's a second-time-arounder." This matter-of-fact comment by a grandmother about her grandchild made a big impression on me. I heard how the little girl had automatically, without being shown, and at a very young age, known how to get dressed, brush her hair, and tie her shoelaces. Since she was the third child in the family the parents had experience of bringing up children, and a pretty good idea of what could be achieved at a particular age. The grandmother accepted as a matter of course that she was looking at a case of pre-knowledge.

On enquiring about this I was told that, indeed, the child remembered these things from her previous life. She had not been meant to die young but had taken a fatal drugs overdose. Because she had been intended to survive into adult life she had reincarnated quickly, within four years of her death.

Even as we conclude one life we will have in some cases predetermined what will happen during our next time on this earth. My husband, who is elderly, regrets that he did not have children. He and his first wife, who was older than he was, were married for many years, but were childless. He even hoped that I might produce, but I was forty when I married, he was very much older, and the thing was not viable so far as I was concerned. I do not believe one should conceive children unless one can have a realistic chance of providing for them well in every way, as active parents and provide a good home environment. My husband was not even going to leave a widow's pension! The idea of dragging a solitary child around, with only an old mother and no proper income, would to my mind have been totally irresponsible.

However, I have been told that in his next life my husband will again be male, and will have children.

I received conflicting messages about when some of my spiritual family would reincarnate. There appeared to be a tendency for it to take longer than expected – though there is no time in the next world – to find the right circumstances in which they could live their next lives.

I was once told that Mr Skinner would reincarnate in March 1998, but it must have been a couple of years later that he actually did so. David, planning to return by March 1999 found difficulty linking up with the ten members of his spiritual group who would need to be with him on earth at the same time, so they could work together.

Great Auntie Louie and Veronica would meet me in the bardo, I have been told. Leopold also had no plans to reincarnate quickly, as he was still recovering from an unhappy life. I was told I would meet my Indian friend who had guided me to a piece of Hindu scripture.

Who believes in reincarnation? Taking religious groups and their beliefs into account more people do than do not. The Christian church decided not to on the strength of a vote in AD 553 by the Second Council of Constantinople. I have heard that the outcome was swayed by the fact that a rather fiesty wife of an influential Roman made known she did not want to believe in reincarnation – and many voted against in the hope of getting preference, in the form of career enhancement, from her husband. Politics was ever so! Prominent Christians who have accepted reincarnation have included Clement of Alexandria and Origen, both 3rd century and St Jerome, 5th century.

I was at a retreat attended by a wonderful Indian Roman Catholic nun who was a mother superior of convent abroad. At one point I mentioned that I knew details about some of my previous lives. Afterwards the lady came running up to me. She said that her sister had had an 'experience'. She had left her village, and travelled for the first time to a more distant town. But on arrival she found that she knew it perfectly – and had a complete memory of it. Clearly, the nun was convinced, and presumably her sister had been, too – that she had lived there in an earlier life.

I have noticed that many Roman Catholics and Jews, who are officially discouraged from accepting psychic phenomena, are having more and more personal memories or experiences which are forcing them to consider the possibility of reincarnation. Genuine enquirers must not be left in ignorance.

The devout American Christian Edgar Cayce, who started off by being very strict in toeing the line of the beliefs of his low protestant church, had to accept reincarnation. The idea is not new, Socrates accepted it as do the members of the world's oldest religion, the Hindus, and all Buddhists.

Whether one believes in reincarnation or not, however, is relatively unimportant. It is what we make of our present lives that matters. The Dalai Lama has said that it is right for some people not to believe in it, as they might discover they have done well in past lives and decide to live on their laurels rather than focussing on what they are supposed to be doing now.

To anyone who wants to argue with me, I would say, "Well, what you or I believe really does not matter. The truth, whatever it is, remains unaltered by what we believe..."

* * *

I hope you have found things in this book which have confirmed for you the vastness and limitless wonder of our immortal existence. Too often we get caught up in our mundane lives and forget that at a profound level our spirit, consciousness, and memory – including the subconscious and unconscious – span many lifetimes and countless experiences. We are what we have been, what we have made ourselves become. We may not be aware of the big over-view of our lives but it does exist, and if we could see it it would enable us to see many apparent problems as necessary and even tragedies would be perceived on a smaller scale. We, and everyone around us, are always progressing, nothing is static.

Please accept, that we both share our humanity and many of life's experiences, some of which have their roots in the so-called inexplicable. Let us accept the latter for what they are, indications there are more things in heaven and earth – wonderful things, souls who love us and care for us, who understand the reality of transcending time and space, and who can transform everything into its perfect state, sickness into radiant health and the desire to hurt into the desire to help. Never forget that while each and every one of us is a unique individual we are all also part of the whole and have access to divine positive energies which are there to benefit all living beings.

If you have difficulty with this concept please keep an open mind. My hope is that, in the near future, you will experience events in your lives which will convince you how much you are a part of the big picture, and that the big picture is there to help you. Accept that you have spiritual friends, and that the afterlife is there for you and those you love just as much as for those who work for you from their spiritual plain.

I thank my guides for the patience and tolerance they have shown me. They have expressed their love, and entrusted me with their Wisdom. Through me they have made their offering – to you.

I often feel that if we had all been raised with an awareness of Eastern religious beliefs we would be more predisposed to accept spiritual matters. As it is I leave you with a quotation from Mrs Mary Baker Eddy, the founder of Christian

Science, one of the very few people from the West who has completely taken on board the enormity of the power of the spiritual:

> Let us feel the divine energy of Spirit, bringing us into newness of life and recognising no mortal nor material power as able to destroy.